ALSO BY PETER DAVIS
Hometown

Where Is Nicaragua?

BY PETER DAVIS

A TOUCHSTONE BOOK
Published by Simon & Schuster Inc.
New York London Toronto Sydney Tokyo

First Touchstone Edition, 1988

Published by Simon & Schuster Inc.
Simon & Schuster Building
Rockefeller Center
1230 Avenue of the Americas
New York, NY 10020

TOUCHSTONE and colophon are registered trademarks
of Simon & Schuster Inc.

Designed by Irving Perkins Associates

Manufactured in the United States of America

10 9 8 7 6 5 4 3 2
10 9 8 7 6 5 4 3 2 1 Pbk.

Library of Congress Cataloging in Publication Data

Davis, Peter, date.
  Where is Nicaragua?

  1. Nicaragua—Politics and government—1979—
2. Nicaragua—Foreign relations—United States.
3. United States—Foreign relations—Nicaragua.
4. Davis, Peter, date. —Journeys—Nicaragua.
I. Title.
F1528.D38 1987   972.85′05   86-29814

ISBN 0-671-54618-X

ISBN 0-671-65720-8 Pbk.

The author is grateful for permission to reprint material from *Selected Poems of
Rubén Darío*, translated by Lysander Kemp, copyright © 1965 University of
Texas Press. Reprinted by permission of the University of Texas Press.

Where Is Nicaragua?

BY PETER DAVIS

A TOUCHSTONE BOOK
Published by Simon & Schuster Inc.
New York London Toronto Sydney Tokyo

Copyright © 1987 by Peter Davis

First Touchstone Edition, 1988

Published by Simon & Schuster Inc.
Simon & Schuster Building
Rockefeller Center
1230 Avenue of the Americas
New York, NY 10020

TOUCHSTONE and colophon are registered trademarks
of Simon & Schuster Inc.

Designed by Irving Perkins Associates

Manufactured in the United States of America

10 9 8 7 6 5 4 3 2
10 9 8 7 6 5 4 3 2 1 Pbk.

Library of Congress Cataloging in Publication Data

Davis, Peter, date.
  Where is Nicaragua?

  1. Nicaragua—Politics and government—1979—
2. Nicaragua—Foreign relations—United States.
3. United States—Foreign relations—Nicaragua.
4. Davis, Peter, date. —Journeys—Nicaragua.
I. Title.
F1528.D38   1987   972.85′05   86-29814

ISBN 0-671-54618-X

ISBN 0-671-65720-8 Pbk.

The author is grateful for permission to reprint material from *Selected Poems of
Rubén Darío*, translated by Lysander Kemp, copyright © 1965 University of
Texas Press. Reprinted by permission of the University of Texas Press.

For Victor Navasky, who first suggested I go to Nicaragua,
and for Roberta Lichtman, who stayed at the end when I no longer could.

CONTENTS

Sing of that Second realm where the human spirit is purged . . .
If within the womb of those flames thou didst abide
Full a thousand years, they could not make thee bald of one hair.
—Dante

Managua, Nicaragua, What a wonderful spot!
There's coffee and bananas and a temp'rature hot,
So take a trip and on a ship go sailing away—
Across the "agua" to Managua, Nicaragua. Olé!
—Albert Gamse

We both made the history of this hemisphere. We must
both remember it. We must both imagine it.
—Carlos Fuentes

NOTE ON SOURCES

THE MAIN SOURCE OF THIS BOOK, as will be clear, is a trip I took to Nicaragua. It was a brief trip, coming at one of the recurring delicate points in the long crisis between Nicaragua and the United States. Later, I made a final visit to calculate changes and clarify positions. Except where the text indicates otherwise, my chief research sources have been the publications of the American Enterprise Institute, the Central American Historical Institute of Georgetown University, and the North American Congress on Latin America. I have also had access to the latter's library. In using material furnished by these institutions, I have ranged a country mile, as it used to be called, from the methods of most of their own researchers and authors. Multitudes of fact, assertion, dispute and sheer fantasy surrounding Nicaragua, each yielding its own layer of interest, have pushed me away from a conventional report. The form this chronicle takes is one I first saw suggested by the historian Richard Hofstadter: "The new genre is part narrative, part personal essay, part systematic empirical inquiry, part speculative philosophy."

INTRODUCTION

Is NICARAGUA the enemy of the United States? The anthem of the Sandinistas, who won the war in 1979 against the Somoza succession, contains the words "We fight against the Yankee, enemy of humanity." There are two ways—many ways, of course, but let's reduce them to two opposites for the moment— to look at that line. The first is that if they call us their enemy, they are our enemy, and we should act accordingly. This is simple, straightforward, without reference to context. The second is that the Somozas made that anthem inevitable, and every Nicaraguan knows who made the Somozas.

Another question: Is Nicaragua a threat to the United States? Two opposite ways present themselves of looking at this, too. The first is that the question is ridiculous. With a staggering economy, primitive technology and fewer than three million people in an area the size of New York State or Wisconsin, an area roughly equivalent to the sum of England and Wales, Nicaragua cannot possibly hurt the United States unless it puts in a Soviet base. The United States has long since made it clear that no Soviet base would be tolerated. Nor can Nicaragua hurt its neighbors as long as the United States guarantees their security. The reverse view is that Nicaragua constitutes a definite threat not only to the United States but to the entire region. If such a small, traditionally pliant country can declare its independence of the United States and get away with this, an entire system of political, military and economic dominion is at risk in the Americas. What then, for instance, happens to Mexico? If the United States cannot "manage," in Henry Kissinger's apt word, its own hemisphere, it loses credibility among allies and clients all over the world. Here, too, is a simple answer, without reference to a context in which such a question may be considered.

Faced with such questions, I have wanted to explore the relationship between Nicaragua and the United States, listen for the meaning as well as the tone of Nicaraguan and American voices, look for the point and counterpoint of a play that oscillates between farce and tragedy.

This book is an attempt to locate context.

Where Is Nicaragua?

I BLOOD

ON A BLASTED CORNER IN MANAGUA, a city which, for all purposes beyond the sentimental need of every people to call some place their capital, ceased to exist after the earthquake of 1972, three white buildings continued to stand until the beginning of 1978. Some pedestrians hurried to them, others avoided them with a sneer or a shudder. The buildings were painted white not because it is popular and cheap in the tropics—yellow and beige and pink resist the daily dust better and look cleaner longer—but because they performed a singular medical function that made a hygienic veneer convenient. Citizens who visited the buildings came to bleed into small transparent bags. The processed results were shipped north, part of the raw materials Nicaragua exported to the United States. American shortages led to brisk trading in one of the few commodities Nicaragua had in abundance. Surely this must be the kind of "illuminating detail" journalists are supposed to look for, the part that reveals the whole. What greater exploitation can there be for an impoverished people than to have their own blood extracted for the benefit of their imperial masters?

Well, yes. But the trouble with everything in Nicaragua is that one detail leads to another, to almost infinite others, until each by itself has only as much significance as a dot in a pointillist painting. The next dot may reject the last and in turn be denied by its successor as part of a series of contradictions and paradoxes that threaten to swallow one another. A clear case of capitalist imperialism or communist oppression, of social progress or economic collapse, need only be turned slightly on its axis in order to be seen as its opposite. It is not that nothing is true in Nicaragua but that the truth dissolves into a collection of meanings whose common thread is their ambiguity. A visit to Nicaragua is a visit to a state of flux.

A priest says the Sandinistas who control Nicaragua are trying to crush the mother church; a nun swears she found God in the revolution. One industrialist accuses the government of stifling free enterprise; another claims the revolution has been good for business. A State Department official condemns the "asphyxiating corruption and oppression" in Nicaragua, but it is the only Central American country where the United States ambassador can go around without bodyguards. The ambassador himself, during my first visit at a critical instant in Nicaragua's relationship with the United States in 1983, was available to a wide range of visitors. He could be found confronting hostile delegations from the United States as well as granting interviews to virtually any journalist who made a determined effort to see him. But he refused to be quoted in the American press, insisting he be referred to as "a Western diplomat." The phrase summons an image, for anyone raised on cowboy movies, of a Texas sheriff not overly shy about reaching for his equalizer. But—again "but," always "but" in Nicaragua—the ambassador gamely appeared on television in Managua in a brisk policy debate with Sandinista officials who outnumbered but diplomatically did not overwhelm him. This took place in December 1983, when it was devoutly believed by many Americans and by most of the three million Nicaraguans that the United States would at any moment invade the country and replace its government.

The threat of invasion has hung over Nicaragua like a heavy cloud that may burst at any moment or else blow away. Percep-

I BLOOD

ON A BLASTED CORNER IN MANAGUA, a city which, for all purposes beyond the sentimental need of every people to call some place their capital, ceased to exist after the earthquake of 1972, three white buildings continued to stand until the beginning of 1978. Some pedestrians hurried to them, others avoided them with a sneer or a shudder. The buildings were painted white not because it is popular and cheap in the tropics—yellow and beige and pink resist the daily dust better and look cleaner longer—but because they performed a singular medical function that made a hygienic veneer convenient. Citizens who visited the buildings came to bleed into small transparent bags. The processed results were shipped north, part of the raw materials Nicaragua exported to the United States. American shortages led to brisk trading in one of the few commodities Nicaragua had in abundance. Surely this must be the kind of "illuminating detail" journalists are supposed to look for, the part that reveals the whole. What greater exploitation can there be for an impoverished people than to have their own blood extracted for the benefit of their imperial masters?

Well, yes. But the trouble with everything in Nicaragua is that one detail leads to another, to almost infinite others, until each by itself has only as much significance as a dot in a pointillist painting. The next dot may reject the last and in turn be denied by its successor as part of a series of contradictions and paradoxes that threaten to swallow one another. A clear case of capitalist imperialism or communist oppression, of social progress or economic collapse, need only be turned slightly on its axis in order to be seen as its opposite. It is not that nothing is true in Nicaragua but that the truth dissolves into a collection of meanings whose common thread is their ambiguity. A visit to Nicaragua is a visit to a state of flux.

A priest says the Sandinistas who control Nicaragua are trying to crush the mother church; a nun swears she found God in the revolution. One industrialist accuses the government of stifling free enterprise; another claims the revolution has been good for business. A State Department official condemns the "asphyxiating corruption and oppression" in Nicaragua, but it is the only Central American country where the United States ambassador can go around without bodyguards. The ambassador himself, during my first visit at a critical instant in Nicaragua's relationship with the United States in 1983, was available to a wide range of visitors. He could be found confronting hostile delegations from the United States as well as granting interviews to virtually any journalist who made a determined effort to see him. But he refused to be quoted in the American press, insisting he be referred to as "a Western diplomat." The phrase summons an image, for anyone raised on cowboy movies, of a Texas sheriff not overly shy about reaching for his equalizer. But—again "but," always "but" in Nicaragua—the ambassador gamely appeared on television in Managua in a brisk policy debate with Sandinista officials who outnumbered but diplomatically did not overwhelm him. This took place in December 1983, when it was devoutly believed by many Americans and by most of the three million Nicaraguans that the United States would at any moment invade the country and replace its government.

The threat of invasion has hung over Nicaragua like a heavy cloud that may burst at any moment or else blow away. Perceptions and judgments are sharpened in such a crisis; praise becomes an incantation, criticism a curse. Putting many of their meager resources into education, the revolutionaries sing proudly of being on the verge of a triumphant conquest of illiteracy among peasants and workers. The middle class complains that the newly literate are taught history, sociology, and economics along Marxist lines. A report of the Americas Watch Committee titled "Human Rights in Central America" concluded that "Nicaragua shows no signs of evolving in the direction of a democratic society in which freedom of expression is respected." Although the Americas Watch Committee softened its judgment in a subsequent report, comparing Nicaragua favorably with the other Central American countries, the tree of Nicaraguan liberty is seldom seen to be well watered. Americans point confidently to our own civil liberties and Bill of Rights as freedom's touchstones for the world. But Nicaraguans are not buying American these days. "Your freedom, sir," said Daniel Ortega Saavedra, then the head of Nicaragua's revolutionary junta and later the country's president, as we talked alone late one hot December night at Government House in Managua, "your freedom is a monster."

Who validates Nicaraguan history? A secret State Department memorandum has a clarifying passage: "Central America has always understood that governments which we recognize and support stay in power, while those which we do not recognize and support fall. Nicaragua has become a test case. It is difficult to see how we can afford to be defeated. Usually it has been sufficient for us to intervene on the sole pretext of furnishing protection to American lives and property." This memorandum, dealing so candidly with "pretext" as a basis for policy, was written in 1927 by Assistant Secretary of State Robert Edwin Olds and declassified in the 1960s. Does current thinking—that of the White House and State Department—repudiate this attitude as unhelpfully anachronistic, or does it reaffirm America's manifest hemispheric destiny? Is Nicaragua the first mainland domino, falling long enough after Cuba to make Fidel Castro's revolution an antecedent rather than a precedent? What is the

Soviet role? Given the actions of the United States as well as Nicaragua's momentum, what are the revolution's prospects? What might an appropriate American response to Nicaragua be? Is there a point, in terms of libertarian expectations, where the Sandinista revolution can be said to have betrayed itself?

The questions seemed pertinent in the United States. In Nicaragua they recede dizzyingly before new questions, an agenda with its own demands, a socialism, for instance, hopelessly married to capitalism. Soaring and plunging, the revolution looks like a kite in an uncertain wind. People live normally, ordinarily—and also on the edge of peril and madness. The cast of characters might be from one of those Renaissance canvases that seem to include everyone in Florence.

What a relief to return for a moment to the simplicity of the Managua blood bank, draining the malnourished prerevolutionary Nicaraguans for the benefit of the rich United States, swollen like a tick from sucking up the life substance of its subjects to the south. Except it was not exactly a blood bank. It was essentially a plasmapheresis center, where the donor's blood, after removal, was centrifuged to separate out the plasma. The packed red cells and other blood components were mixed with saline solution and reinfused into the donor. The plasma itself was shipped to the United States.

According to a hematologist who received the plasma in New York City and a research chemist who inspected the plasmapheresis process in Managua, the center's health standards were the highest of any such facility in the world. The plasma produced was superior (with less risk of infectious hepatitis, for example) to what could be obtained from comparable centers in the United States. The three white buildings in Managua contained 250 beds and were capable of handling fifteen hundred donors a day. When the operation was at its peak, twenty thousand liters of plasma were shipped to the United States every month, approximately seven times as much as that produced by the average center in a big American city. The huge volume held the price of plasma down in the United States and made it possible for patients in charity wards to have operations and medical treatment that other-

wise would have been completely out of their reach. Nicaraguan plasma kept American hemophiliacs, who at that time were almost completely dependent on a steady flow of blood, from having to pay with their lives for lapses in our own social policy and individual generosity.

The Nicaraguan donors were attended by twenty-four doctors and received better medical care than that provided at plasmapheresis centers in New York, Chicago, or Los Angeles. Because of malnutrition in Nicaragua, relatively high percentages of volunteers were rejected each month; they were given free food and a supply of vitamins, with instructions to try again the following month. Those accepted as donors were fed a hot meal after their plasma donation, and they were paid the equivalent in Nicaraguan córdobas of what their counterparts at American commercial plasmapheresis centers were then receiving in dollars. The pay, of course, was the reason the center attracted so many donors among the unemployed from all over Nicaragua. The córdobas amounted to wages for the wretched, and the plasmaseparation process had so little effect on their health that they were able, like volunteers in the United States, to donate as frequently as twice a week.

Then everyone was served: Nicaraguans and Americans each got something they desperately needed.

But there is one more detail. The Managua center was jointly owned by an exiled Cuban doctor and by Anastasio Somoza Debayle, dictator of Nicaragua and third in his family, after his father and brother, to hold that post with the political and economic support of the United States. Although Somoza and the Cuban exile, Dr. Pedro Ramos, did pay the donors between $5 and $10 for each unit of plasma, they sold it for a greater than 300 percent markup. For twenty thousand liters per month at approximately $50 per liter, the yearly take was around $12 million. Somoza, bleeding his own people, had turned his country into the ultimate family business. When *La Prensa,* the Managua newspaper that once opposed the Somozas and later opposed the Sandinistas, ran a series of articles in 1977 denouncing the traffic in blood, Dr. Ramos sued its editor, Pedro Joaquín Chamorro, for libel. He lost the suit and moved to Miami. In January 1978, Chamorro was assassinated, and a captured hit man identified Ramos as having put out the contract.

Managua erupted. Opposition to Somoza had been led by the Sandinistas, but their support was fragmentary. Now the opposition suddenly became much more broadly based as it coalesced around the death of Pedro Joaquín Chamorro. Forty thousand enraged mourners followed Chamorro's casket from his house to *La Prensa*. Part of the crowd split off and surrounded the plasmapheresis center. A full year and a half before the triumph of the Sandinista revolution, furious Nicaraguans set fire to the plasmapheresis headquarters and burned it down. Somoza lost a business and his customers lost access to 15 percent of the world's plasma supply. The Nicaraguans' name for the center they destroyed was *casa de vampiros*.

II STOCK FOOTAGE

BY DECEMBER 1983 the United States and Nicaragua were trading accusations every day, and every day confirmed the imminence of war. For the United States, the Grenada landings had been accomplished so cheaply and effectively that invasion was spoken of in Washington as the strong right arm of foreign policy. For Nicaragua, each threat from the North fortified the position of hard-liners among the Sandinistas who felt war was inevitable. Each side was having fantasies about the other.

The United States government saw Nicaragua variously as a case of gangrene, or cancer, or as a dagger pointed at the Río Grande. This was not a new fantasy. The vision of hemispheric menace to the United States has existed at least since the Monroe Doctrine was issued in 1823 with the primary intent of keeping European powers from further colonization of the New World. But the vision contained a contradiction. While their country was a menace, Nicaraguans themselves were seen as barely able to tie their shoelaces, much less run their own affairs.

On their side, Nicaraguans saw the United States as an omnipotent Jove liable equally (and also contradictorily) to hurl thunderbolts from the north and to quiet the noisy affairs of the smaller, poorer countries in the equatorial sun. This vision of American power may be more in accord with international reality than the American vision of a gangrenous Nicaragua, but it led to the paranoid conclusion within the Sandinista government that domestic opposition was inevitably associated with treasonous CIA conspiracy. It also led to the impression that the United States can work its will in the world simply by flexing its muscles. Waiting for the United States to make up its mind was so ingrained in Nicaraguan life that from left to right in the political spectrum a national inferiority complex could be discerned.

The southern fantasy of northern omnipotence, like the northern fantasy of threat from southern independence, did not originate with the Sandinistas in 1979. As early as the 1820s the citizens of the Central American Federation, newly freed from Spain, began to look to the United States to settle their disputes and buy their raw materials. For the next century and a half, the outlines of the relationship between the United States and Nicaragua seldom blurred. With exceptions that proved brief, Nicaragua accepted its dependency the way its neighbors did theirs. When the Sandinistas finally overthrew the Somozas in 1979, they took control of a people ambitious for independence from the United States but far more accustomed to dependence.

Looking at Nicaragua in the 1980s, any American government would find itself contending with shadows in a dark thicket. Does this Central American backwater, in the flow of its revolutionary tide, threaten to wash over us if we don't dam it? Or does Nicaragua reflect our own spent country come of middle age, waiting for a second wind, wondering what to do with itself? If Dante, who knew a midlife crisis when he saw one, could return to make his journey through Central America, El Salvador would offer him at least snapshots of *Inferno*. *Paradiso,* despite Costa Rican aspirations, would be served up only by Club Med. For *Purgatorio,* the hope, torment, disappointment, promise and uncertainty belong to Nicaragua.

Preparing to go to Nicaragua, I visited a film library. Since pictures convey, however momentarily, a sense of being somewhere else, I hoped to get a feel for the people and terrain of a country I had never seen. The newsreel collection and television stock footage were a sampling of what Americans had been shown of Nicaragua over the years. In the initials favored by scriptwriters and the card-catalogue summarizers at the library, what I was treated to was the American POV.

"Dateline, Nicaragua, 1926" was the earliest American point of view, with narration laid in years later, after sound had been added to motion pictures. Marines are shown landing in Nicaragua, described as a "small but strategically located country" that has become a "hotbed of changing political power and open revolution." The narrator telescopes several events and years. He describes President Calvin Coolidge sending Henry Stimson (later Herbert Hoover's secretary of state, and still later Franklin Roosevelt's secretary of war) as his special envoy to make peace between the warring Nicaraguans. A formally dressed Stimson arrives in Managua, full of the take-charge energy of an official from up north. To see him is to feel that Manifest Destiny and the Monroe Doctrine are all that occupy his mind. The pictures project a man of duty and principle, a can-do man, contrasting with his relaxed hosts who wear rumpled clothes and look, when compared with North American custom, as though they are on permanent vacation. Through Stimson and the Marines, the narrator says, "the United States proved once again its dedication to peace and freedom around the world."

Stimson worked quickly. In his memoir of this mission to Nicaragua, Stimson recalled his meeting with the principal Nicaraguan rebel, General José María Moncada: "In less than thirty minutes we understood each other and had settled the matter. . . . He then returned to his army and on the following day I received a telegram signed by him and by all his chieftains except Sandino formally agreeing to lay down their arms and asking that American forces be immediately sent to receive them and 'guarantee order, liberty, and prosperity.' . . . The only exception was Sandino. . . . " Stimson was referring to one of Moncada's generals, Augusto César Sandino, who refused to accept a settlement he regarded as making Nicaragua a protectorate of the United States. He promised to rebel against foreign domination.

The key feature of Stimson's peace treaty provided for the establishment of a National Guard to be trained by Americans.

In 1927, "Revolution brings U.S. Marines to Nicaraguan soil." The Marines have begun their six-year hunt for Sandino. By now they have local help, with the card catalogue describing a "pan shot of loyal native troops carrying wounded soldiers along street," followed quickly by a "semi-close shot of a revolutionist sharpening a machete." In 1928, President-elect Hoover goes to Nicaragua and is greeted by President Díaz, whom Stimson had placed in power during *his* visit, though that information is left out of the visual story. Adolfo Díaz, who has been brought to power several times by the United States, looks grateful, and the recently elected, un-Depressed Herbert Hoover looks sure of his ability to engineer the Central American republics toward stable democracy.

An earthquake strikes in 1931, and "natives salvage their belongings from the ruins of still-smoldering Managua." The natives are not left to fend for themselves since there happen to be "a thousand U.S. Marines stationed in the city helping to restore order following the shock and fire which turned the town into a roaring inferno." In a "Remember When" newsreel of the 1930s, Gabriel Heatter looks back nostalgically—"You remember the bandit rebel Sandino"—and shows a picture of a worried-looking man in a white bandanna doffing his white sombrero for the camera. Sandino is surrounded by civilians in ties and appears uncomfortable, but he manages to smile. It is the shy smile of an uneasy man whose wary, unsmiling eyes declare his wish to be elsewhere. Gabriel Heatter says no more about him. The Marines never do catch up with Sandino and eventually leave Nicaragua in the hands of the National Guard and its leader, Anastasio Somoza García. To close out the 1930s, President Roosevelt welcomes Anastasio Somoza García, Somoza I, who by now has long since dispatched Sandino, into the White House. All smiles, both leaders sporting the jaunty FDR cigarette holder. If FDR said in private, "Somoza may be a son of a bitch, but he's our son of a bitch," this was not part of the image presented to the American public by the White House press corps. For the press as well as the Administration's protocol specialists, the occasion was regarded as a dress rehearsal for the king and queen of England, who followed Somoza I to the White House in 1939.

At an airfield in 1943, President Calderón of Costa Rica alights from a Cadillac limousine and waits while Somoza I, now in a general's uniform, climbs out after him. It is Somoza's birthday, and an honor guard attends, ready to salute him. Somoza has swelled toward blimphood in the newsreel, and Calderón of Costa Rica watches as though he cannot believe that so much man can get out of a single car even if it is a limo. As Somoza strains to get out the Cadillac's door, the camera notices that he has, curiously, an iron cross similar to the Germans' on top of his hat. Somoza finally makes it out of the car. Bemedaled, be-ribboned, Somoza smiles and the family double chins assume sausage proportion. Gold braid drips from his uniform as he salutes the honor guard, who troop by him with bayonets on their rifles. They are doing a goose step they did not learn at Fort Benning or Camp Lejeune. In succeeding decades, hemispheric historians have speculated on Latin dictators' affinity for the Axis cause. Did Somoza secretly want the Germans to win? Was that his generation's, and class's, fantasy of independence from the United States? Did the dictator hope to trade his status as American puppet for that of a Nazi proconsul in the Western Hemisphere?

It was not to be. In 1954, "U.S. Air Force planes make a historic goodwill flight through twelve 'Good Neighbor' nations of Central and South America." Though this is not mentioned in the newsreel, six weeks before the goodwill flight the CIA had overthrown Guatemala's president, Jacobo Arbenz. While the narrator praises his loyalty to the United States, Somoza I and his wife greet the American pilots who have descended on Managua.

But nothing is ever so orderly and reliable in the Latin countries. Somoza I stares upward with his glassy eyes in 1956 while lying on the floor after being shot by the poet Rigoberto López Perez during a reception. In 1956 it is still possible to believe assassinations do not happen in thoroughly civilized countries.

But Nicaragua recovers with a smart show of continuity; Somoza's son is ready to take the helm. Luis Somoza—Somoza II—is an agronomist by training and choice, and he is shown advising farmers on crop production. His brother, Anastasio, is shown in uniform, more like his father than Luis is, emerging in the 1960s as a Central American strongman. In 1967, a television newsman asks Anastasio Somoza Debayle, during his own first election campaign, if it is true he has jailed his principal opponent. "My opponent is a funny man," Anastasio answers in perfect English, inflected only as much as Ricardo Montalban's might be. "He encouraged his followers to subversion and a firefight. The authorities had to put him in jail to keep order. Now, closing the newspaper is not wise, but Nicaragua is a very special place—the paper is used for subversion, so it had to be closed. Many of the people in the firefight were trained in Havana, some in Moscow. What are we going to do? We have to fight Communism." The election over, he becomes Somoza III.

The genial Luis Somoza is stricken with a heart attack. President Johnson, who knows about heart attacks, sends his own specialist. Luis Somoza dies, but his brother has already taken his place. The dynasty achieves its fullest flower.

In 1972, Somoza III welcomes Howard Hughes to Managua, but the photo opportunity is unsatisfactory because Hughes refuses to come to the press conference. In the posh Hotel Intercontinental (the reclusive Hughes would not leave his penthouse suite to come downstairs), Somoza announces, "He's my guest. If I don't see him it's okay. Maybe he doesn't want to be seen for many days or many years." Somoza's chins recall those of his father. His West Point ring seems to weigh down his pudgy hand. When he smiles, which he frequently does, the back part of his cheeks almost obscures his ears. But he is also, in his way, sensual, with curving, expressive lips, eyes that command and plead at the same time. He can probably outdrink anyone in Managua all night and still show up in a dark suit and white shirt with a red-and-green tie for this conference with the international press. Hughes, however, is more than even a well-trained dictator can handle. Somoza reads a letter from the financier that ends by saying, "I look forward with pleasure to our future contacts," but he never says they will be in person, which in fact they never were.

Hope Somoza, the dictator's wife, arrives at the airport in Managua to meet her husband, who is returning from a state visit to Panama. On the tarmac a band plays while an honor guard stands at attention. Somoza's personal jet lands. The band plays, the guard struts, Somoza descends the ramp. The camera looks for Mrs. Somoza but does not find her. The narrator goes on with his story about Somoza's friendship mission to Panama. What Managua learned the next day, but American network audiences did not, is that just before Somoza's own plane landed, a regularly scheduled Pan Am flight arrived from Panama. When she saw her husband's mistress, Dinorah Sampson, get off the Pan Am flight, Hope Somoza shot out of the airport in her Mercedes.

The 1972 earthquake strikes and the son of Somoza III, slated to become Somoza IV in time, is called down from Harvard to manage earthquake relief. The young Somoza looks very tired and has obviously been working long hours. Refugees walk by him as he tells the interviewer, "We have the distribution problems solved now. The reason I have been put here is we want to keep the distribution honest." In the next shot he gives an order in Spanish to a senior officer; what the younger Somoza does not see, but the camera does, is that the officer snickers. "Keep the rice and beans coming," young Somoza says to the American television audience, "because that's what we all eat."

"I'd like to take this opportunity," says the senior Somoza, wearing tinted glasses and five stars on his uniform, "to thank the U.S. government, President Nixon, and the good-willed people of the United States." Over a picture of a man hitting a home run, the narrator announces that Roberto Clemente, the Pittsburgh Pirates' star outfielder, is missing and presumed dead when his privately chartered plane, flying earthquake relief supplies to Managua, has disappeared.

A crowd chants "So-mo-za" repeatedly, accompanied by a huge demonstration featuring horns, drums and marchers. The crowd cheers when firecrackers are set off, cheers louder when the dictator appears and calls them his *amigos* to whom he is bringing *democracía.* He is a little less fat than at the Interconti- nental, hair all black, totally in command. Hope Somoza is by his side. She is beautiful in a pouting, upper-class way, with lonely eyes, her mouth showing lines on either side falling down to her chin. She looks uneasily at the throng. She is dressed loyally with the red scarf of a Somoza supporter around her neck, but it is slightly out of place with her gold earrings and Balmain dress. The wife of a politician, she is close to power and power- less. She smiles momentarily at someone in the crowd—a sister, an oligarch's wife, a lover, someone who almost understands what she is going through? Does she wait on his mistresses, see them out the door, arrange their abortions in Miami? There is no misery, for Hope Somoza, like misery clad in silk. The dictator finishes declaiming about *libertad,* and the crowd again chants "So-mo-za!" Every one in the picture claps except one body- guard and Hope Somoza.

By 1978 Somoza III is graying, thinner though still pudgy, and his eyes sag. In his early fifties, it is not clear if he is more debauched or careworn, but his shoulders slope and his carriage is that of a man in his late sixties. The narrator says a revolt is in progress against the Somoza rule. A correspondent asks Somoza how he feels about the assassination of the editor of *La Prensa,* Pedro Joaquín Chamorro, killed after his newspaper exposed the profiteering of Somoza's plasmapheresis center. "We knew Pedro Joaquín as an adversary. He was a good enemy to have, though some of his writings were caustic." Somoza adds that the presumed ringleader of the assassination, Dr. Pedro Ramos, the Cuban exile who ran the plasmapheresis center in Managua, is now an American citizen living in Miami and would therefore pose a complicated problem in extradition. He does not add that he was Dr. Ramos' partner in the plasmapheresis center.

Later in 1978, Somoza speaks to a small crowd of his support- ers from a wraparound bulletproof transparent shield that distorts his features. In one shot his mouth looks like a tunnel, his eyes like those of an exotic tropical fish. Hope Somoza is no longer by his side. In the front row of his supporters, looking proud of herself and of Somoza, is Dinorah Sampson. She has smiling eyes, bedroom eyes they were once called, and is younger than Hope Somoza, whom she has outlasted. (Mrs. Somoza has removed to Florida, New York, and London.) Somoza is too decayed for the Latin lover; he is ready for character parts. In fact, he is ready to play the dictator trying to hold on. He shouts, proclaims, promises, pleads. The choice is *democracía* or *comunismo*. He finishes, and the crowd begins its chant for him, but he does not wait. In seven remarkable seconds of screen time, Somoza dashes from his bulletproof shield to his bulletproof limousine. The next shot shows upper-middle-class housewives demonstrating against the regime as soldiers throw tear-gas canisters at them. In an interview, Somoza says, "Our country needs a civil war like a hole in the head."

Led by the Sandinista Edén Pastora Gómez, who calls himself Commander Zero, a squad of revolutionaries storms the National Palace and holds sixty-seven Nicaraguan congressmen and one thousand government officials hostage. Against the advice of his generals, Somoza negotiates and releases fifty-nine political prisoners, publishes the Frente Sandinista de Liberación Nacional (FSLN) program, and pays a ransom of $500,000. The camera shows a yellow school bus on its way to the airport with political prisoners, who will be flown to Havana. The FSLN leaders in the bus wave to a small crowd outside; a few in the crowd cheer and wave back. Among the released prisoners is Tomás Borge, last surviving founder of the FSLN.

In an interview later in 1978, a newsman asks Somoza how he feels. Somoza is sitting down, sallow. "I feel better than I did before the heart attack," he says. An American announces to the camera, "My name is Norman Wolfson, and I'll be working with the president as his press secretary."

Outside for an early-morning photo opportunity, Somoza takes an exercise walk around the driveway of his bunker in Managua. He wears tennis whites. Even in the walled bunker, he is accompanied by a bodyguard with bulging latissimis dorsi. The bodyguard is red-haired and wears gold dog tags. To show how healthy he is, Somoza pounds his chest with the hand carrying the West Point ring. He is said to be the only West Pointer ever to receive an entire army as a graduation present. (Before West Point, Bernard Dietrich notes in his valuable biography of the family, Somoza went to La Salle Military Academy on Long Island, where his classmates referred to him as a spic. He apparently believed them. When in power, he saved his contempt for his Nicaraguan advisers, preferring the company of visiting Americans.) Somoza, jowly but tall and erect, circles his bunker driveway and tells the network correspondent that he does this for forty-five minutes every morning. He does look slimmer than the pictures have ever shown him. A dwarf comes with a towel; he leaps to pat the sweat off his master's brow. Somoza has lost enough weight so that his flesh has begun to look like folds of a curtain that has too much material for the size of the window it is covering. "The issue in Nicaragua today is the survival of democratic government in this country," Somoza tells the correspondent. "My ideals are basically the ideals the average North American has, and Nicaragua has similar interests to the United States. The Somoza of 1936 is not the Somoza of 1978." He sees his brother, father, and himself, then, as one person who has changed and grown over the years. In the early-morning light he looks exhausted.

Wearing a civilian suit with a white handkerchief peeking smartly out of the left breast pocket, Somoza hurries from his limousine into a military hospital to visit his wounded. In the ward he comes to a young soldier who sits right up in bed and tells his leader he is not too bad, but in the next bed a National Guardsman's leg is almost torn off. Somoza looks pained and tells him, "Keep going, *amigo.*" In the next shot, he hugs a boy with many holes in his bare buttocks and one of his legs. A soldier congratulates Somoza, who thanks him for his sacrifice. The next man says he was wounded in Chinandega, the man after him was shot in Matagalpa, the next man in Rivas. The enemy is getting closer; all of these towns are less than sixty miles from Managua. The Chinandega man has seven bullets in his arm. Somoza asks if he is in pain and he says no. He pats the man on the foot gently and moves on to bestow his gratitude among the boys and men who have been hurt trying to preserve him in power. Watching these scared young Nicaraguans, it is impossible not to wonder what has become of them. Are they in the mountains with the counterrevolutionaries or home cheering for Tomás Borge and Daniel Ortega, or building houses or plowing a furrow somewhere, or simply dead?

An interviewer asks Somoza about allegations of atrocities by the National Guard. It is May 1979. "The National Guard is a professional institution. They are trained and educated ninety-eight percent by the United States of America. They are people who believe in democracy." The interviewer asks how Nicaraguans become Guard members. "They are not pressed into service. This is a voluntary organization. They need to eat. They need clothing and shelter. So they come into the National Guard."

A network cameraman has found eleven dead bodies by Lake Managua. The correspondent tells us they were killed by the National Guard, which then burned the bodies. Behind him smoke rises from a rib cage; behind the rib cage several partial skeletons still have their hands tied behind them; behind the skeletons is the lake. The correspondent explains that the black smoke off to one side is not from the bodies themselves but is instead caused by tires and other rubber materials burned by the National Guard in an attempt to overwhelm the stench of burning flesh in Managua. At a cocktail party for the press and networks, Somoza tells a correspondent, "They think I'm some kind of ogre. I'm really not, you know. We have our faults here, we don't deny that."

Bill Stewart, an ABC News correspondent in Managua, is commanded by several National Guardsmen to approach them and kneel. He does so while his cameraman continues filming from perhaps twenty yards away. A Guardsman orders Stewart to lie on the ground and stands directly above him. When the Guardsman shoots Stewart through the head, causing his body to make a bouncy little flutter before lying still, the camera jiggles but does not stop recording the scene. Somoza looks somber at his press conference. "I have already ordered a full investigation of this painful and dreadful incident, and I assure you that the individual or individuals responsible for it either by actions or omissions will receive the full weight of the law. I have been advised that film of this tragic incident has already been exhibited in the United States and perhaps the rest of the world."

The FSLN is welcomed into León, a university town and Nicaragua's traditional city of intellectual ferment. Two flatbed trucks carry several dozen happy Sandinistas in their red-and-black scarves. They are cheered by people who throw flowers at them. The camera cuts inside to what looks like the meeting room of a board of directors. The new ruling junta sits soberly in a line of high-backed chairs. Daniel Ortega's hair is mussed and he looks suspiciously at the camera, perhaps uncertain as to whether he welcomes it into his life or not. Tomás Borge demands the surrender of the National Guard. In Managua, Somoza tells several correspondents, "León is the first city on the mainland of America under Communist rule." One of the correspondents asks him about the attitude of the United States. "I don't know how the United States is feeling toward my government, so whatever I'd tell you would be nonsensical."

In Cuernavaca, former President Nixon visits the former shah of Iran at a stately red-tiled villa of pink adobe. Posing with the shah on the steps of the villa, Nixon tries to make small talk but gets no reply. Nixon waves at the camera. The shah, already very sick, smiles his pained smile and keeps his hands behind his back. Empress Farah stands next to the shah, expressionless. The camera cuts to Nixon alone, outside the villa. He is asked about developments in Nicaragua. "You don't grease the skids for your friends," he says. "The choice we face is not between President Somoza and somebody better but between President Somoza and somebody much worse."

Behind his tinted glasses, Somoza blinks frequently and gets his mouth to smile, listening patiently to questions. He wears a short-sleeved blue shirt. "I have fought Communism for thirty years," he says. "I have been affected by foreign forces—Cuba, Costa Rica, Venezuela, Panama. There is no parallel in the history of the Americas where countries have ganged up against another country like they have ganged up on me." He makes no distinction between his country and his person. He is asked if he includes the Carter Administration as part of the conspiracy against him. "I refuse to criticize the United States." He is asked where he is going. "I cannot say." He sighs. "I want to appeal to the American people and tell them that if Nicaragua goes to the Communists, you will have them right next door at the Rio Grande in a few years. I am not trying to make a case for me because my fate is already sealed."

In the middle of the night on July 17, 1979, a black limousine is barely visible hurtling past the camera. The narrator says that President Somoza is on his way to the airport. Estimates of Somoza's personal fortune range from $100 million to $500 million. In a small truck are the coffins of his brother and his father. The presidential jet takes off for Miami carrying all three Somozas.

Two days later, a crowd estimated at 200,000 jams into Managua's central plaza between the National Assembly building and the cathedral destroyed by the 1972 earthquake. "Nicaraguans hail the victorious Sandinistas and wonder what the future will bring."

Black-and-white footage from Paraguay in September 1980 shows the remains of a limousine that has been destroyed by bazookas. There are no remains of Anastasio Somoza to be seen since his entire body has been blown apart. Standing by the destroyed limousine, Dinorah Sampson, who has rushed to the scene from the home she and Somoza shared, yells at the camera to go away.

III   WHERE IS NICARAGUA?

A MIRROR IS almost the first object a visitor comes in contact with in Nicaragua. Above each customs booth at Sandino International Airport a mirror perches, tilting downward over the heads of arriving passengers, enabling the customs officer to look at people's lower extremities if that is what he wants to do. Perhaps he is helped most if he is doing a class analysis of the footwear sported by guests coming to interrogate or adore his revolution: cycle boots, brass-buckled Guccis, scuffed Adidas. The impression of surveillance is fortified by a sign on the booth quoting General Augusto César Sandino's advice to be on the lookout for *los imperialistas yanquis*. The mirror is straight from East Germany, which has provided technique and training to the Sandinista security apparatus. But the customs officer is not East German. He is rumpled and smiling, he is puffy with midnight sleepiness, and he is, if ethnic generalizations can still be applied without insult, very Latin. "*Bienvenido*. Enjoy," he says.

Above the baggage inspection ramp a sign said, in English, "Welcome to Nicaragua. You'll love it." An official was inspecting a porn magazine he had found in the luggage of the passenger ahead of me, a Nicaraguan returning from Miami. After he gave the magazine back to its owner, he conscientiously searched my belongings before waving me through. Suspicious that everyone was an agent for us or them and worried that the widely predicted invasion was about to begin, I glanced furtively at the night sky for planes or parachutes before sharing a cab with two Americans who spoke with slight Spanish accents. They said they were businessmen from Iowa, tire retreaders come down to do some merchandising in Nicaragua. Of course, and next week cabbages will sing. Can't the Company think up a better cover than that? Still, all the way into town they kept up their chatter about the Nicaraguans needing retreads since they could not afford to buy new tires. Who knew?

By all the norms and wicker of the international hospitality industry's tropical division, Hotel El Camino Real is easily Managua's best. First World luxury set in Third World ambience, fashionably elevated bar above a large clean pool, tennis courts, private jogging course, rooms so relentlessly air-conditioned they rebuke the entire country that surrounds them. El Camino's problem is that it is situated so close to the airport it has more to do with entering or leaving Nicaragua than with actually being there. With the choice narrowed, the bulk of the international news-gathering community, except for ABC News which secretes itself at El Camino, turns to the prerevolutionary, pre-earthquake trapezoidal hive called the Intercontinental. It is the Elaine's of Central America. The Intercontinental buzzes with journalists, photographers, TV crews, presumed agents, visiting U.S. officials in-country for a quick briefing but not important enough to stay with the ambassador, town gossips, Marxist theoreticians delivered straight from La Coupole along with their Gauloises, revolution groupies, Sandinista press officers and poets, black marketeers, idealists gathered for one more chance to remake the world.

Rising in tiers like a Mayan pyramid, the Intercontinental sits on a sloping hill above what would be downtown Managua if there were still a town to be down in. Because of the hill, the hotel seems much taller than its nine stories. Although the Intercontinental is even less representative of life in Managua than the Helmsley Palace is of life in New York City, its magnetism for such a diverse congregation allows it to reveal certain of the revolution's sliding, free-form realities.

The night I arrived, Orson Welles was crowding out all other objects on the small television screen in the bar. As in many American bars, the sound was turned off while the set stayed on for the sake of the pictures, providing the comforting mirage of more people in the room having a better time than was actually the case. Orson Welles in *A Touch of Evil*—murder and intrigue between gringos and Latinos—was followed by a trailer for a forthcoming *Lou Grant* episode, then *Laverne and Shirley.*

Two young men came in from the pool, where there was a big party with spirited dancing. The music from the loudspeakers around the pool almost drowned out the Nicaraguans when they asked what I was doing in their country.

Periodista, I said.

"Oh, a journalist."

Sí, I said, not quite ready to give up and speak my own language.

"Yes," they said. "Did you come to see the revolution?"

Isn't that why everyone comes now?

"Do you like it?"

I don't know. I've only been here ten minutes. Do you?

Wait a minute! One of them was crying. "No," he said, "it's not for me. It's good for some people, not for me."

He was eighteen, or thirty. It was dark in the bar, but the tears shone on his face and he tried to sniff them back.

Why isn't it good for you?

"It's not mine, it's not my dream, this revolution. I want to love it, and I can't."

On the television screen, *Laverne and Shirley* gave way to the FSLN logo: *Todas las Armas al Pueblo.* "All arms to the people" is the literal translation. "Learn to live with contradiction" would be the looser construction. The old mixed signal, an American sitcom followed by a Sandinista slogan.

Outside by the pool, young Nicaraguans were flinging themselves around with what I took to be a Central American version of reckless abandon. Where were the bomb shelters, the trenches? Where was the country under siege? Is this what I was so scared of? These people were enjoying graduation night, maybe the first Christmas ball of the season. It was hot, at least eighty degrees, and the sound system blared "Maniac" from *Flashdance* while the poolside party jumped and swarmed. Behind the dancers a wall perhaps fifteen feet high protected the Intercontinental from what used to be Managua. An ABC News crew came out onto the terrace and briefly filmed the dancers, throwing their shadows up against the wall with a Sun Gun light that gave the cameraman the exposure he wanted. They would need only a little footage. "Meanwhile, in beleaguered Managua at the center of the political storm, pre-Christmas revels go on as usual among the dwindling middle class." Elvis came on with "Hound Dog"—"You ain't never caught a rabbit and you ain't no friend of mine"—and the dancers' silhouettes kept time with one another on the wall.

I wondered what the U.S. Army Rangers would look like climbing over that wall in assault force. They would be followed by the Marines, of course; fifteen-foot walls are nothing to those guys. Together again, the same winning team that brought you Grenada. Now in living color. The press couldn't be barred from this one because the press was there first, charting the fall of Somoza day by day and then the rise and presumed fall of the revolution. By unintentionally sacrificing one of its own on camera—ABC's Bill Stewart—the press might even have hastened the departure from Nicaragua of Somoza III. The press was waiting now, searching everywhere for signs that would proclaim the imminent invasion by the United States or the internal collapse of the Sandinistas. Tiring of its vigil, NBC News went up to bed, the dancers oblivious, grinding Latinly on.

The Intercontinental affords a view of Managua, and beyond it Lake Managua, that is deceptively lush and peaceful. The palms, the rainbows of flowers, the poinciana and mimosa trees, and especially the weeds grow back so quickly it is hard to tell that beneath the foliate camouflage is a destroyed city. Since the hotel is a cluttered pleasure to live in, it, too, becomes a kind of disguise for what lies beyond. When the hotel is good it encourages sloth totally incongruous in revolutionary Nicaragua; when it is bad it elicits fantasy.

A clerk who feels like it can dole out a cell of a room, and I was at first given one of these. I remembered a facsimile of the Ugly American speech I once heard ranted in Havana: Look, señorita, I've seen better countries than yours blow away like dust when a determined U.S. president wants to stop the spread of anything farther to the left than a pink sunset. Iran 1953. Guatemala 1954, honey, Dominican Republic 1965, Chile 1973, don't forget it. El Salvador today. Bay of Pigs 1961, we got stopped on the one-yard line only because our nerve failed. Okay, okay, Saigon 1975, we wouldn't walk the last mile. But this is our backyard, sweetheart, always has been, always will be. So if you want your little fight-for-life reported favorably you'll bloody well give me a bigger room. The Pegler school of journalism. At the Caravelle in Saigon, the biggies, the combat freaks, the press vets, the World War II and Korea aristocrats would sit in the bar on the top floor telling stories of real wars and complaining that Vietnam wasn't worth their attention even though we *were* winning. Later on at the Intercontinental, I did see a reporter give a patented Ugly American performance that froze the entire lobby. In my case they choked off protest abruptly with the Commie ruse of a bigger room.

Fantasies disappear at the Intercontinental's front door. With the country on a wartime footing, armed police, militia, or members of the regular army were posted in various spots around Managua, some obviously strategic, others apparently random. A block from the hotel on my first morning in Nicaragua, I was halted by a soldier with a rifle. The rifle was strapped loosely around his shoulder and he was smiling, but unaccustomed to being stopped by people with guns, I put my hands up. He fiddled with the rifle barrel playfully as he asked for identification, idly sticking a finger down the muzzle. For a reason I did not then comprehend but shortly would, I had an impulse to tell him to be careful, that thing was not a toy. But I shut up and produced a passport and press card. The soldier fingered his rifle a little more and called over his superior, who was standing a few yards away. The senior authority looked at the identification, grinned, and told me I could go.

The crisis behind us, I decided to ask them how old they were. When they answered I understood why I had wanted to warn the first soldier about the lethal properties of his weapon. The one who had stopped me was thirteen, the one in charge seventeen. The thirteen-year-old was carrying a Russian BZM-52, the seventeen-year-old an AK-47, the standard Russian combat rifle used by the Nicaraguan army, known to everyone as an Ahka. Francisco, the younger soldier, was eager to be liked and seemed ready to ask for a candy bar, but glancing at both his uniform and his superior he restrained himself. He said he had worn the uniform and carried the rifle a little less than a year. Javier, the older boy, had been practicing with his Ahka for two years and hoped someday to become a carpenter. "When President Reagan lets us study and work," he said, "instead of defending our homes."

"We know the American people want peace," Francisco said, "if only your leaders would permit this." It was as though they believed the United States government is no expression of the national will but something imposed from above or outside, as governments in Nicaragua traditionally had been. In encounters with hundreds of Nicaraguans I met only one, a Special Forces soldier in the north, who believed American citizens are responsible for our government. Everyone else put average Americans on a pedestal above the government. Everyone else blamed the Administration, often Ronald Reagan himself, for policies that have placed as many as 7,000 American military personnel in Nicaragua's northern neighbor, Honduras, hostile armies of counterrevolutionaries on both their Honduran and Costa Rican borders, American warships on their Atlantic and Pacific coasts, and for an economic strategy that cut off Nicaragua's credits from the United States and denied it the opportunity to borrow from the International Monetary Fund and regional banks. Everyone else, beginning with these two teenagers, Francisco and Javier, exonerated the American people, with whom they said they wished only to be friendly, for the acts committed in our name by our leadership.

More than 90 percent of Nicaragua's population live in the western portion of the country and are descended from the Spaniards, who first settled the area in 1524 and ruled until 1821. Most Nicaraguans are mestizos, of mixed Spanish and Indian ancestry. But approximately sixty thousand Miskito Indians, never assimilated into the Spanish society of the West, live on the East Coast, along with several thousand other Indians and Caribbean blacks. Spain, which periodically came over the mountains and through the jungles to what became known as the Miskito Coast, never fully succeeded in conquering the Indians. If the eastern part of Nicaragua acknowledged any colonial power, it was England, which traded and pirated along the East Coast, never Spain. The word for Spaniard in the Miskito language is the same as the word for enemy.

Against the background of hostility between the two peoples and the two coasts, the Sandinistas pushed quickly to the Atlantic after their victory in 1979. By the mid-1980s, they admitted making mistakes in their treatment of the Miskitos. These were due, the Sandinistas said, largely to their overzealousness in trying to incorporate the Indians into the revolutionary process and to their lack of understanding of Miskito culture. Racial and ethnic prejudice undoubtedly was present as well; one does not have to venture far in Nicaragua to hear Miskitos described as lazy, dirty and backward. There is also some Catholic bias against the Moravian Church, the Protestant denomination most Miskitos belong to.

Sandinista abuse was accompanied by American propaganda. According to human-rights groups, radio broadcasts and leaflets from Honduras told the Miskitos the Communists were coming to bury them alive, prohibit their religion and language, steal their land and send their children to Russia. Numerous Miskito villagers expressed a fear, implanted by the counterrevolutionaries, that the Sandinistas' liquid polio vaccine would make them sterile. It was even said to be a potion containing the urine of Fidel Castro. The result of the propaganda and the Sandinistas' own mistreatment was a migration—at times almost a stampede—of Miskitos northward into Honduran refugee camps. The Miskitos have historically been spread out over both Nicaragua and Honduras. Between fifteen and twenty thousand Indians, perhaps one third the Miskito population, left Nicaragua in the early 1980s. After a couple of years in the Honduran refugee camps, several thousand drifted back.

One morning during my first week in Nicaragua a woman from the government press office, which the Sandinistas had shrewdly deposited, like a fishnet, in the Intercontinental, asked if I would go to the East Coast with three hundred Miskito Indians who were being repatriated. The Miskitos were essentially POWs granted amnesty in the hope that they would stop fighting the government.

Sandinista officials said the new Miskito villages were protected by government troops, secure from attacks by the counter-revolutionaries, *los contras*. The Indians would be free to build new lives for themselves. I felt I had too much to do in the far busier and more crowded west to join what smelled like a press junket to what sounded like a bunch of strategic hamlets, so I turned the trip down. Other Americans, however, including a lawyer visiting Nicaragua to investigate human-rights violations, went along and remained eight days on the East Coast with the Miskitos.

When they returned to Managua, they told of a thinly populated, exotic Miskito Coast, where coconut palms sway over villages of houses on stilts. They were able to reach some of the settlements only by boat. In several of them, books and doctors were unknown until the Sandinistas brought them. By the standards of the American visitors and their Nicaraguan guides, the older communities were filthy, with people often defecating upstream from where they did their laundry. There was a kind of random farming and fishing but almost no other organized economic activity. Into these conditions the government was trying to insert itself—through hygiene, modern crop techniques, inoculations for children, literacy. But the Sandinistas were often doing this with a heavy hand.

At the newly created community of Tasba Pri, described by one of the Americans as a Levittown on stilts, the principal complaints were homesickness and poverty. Having been forcibly moved approximately seventy miles south from their original land along the Río Coco, the river separating Nicaragua from Honduras, the Miskitos wanted simply to go home. Although it was possible to farm at Tasba Pri, the Miskitos were not finding the land nearly as fertile as it was along the Río Coco. *"Esta tierra es mala,"* one of the Americans heard repeatedly: This land is bad.

In an older village the Miskitos were resettling into new homes after previously being evacuated by the Sandinistas in order to deny a haven to the contras. The Miskitos were glad to get home, and their new government-built houses were better than the shacks and lean-tos they had left. But a number of them were afraid of the government because of its past treatment of them; the Americans found that when they used a Sandinista interpreter who spoke Miskito, the Indians were less communicative than when they used a Miskito interpreter who spoke English. The Miskitos told the Americans of harassment, unexplained arrests and rough handling by the government soldiers. In Walpasixa, a small settlement along the coast, the Sandinistas arrested half the men and carted them away. Later they were brought back. No one knew why the Sandinistas left the other half alone.

Many Miskitos had once worked for American lumber companies, which arrived in the 1930s, took all the pine they could find and got out in the 1960s. Some of the Indians had not been employed since the lumber companies left, but it was common for them to have American names and memories of better times, or at least of steady American pay. In successive villages one of the Americans met Miskitos named George Washington and Abraham Lincoln. Washington hated the Sandinistas; Lincoln was satisfied with them.

Both in Managua and along the East Coast, the government was making efforts to end the mistreatment of the early 1980s. In

one military zone, forty-two Sandinista soldiers were found to have committed what the court called "grave abuses" against the local Indian families. The forty-two were given prison sentences of up to thirty years (the death penalty was abolished by the Sandinistas). Later, beginning at the end of 1985 and continuing through 1986, the Nicaraguan government permitted large numbers of Miskitos to return to their old homes along the Río Coco, virtually on top of the Honduran border. Like so much else in Nicaragua, the new policy went in two directions; it won friends for the Sandinistas and also provided their enemies with new recruits.

In addition to punishing those commanders found guilty of cruelty to the Miskitos, the Sandinistas backed off from their earlier efforts to integrate (as they put it) or forcibly conform (as their critics put it) the Miskitos with the rest of Nicaraguan society. The Americas Watch Committee, with a history of being highly critical of the Sandinistas, found "important improvement" in their relations with Miskitos after 1985. The greater continuing problem is what happens to a culture and its members when war causes repeated uprooting. Those who visit the Indians often return with descriptions of individuals withdrawing into cocoons of despondency.

From a CIA perspective, the Miskitos and the East Coast are the Vietnamese Montagnards and the Central Highlands redux. The area in northeastern Nicaragua where many of the Miskitos live is actually called the highlands. Since Miskitos have always been estranged from whatever government was in Managua, as the Montagnards traditionally ignored Saigon, they are perfect marks for an enemy intelligence agency to recruit and run for a while, then drop when they are no longer useful.

Just before Christmas one year, an American Catholic bishop named Salvator Schlaefer, who had lived in Nicaragua for thirty-eight years, accompanied several hundred Miskitos north into Honduras, presenting the counterrevolutionaries with a considerable public-relations victory. Some of the Miskitos were armed members of the Misura, which was the Miskito affiliate of the contras and was supported by the CIA; others were reported to have gone north reluctantly, bewildered at being moved one more time. The rumor around Managua was that the Misura members had got lost in the jungle on their way to raid one village and wound up in another. This village contained Bishop Schlaefer and an American Catholic priest, Wendelin Shafer, who said later that he and the bishop happened to be visiting the Miskito village when the contras arrived to take everyone north. In Managua, trying for their own public-relations success, the Sandinistas reported Bishop Schlaefer had been killed by counter-revolutionaries. After three days' march, the Miskitos and the churchmen arrived safely in Honduras. Bishop Schlaefer was evacuated to the United States in time to spend the holidays with his mother in Wisconsin and receive the winning-coach-in-the-locker-room phone call from President Reagan on Christmas Day. Over the enterprise there hung confusion, missed opportunities on both sides, conflicting loyalties, and the whiff of a bungled CIA operation that accidentally succeeded. The following month, Bishop Schlaefer returned to work in Nicaragua, where he has remained ever since.

The Miskitos are important both as individuals and as a conscience for the Sandinistas. What will the revolution do with its weakest link? The question still remains unanswered. But although they need to consolidate and develop their territory in the east, the Sandinistas' primary concerns are on the other side of the country, where most Nicaraguans live. The war and the revolution will be won or lost in the west.

IV LEÓN AND CORINTO

TO TAKE A BETTER LOOK at the country and its revolution, I left Managua, heading for the old university town of León and the principal Nicaraguan port, Corinto.

Inside Managua, where government programs and control are strongest, it is often difficult to tell the difference between intention and accomplishment. A proclamation can engender so much enthusiasm that the project itself appears to be working. But like other large cities, Managua is a center of sophistication and jaded sensibilities, which means that skepticism about the revolution is also easy to find. Outside Managua, in the countryside, Nicaraguans tend to be neither cheering nor booing but simply coping. Here it is easier to get a sense of how the revolution is doing in its struggle against poverty, the contras and the tenacity with which some Nicaraguans cling to their prerevolutionary ways.

After Managua, the largest cities in Nicaragua are León, with 80,000 people, and Granada, with 55,000. (Managua itself had approximately 500,000 people in the early 1980s; after a rapid influx of refugees from the countryside, its population was said to have doubled by the end of 1986.) Population figures in Nicaragua are casual estimates—at times extremely casual, varying widely—because no census has been taken since the early 1970s. One of the problems the Sandinistas faced in organizing the country administratively and preparing for elections was that no one had a clear idea of who or where the potential voters were nor how many of them existed. The total population is variously reported between 2.8 and 3.2 million. Most Nicaraguans are still close to the soil, no more than a few miles or a single generation away.

Fifty-five miles northwest of Managua, León was the capital of Nicaragua from its settlement by Spaniards in 1524 until 1858. The small city, with low adobe houses, red tiled roofs, narrow streets and generous plazas, recalls sections of any Spanish American seat between Santiago and Santa Fe. León had the first university in Nicaragua and was a center of revolutionary ferment for the Sandinistas as well as for diverse radical movements before them. The old Liberal Party based itself in León, though the label carried less of an ideological than a sectional meaning. (Each of the Somozas was a Liberal.) León's traditional competitor was Granada, stronghold of the Conservative Party, forty miles southeast of Managua and founded the same year as León. Granada's Conservatives never accepted the primacy of León's Liberals, and the two cities—led by their political parties—were often at war. Largely as a result of a bizarre episode involving two Americans, León and Granada gave up their prominence in the 1850s and Managua, a cowtown in the hottest, lowest part of the country, became a compromise capital.

The episode is seldom remembered by Americans, never forgotten by Nicaraguans. Except that it set the tone in U.S.-Nicaraguan relations for the next century, the confrontation of William Walker with Cornelius Vanderbilt would have been an endearing duel between two different kinds of pirates. William Walker's singular contribution to history is that he conquered Nicaragua in the 1850s, conquered it not for the United States but simply for himself. The Liberals of León had invited Walker down to reinforce them in one of their wars against Granada's Conservatives. When he won, they could not get rid of him.

Walker burst out of Nashville, Tennessee, in a hurry and by

the time he was thirty had already enjoyed impostor careers as a doctor and lawyer while he did a little journalism on the side. He found his true calling as a "filibuster," a word applied to buccaneers along the Spanish American coasts before it came to mean nonstop talking to thwart legislation in the U.S. Congress. Hearing of Walker's exploits as a paramilitary adventurer in Mexico, León's Liberals asked for his help in 1855. With fifty-eight American mercenaries, whom he called his "immortals," and a new type of quick-action rifle, Walker captured Granada and set up a new regime. Officially, the United States government disdained him at first, but newspapers celebrated Walker as "the gray-eyed man of destiny." To a segment of the public he became an authentic American hero. Walker was master of Nicaragua, but he needed recruits from the United States to fortify his kingdom.

Cornelius Vanderbilt at this time operated a steamship line to bring easterners to look for gold in California. Displeased by Panama's malarial jungles, Vanderbilt planned eventually to put a canal across Nicaragua, but in the meantime he was running an ingenious ocean-river-lake-land-ocean service at a $2-million-a-year profit. Passengers sailed from New York to the East Coast of Nicaragua, where they were put aboard riverboats that carried them up the Río San Juan to Lake Nicaragua. Ferries took them across the lake to its western shore, where they would hit dry land for the first and only time. Twelve miles from Nicaragua's Pacific coast, Vanderbilt's commuters were put aboard sky-blue carriages with fringed canopies for the short journey over the only macadam road in Central America. Steamships from Vanderbilt's Pacific Line took them on the final leg to San Francisco.

Vanderbilt brought Walker's recruits down from New York free of charge (the gold rushers paid a $135 deck rate for the passage, more if they wanted cabins), and Walker was soon powerful enough to disregard his Liberal hosts in León. Proclaiming his new country a democracy, he called for a referendum on his stewardship. He controlled voter registration, the ballot boxes and poll-watching. According to the Central American Historical Institute at Georgetown University, "Long lists of nonexistent voters were drawn up to convince Nicaraguans and, more importantly, Americans of the widespread participation in the exercise." On June 29, 1856, at the age of thirty-two, William Walker —to the amusement of North America and the embarrassment of Latin America—was elected president of Nicaragua. The United States, under President Franklin Pierce, quickly recognized Walker's government and had its minister present credentials to him.

At this point, having gained all he originally aspired to, Walker went into his self-destruct mode. He decided, as a southerner, that slavery was indispensable to the development of Nicaragua. Wanting help from what would shortly become the Confederate States of America, he petitioned Congress to admit Nicaragua to the Union as a slave state. "The necessary consequence of the triumph of free labor will be the destruction, by a slow and cruel process, of the colored races," Walker wrote. "The labor of the inferior races cannot compete with that of the white race unless you give it a white master to direct its energies; and without such protection as slavery affords, the colored races must inevitably succumb in the struggle with white labor."

Slavery had been abolished in Central America upon its independence from Spain in 1821. The original Central American Federation soon broke into disputing chieftaincies, and Nicaragua had become a separate country in 1838. But in 1856, with his proclamation of slavery in Nicaragua, William Walker reunited Guatemala, El Salvador, Honduras and Costa Rica, if only for a historical moment, in their determination to get him out of Central America. They might have succeeded by themselves, but Walker gave them invaluable help. He canceled Cornelius Vanderbilt's license to run a transit company across Nicaragua and seized Vanderbilt's Nicaraguan assets. This was no way to treat a benefactor and particularly no way to treat the Commodore, as he was known. In a contest of greed, Walker was an amateur challenging one of the century's versatile professionals.

Vanderbilt, who loved power as much as Walker and knew a great deal more about it, financed his own fighting force to join the Central American countries. He then talked the British navy, which owed him a favor for protecting British interests along

Nicaragua's East Coast, into contributing part of its Caribbean fleet. Finally, he obtained the United States Navy's agreement to send a detachment of Marines to help out against Walker. Suddenly Walker was the underdog. He and his immortals tried to fight on several fronts but were driven from Nicaragua in 1857.

Walker was able to raise money in the United States for two more filibustering expeditions to recapture what he regarded as his lost kingdom. Both failed, and the second time, in 1860, Walker surrendered to a British warship on the captain's promise that he would be sent home to the United States. The British captain, however, turned Walker over to the Hondurans, who had a firing squad make sure the man of'destiny had mounted his last filibuster. By this time tracks had been laid across Panama, and the new railroad paid Commodore Vanderbilt $500,000 a year not to operate his Nicaraguan transit company anymore.

When the Marines helped remove William Walker from Nicaragua, it was the third time they had landed in the country. Between 1852 and 1933, the Marines landed fourteen times in Nicaragua, staying for durations of as little as five hours and as long as six years. Usually, according to Captain Harry Allenson Ellsworth, a Marine Corps historian, they were in Nicaragua "for the protection of American lives and interests." On one occasion all they did was guard an American mining company where workers were threatening a strike. Another time they stayed only long enough to burn down the East Coast town of San Juan del Norte (also known as Greytown) because—seven months earlier—the American minister to Nicaragua had been kept there overnight against his will before being released in the morning. Most of the Marine landings involved the support of one Nicaraguan faction against another, which had been, after all, the purpose of William Walker's own original mission to León.

William Walker and Commodore Vanderbilt, though each in his way was a renegade operating a personal foreign policy, forecast an American attitude toward Nicaragua that lasted more than a century. Statecraft was reduced to business, business to exploitation. Where economic interests were not the determinant, geopolitical fears were. United States policy was guided less by Jefferson's devotion to life, liberty and the pursuit of happiness than by his assertion, after leaving the presidency, that "America has a hemisphere to itself." The American ambassador to Nicaragua became at times a virtual governor-general. The State Department's own thinking on Central American diplomacy was displayed by Assistant Secretary Robert Edwin Olds in his memorandum on Nicaragua in 1927. "Geographical facts cannot be ignored," Olds wrote. "Our ministers accredited to the five little republics stretching from the Mexican border to Panama have always been more than mere diplomatic representatives. They have been advisers whose advice has been accepted virtually as law in the capitals where they respectively reside."

Early in the twentieth century, a nationalist leader, José Santos Zelaya, cooperated with the British in a plan to build a railway that would compete with the still-unfinished Panama Canal. Washington declared him a "destabilizing" influence and had him replaced in 1909. Thereafter, except for brief intervals— holidays for the Nicaraguans, furloughs for the Americans—the United States Marines were in Nicaragua until 1933. What was stability for one side was oppression for the other. During the final six years of their occupation, the Marines chased General Augusto César Sandino while they trained a domestic constabulary, the National Guard, to take their place. When they could not catch Sandino, whose social ideals and success at resisting the Americans provided the inspiration for the Frente Sandinista de Liberación Nacional a generation later, the Marines left. Then came Somoza I, who had Sandino assassinated, followed by Somozas II and III, lasting until the Sandinista insurrection of 1979.

The fall of William Walker deprived León of its status as capital, but the city still has the dignity of a gracefully retired athlete. Its eighteenth-century cathedral, the largest in Central America, is said to have been built by mistake when the design for an elegant cathedral to be constructed in the gold-rich capital of Lima, Peru, was mixed up aboard ship with the plans for a more modest church in León. Somoza I was married in the cathedral. Rubén Darío, Nicaragua's national poet, is buried in it. The cathedral preens over León with an opulence that refutes the revolution, and confirms it.

While I was in the cathedral one morning, a sound truck drove by, blaring instructions for a civil-defense meeting where trench-digging, firefighting and evacuation techniques would be taught in preparation for the Yankee invasion. The announcer, visible in the front seat of the truck, emphasized that the meeting would begin at nine o'clock. It was then a little after ten-thirty. This is called *hora Nica,* Nicaraguan time. Meetings not only start late, they occasionally do not take place even on the day they are scheduled. The sound truck proceeded around León, past an open bazaar, shops, the venerable university and signs advertising Pepsi, Coke, Black & Decker tools and "Death to hoarding and speculating." More mixed signals from a mixed economy.

Across the street on one side of the cathedral is an adjacent pair of political statements, characteristic of Nicaraguan cities. First, there are the gutted remains of a department store bombed by Somoza's National Guard during heavy fighting in 1978. Twisted metal girders are all that separate the earth from the sky. Next to the former store is a tiny plaza with enlarged photographs of the revolutionary heroes Sandino and Carlos Fonseca, and of the martyr Rigoberto López Pérez, the poet who shot Somoza I in León in 1956. "I'll give this country peace if I have to kill every other man in Nicaragua," Somoza I had said before his own turn came.

On the other side of the cathedral is the Colegio La Asunción, formerly an elite parochial academy for girls, now a girls' public school. The curriculum is no longer dictated by the church, but when I was there the school had not exactly embraced the revolution either. Two teachers and a school secretary I spoke with thought the Sandinistas were going backward. One of them left shortly after we began talking—"Wait, I'll show you what I mean," she said—and reappeared with a block of unrefined brown sugar. "See this? That is what we have to eat now."

Regardless of whether North American health chic stipulates raw sugar, the Nicaraguan middle class always insisted on refined white sugar, and this science teacher could no longer buy it.

The two teachers described themselves as liberal but not of the left. They were pleasant and perplexed. "Even with the hostility of the United States," one of them said, "there should be more progress this many years after the triumph. The government has good intentions, but it is on the wrong path. The Sandinistas give us no way to organize a campaign against their own mistakes."

"When someone has told you three or four lies, the fifth time you don't believe him," the other teacher said. "Nothing good can come of voting in such circumstances. There is not enough freedom. You can't even chop a tree down without permission. This is no atmosphere for organizing a democracy. Why don't the Sandinistas behave better to get the economic aid from the United States restored?"

"We are not contras," the first said. "We want what is best for our *país,* our country, our *patria.*"

A nun sitting on a bench nearby looked up at the teachers and the secretary, then returned to her Graham Greene paperback, *La Fuerza y la Gloria.*

The secretary had once been a student at the school, and her small, tidy features drooped when she talked about the revolution. "I can't complain for myself," she said, "but the lack of freedom hurts the production of goods. You don't have to be an economist to see the economy is worse now than ten years ago. Because of the United States, we have to have so many people involved in defense we can't produce what we need. Some of our teachers have to go pick cotton on their holidays. That's not a proper activity for a teacher. I hated Somoza. The Sandinistas seemed like saints to me when they first came. But they let me down, and they don't show proper respect for the United States. They should change, be more friendly to your country, give no excuse for the United States to attack us."

The nun looked up again as she turned a page.

"When the Pope came here this year," one of the teachers said, "it was a very painful experience."

The nun smiled and nodded to herself.

"It was *doloroso*," the secretary said. "He was insulted by Sandinistas waving their red-and-black flags right here in the cathedral square, while he was treated well at the leftist university. How can you figure that? All right, some of my family are Sandinistas. My brothers pound the table, my father pounds the table. My mother cries. We fight about it, but we're still a family."

The teachers and the secretary left for lunch, and the school door was closed behind me for the midday break as I walked out. But there was a window in the door, barred with thin whitewashed wooden dowels. The little window opened. I had forgotten the nun. She appeared, spectral in the shadows behind the white bars. *"Por favor, señor,"* she said, "we do not all feel like that."

All I could see of her was white—her face, her nun's coronet, her plain T-shirt. "First, the Pope," she said. "I love him, and the *campesinos* I work with were very happy to have him visit. But he was poorly advised. Sixteen Christian boys from the *milicia* were buried the day before the Pope came. Their mothers asked the Pope to say a prayer for them. He refused. Something for these young *compañeros* killed on the border fighting *los contras*. Just one word. No. In Costa Rica he said he came to listen to the cries of the people. Here he spoke only of the need for unity in the church. In the way the church can sometimes be, he was too dogmatic."

The nun opened the door and came out on the school steps. She was Sister Ana María Macias, a social worker originally from Spain, now thirty-six and a Nicaraguan. She had prominent bones and eyes, and her strong nose managed to suggest both a peasant and an aristocrat. After the revolution she became treasurer of a farm cooperative. "Beans, corn, rice," she said. "I organize the selling of our produce to the markets, and I try to manage the money. Before, the farmers could get loans only from big landowners who charged over fifty percent. A whole family could work for a year and only make enough to buy ten pounds of salt. The system was structured to make them peons. Now the farmers get loans at eight percent and they own their own land. Is that Communism?''

Sister Ana María had left Spain in 1974, intending to stay two years in Nicaragua. She was not one of the church workers caught up in the Sandinistas' struggle, but as the fighting spread her sympathies for its victims became stronger. "In the time of Somoza," she said, "soldiers were everywhere and you could not look at them, not even a nun. They would do anything to you that amused them. When Chamorro, the publisher, was killed in 1978, it could be worth your life only to walk past the headquarters of the Guardia here in León. Holy Week was full of terror. On the Monday before Easter, the Guardia killed three boys right in front of the church. The rest of the week, disappearances every day.

"But now, see the *vida nueva,* see the betterment. Priests and nuns in Guatemala and El Salvador are killed for doing the kind of work with *campesinos* I do here. The soldiers come up to me on the street and shake my hand. There are shortages in some areas, but the revolution never promised Italian olive oil and French wine. It's true some Nicaraguans like my friends in the *escuela* here are very offended to have to eat brown sugar—I think we can live through that. The poor people have the necessities they never dreamed of before.''

What Sister Ana María does not admire about the Sandinistas is the way they treat their opponents. "I don't like the neighborhood surveillance groups who harass people they don't agree with," she said. "I don't like the signs that say, 'Counterrevolutionaries, ten thousand eyes are watching you.' When people disagree with the government, they often try to be funny about perhaps going to jail. The fact is they do not go to jail, but the possibility is in the air enough so that they have to make a little joke about it. I do not like this at all, but it is the tail of the revolution, not its body. The body is healthy and growing. Tell the United States government, *por favor,* it's all right not to help Nicaragua, but at least don't help the contras. Two of our boys from the farm have been killed on the border. We won't let them die in vain.''

• • •

I continued on to the port of Corinto, thirty-five miles west of León. On at least a half-dozen of the occasions when the United States Marines have landed in Nicaragua, Corinto was their port of entry. After the murder of Pedro Joaquín Chamorro in 1978, Somoza III told a hostile crowd in Corinto, "I am a politician; I can be killed too, you know." The crowd found this reassuring and hooted their dictator. Before the revolution, sailors would get off their ships in Corinto, hire Nicaraguan bodyguards known locally as cowboys and make the round of bars, card games and brothels without fear of being rolled. Although the Sandinistas have tried to eliminate prostitution and gambling, Corinto is still a busy little port city with a market in practically everything. The revolution has not changed the face of the port, but the CIA has.

Corinto is on an island and handles 60 percent of Nicaragua's foreign trade; both facts make it an attractive target for sabotage. Its harbor has been mined by the CIA, though shipping traffic continues. The contras had tried several times to blow up the main bridge to the island but at the time of my visit had failed. The CIA did not fail, however, in its night raid on Corinto's oil storage depot two months before I was there. The contras had been unable to penetrate the port's defenses with either planes or small ships, so the CIA sent its own speedboat into the harbor. The oil depot was shelled from the speedboat for perhaps three minutes, after which the boat escaped. Four diesel-fuel tanks were hit directly. The explosions started fires which eventually destroyed eight tanks and their fuel lines, a loading crane, two molasses storage tanks, a concrete wall, two small buildings and a large warehouse with all its contents, which included coffee, beans and shrimp. Three million gallons of fuel were lost.

The following day, a group of counterrevolutionaries were captured near Corinto. They said they had been trained to make the assault on the port but when they had not been able to accomplish it in three attempts, their CIA instructors had done the job themselves. According to the captive contras, the speedboat had a 325-horsepower engine and used 60-millimeter shells.

The storage depot was moonscape, sheet metal twisted into

five acres of the more playful varieties of pasta. Red and green paint, having passed through the stages of boiling and peeling, lay in flakes on the ground. The fire had burned for forty-eight hours and was finally contained by sophisticated equipment sent from Mexico, Venezuela and Cuba. When I was there, planes from Honduras had come in low under the Nicaraguan radar for three days in a row. They strafed the port and were driven away before they could do further damage to the oil tanks. In international law, that might be called repeated violations of airspace accompanied by unprovoked acts of war; in the intelligence community it is known as keeping in touch. Pointing out the ruined Exxon tanks, a welder at the depot said, "See, business too must make its sacrifices for democracy."

Irving Ramos, a nineteen-year-old who said he had a seventh-grade education, was piling rubble in the depot, which was still being cleaned up two months after the attack. He had come home recently from military duty. "Nicaragua can't afford to throw away any metal, so we stack it carefully," Irving Ramos said. "What you have to try to understand is that the Nicaraguan government works for the *campesino* now instead of the other way around, like it used to be. Your war is good for nothing. If you can't send peace, at least don't send bombs. If you don't send bombs, maybe you'll send books. What about Salinger? I get off early if I go to night school."

On the way out of Corinto, I drove past the statue of a boy holding the giant letters A, B, C, D. The literacy campaign. Across the bridge to the mainland, in the twilight, I was stopped by the blinking red lights of a slow convoy of Soviet tractors, unloaded that afternoon in Corinto. When I could pass them, I came to a caravan of Toyota pickups, also new. In front of the Toyotas were Soviet trucks and two Soviet ambulances. Just before the town of Chinandega, where I turned south to get back to Managua, I came to a field hospital built by the Russians, most of it under tents, staffed by Russian doctors. The Soviets could do as they pleased in Afghanistan, or with Russian Jews, and it made little difference in a Third World country eight thousand miles away. The penicillin they provided the Nicaraguans had the same molecular structure as that which the United States had stopped sending.

The way the United States and the Soviet Union were behaving toward Nicaragua was a reminder of the fairy tale about the wind and the sun. The two of them look down at the earth and see a freezing man walking along, wearing an overcoat. They devise a contest to see who can get the coat off the man first. The wind blows hard and almost whisks the coat right off the man's back, but he grabs it and hugs it tightly around him. The wind swirls, huffs and puffs some more, but nothing works. It is the sun's turn. He shines brightly for a few minutes. The man removes his overcoat and continues walking.

The question was, Why did the United States have to be the wind in this story?

V THE LAST MARINE

SEARCHING FOR SANDINO: Doddering but still ceremonious, First Lieutenant Stanley D. Atha, USMC, Retired, moved around his small airy home very delicately. He had something important to find but could not for the moment remember what. From the living room to the dining area into his crowded little office and back to the living room, his movements had purpose, though they were unsteady. His home was close to its neighbors on a pleasant street lined with shrubbery and flowers in a Managua neighborhood of louvered windows and plywood front doors that looked like a working-class suburb of Houston.

He was somewhat too tall for his surroundings at six feet one, perhaps half a foot taller than most of the Nicaraguans among whom he has lived for nearly sixty years. But he stooped only a little and was courteous to a fault. He smiled with his memories. "By the time I was eight years old I was walking three miles to school from our farm in West Virginia," he said. He continued with his slow deliberate motions, going through his bureau drawers and then a file cabinet. "What did I tell you I was hunting? Oh yes, I recollect. It's here somewhere. We lived near a coalmine shaft and when it got too sooty we moved farther up the run

—the creek—where it was healthier for our chickens and seventeen cows. We kept the cows for butter and the chickens for eggs, so we liked to call my good old dad a butter-and-egg man, though he was just a poor farmer like all our neighbors. All that stuff is around here, just a matter of laying hands on it. I'd like to say I finished high school before I joined the Marines, but really I didn't."

Stanley Atha was patient with his infirmities, his principal companions now except for his Nicaraguan wife. Like many people past eighty, he was on more familiar terms with the distant than the recent past. What he forgot most frequently was the language he was speaking. Some limiting authority, some brake on his powers of expression, had been released, and he flowed unobstructed between English and Spanish. Stanley Atha, born almost with the century, moved from his file cabinet to his closet, piled with books and boxes and photographs.

"We'll get it," he said. "I left the run at seventeen to join the Marines, who I told I was eighteen. After Parris Island they had me doing carpentry in Washington, D.C., until Henry Stimson signed the treaty with Nicaragua; I was part of the contingent of Marines who were sent in to organize a National Guard to keep the peace."

He went from the closet back to his desk, picking through a bottom drawer. "So I left New York City on the S.S. *Columbia* in 1926 and took seventeen days to sail down through the Canal to Corinto. They sent me first-class, of course. I was an officer."

He was back in his closet again. "There was only a cart road at Corinto, but then I caught the train at Chinandega and came on down through León to Managua. I checked into a boarding-house with three other Marines across the street from the old Gran Hotel, which was wrecked in the first earthquake of '31. The only warning we had was a little tinkling of one chandelier, and by the next morning the whole city was a ruin. But that was later, wasn't it? Anyhow, here it is."

Stanley Atha was pleased with the Thom McAn shoe box he had been looking for. He opened it to display a collection of insignia, medals, coins, reports, letters, sepia photographs of uniformed Marines with short mustaches and shorter sideburns, later photographs of men in sombreros with women in shawls. "It's all in here. I made carbons of my reports. Chasing Sandino."

Chasing Sandino was how the U.S. Marines occupied themselves in Nicaragua between 1926 and 1933. It was taken seriously and many died, but it was also a form of sport. The Marines had contests to see who could get over the most hills, mountains, gorges and ravines the fastest in their pursuit. They would hear he was in a village or had camped near a river, but by the time they got there he was gone. For once, the word "native" was applicable and undemeaning. No one knew the back country of Nicaragua like a native, and no native made more effective use of his knowledge than Augusto César Sandino.

Sandino was then in his early thirties. As the illegitimate son of a Liberal Party landowner and an Indian peasant, he grew up both rich and poor in Nicaragua. After a fight in a bar that left one man dead and the police after him, Sandino escaped to Mexico in his twenties. He worked for about a year in the oil fields at Tampico, where he also began to read about revolution. Returning to Nicaragua, he became a soldier in the Liberal army and soon had a contingent of the army under his leadership. When the Liberal General Moncada made the agreement with Henry Stimson to forge a Liberal-Conservative coalition to govern Nicaragua, Sandino refused to lay down his arms, accusing Moncada of having sold out Nicaraguan independence to the Americans. The United States Marines then began the process of trying to subdue Sandino's army as the last remaining obstacle to peace in Nicaragua.

In 1928, after months of tracking him, the Marines trapped Sandino at his mountain fortress, El Chipote, in the department of Nueva Segovia in northern Nicaragua. "We had him pinned up there, no question about that," Stanley Atha said. "We could have done great things with radio contact." Other accounts of the Marines' siege of El Chipote fill out Lieutenant Atha's, essentially substantiating his memory. Lieutenant Atha had been in Nicaragua two years by then, but although the Marines were using airplanes by 1928 they did not yet have good portable two-way radios. El Chipote was about twenty miles south of the Honduran border, and one of the fears the Marines had was that Sandino and his forces might escape to Honduras, where the Marines had no license to follow. With Sandino and approximately three hundred of his troops surrounded, the Marines steadily and cautiously advanced toward El Chipote over a period of two months. They destroyed hillside villages on the way if these had been reported to supply Sandino.

"Now, I wouldn't burn a village," Stanley Atha said. "Not ever. It happened, but it was never done by me or anyone under my command. We had a Lieutenant Pennington, there's no denying this, who was put in charge of the garrison at Matagalpa. He cut off the heads of six bandits and held the heads to be photographed with them. I have one of the pictures—there, see, he holds them by the hair. Now, no Marine officer in his right mind is going to do that. Pennington said he did it to disprove the local charge in Matagalpa that when the Marines and bandits met in combat, the bandits ran one way and the Marines ran the other. The Marines were very mad at Pennington, and the commanding officer in Managua yanked him right out of Matagalpa. I was sent to relieve Pennington and took over as the commanding officer of the Eighth Company in Matagalpa. It was a big job. I had troops in a number of outposts, and some of the best were native Nicaraguans.

"I'll tell you what I *would* do. I always paid for information if it proved to be true. If it was not true, I wouldn't allow anyone to touch the informant, but I'd never pay any attention to him later on. Someone else from another company might give him hell, not me. Anyhow, tracking Sandino up his mountain, all our information from locals, all the scouts and all the spies reported that Sandino was fortified at El Chipote. When we got near the top at last, the planes came in."

The airplanes Stanley Atha referred to were Voughts and Corsairs engaged in some of the first aerial bombardment in history. Dogfights between German and Allied planes took place in World War I, but bombardment from the air began in the next decade.

Marine planes had already attacked Ocotal when Sandino's forces tried and failed to dislodge the Marines from the town. At El Chipote, the top of the mountain was bombed by planes while artillery was pounding from below as soon as it came within range of Sandino's headquarters.

"You know what happened when we reached the *pico*," Stanley Atha said. "At the top was nothing, not a machete, not a dead mule. We all had fleas—ha, ha—that was what we had to show for our assault on El Chipote. Sandino had decamped maybe a week before we got there. He left by way of a trail that led to a pass that took him into a canyon we had not known existed. We had him surrounded, but we were guarding the north especially, because he had tried to take Ocotal before and that was to the north, and we thought he might try to go on across into Honduras. So of course he slipped out on *la carretera del sur,* the southern route, and the next we heard of him he had set up shop in San Rafael del Norte, a good thirty miles south and maybe five days' march for us over poor roads and forested terrain. During the rainy season the mud would be two feet deep on the roads. But Sandino had other ways to go. All we captured was a mountain. Coming down from El Chipote, I'll tell you we did not pay informants."

The Marines never found Sandino, but the search kept on for another five years. Time has gilded the search, for both the hunters and the hunted. Numerous Nicaraguans still claim to have served with Sandino. One was a mess sergeant, another ran errands for Sandino's wife, a third escaped from Ocotal when the Marines drove Sandino out. The claim alone confers an aura most Nicaraguans cherish. Tomás Borge swears his father was a bugler for Sandino. Daniel Ortega's father is said to have written pamphlets for the Sandino forces. In Estelí, later, I met a man almost as old as Stanley Atha, a formal old man in a tattered but neat suit and a frayed tie, who professed to have been Sandino's favorite guitarist. But perhaps perversely, I felt I had gotten closest to Sandino in the presence of his old enemy, Stanley Atha, for whom the past had become a kind of movie ready to be rerun whenever someone bothered to switch on the projector to his memory.

"My last patrol was in '32, and it was almost my lost patrol," Stanley Atha continued. His years of searching for Sandino blended over the decades into a romance for Stanley Atha, but his narrative reveals what foreign troops with superior technology are up against in unfamiliar territory where the natives protect the poorly equipped insurgents. When Stanley Atha talked about Nicaragua in the 1920s and '30s, he could have been talking about Vietnam in the 1960s and '70s, or he could have been describing Afghanistan in the 1980s.

"We were using cattle sellers as spies, because they moved around from town to town so much they were regarded as good sources of information—not always reliable but always full of stories. We were heading out against real bandits as much as against Sandino. That's what people forget. The bandits were all over the place in those days in Nicaragua, like they used to be in our old West a hundred years and more ago. Sandino himself was no *bandido*, not by a stretch. *Bandidos* never commanded the loyalty, never had people voluntarily giving them food and animals for the soldiers. There was a colonel in Sandino's army by the name of Porfirio Sánchez, this was well known. Sánchez went into Yalí ahead of Sandino's main force one time and requisitioned supplies without paying for them, just forced people in the town to turn over whatever they had. When Sandino heard about it he tried to have Sánchez shot, but Sánchez got wind of it and escaped. Sandino paid as he went, and when he couldn't pay he gave people notes and sent someone back to pay them later. That was not a bandit, which we had plenty of, believe me, and I caught my share.

"A flood had practically knocked down a bridge over the Río Coco just below Ocotal. Ocotal was under siege, and my last patrol was to bring 176 Nicaraguan recruits to relieve the Ocotal garrisons. A Marine scout coming south met us and warned us not to try to use the bridge because it was as good as washed out. Well, that was the only way to go, and we had to go there, we had no rafts or suchlike, so I gave the order to stay ten yards apart on the bridge, not to put too much weight on it at once. I put my sergeant and my second lieutenant in the lead and I brought up the rear to make sure they all got across. When I got to the middle the bridge began to sway like it was doing the tango, and I figured we were all going in, those of us still on the bridge. But the bridge held, don't ask me how. As I stepped off the bridge, so help me, the whole thing collapsed into the Río Coco. But I got my 176 men across.

"From Ocotal I had to continue on through Nueva Segovia garrisoning these towns against the small bandit groups and also against Sandino. We had great success against the bandits. By the time I got word Sandino's army was in the vicinity, my patrol was down to twenty-five men, because we had left most of the others at Ocotal and the small towns we were garrisoning. We found a boy who had some food and who agreed to tell us where Sandino's forces had bivouacked. I never used force to get information, because that kind of information wasn't worth much. This boy directed us to a spot within five hundred yards of where the Sandino group was camped. There were over a hundred of them and only twenty-five of us, but I knew a number of them would be camp followers and *juanas*—that's women who traveled with Sandino. And we had rifle grenades.

"It was night, and we couldn't attack what we couldn't see. We lay on our stomachs and estimated our distance and what we had to do as soon as dawn broke. The rebels were on a rise above us. In the middle of the night it rained barrels, I thought we'd float away. Then I slept a bit but was wakened suddenly by a snore loud as a chain saw. I said to myself, that's not Slattery. He was my second lieutenant and he slept like a mouse. So I looked around to see who was doing this tremendous snoring. It was an old sow that had crawled into our tent to keep dry. Didn't stink too much, so I let her stay there.

"At first light, I ordered everyone up and on the attack. Let's rout 'em, I said. We fired our rifle grenades into the rebel camp. They hollered and we give 'em hell. They set up a machine gun on a ridge above us, and they opened up. We had good cover and weren't getting hit, but we couldn't advance. We had surprised them, but we were losing our advantage while their machine gun worked. So I took a squad of five and left Slattery behind to give us cover with the rest of the Nicaraguan troops. My point man and I had repeating rifles and we combed the ridge with them. Silence. We went on up and it was empty, no killed or wounded, no machine gun. They went up to Río Negro, I figured, and we had a garrison about fifteen kilometers up, but we had no way to let them know what was going on.

"A little later we captured a boy who was bringing meat to the rebels. We told him to keep going and we'd follow him. He didn't know who to be more scared of. After he'd gone up the Río Negro a few miles we sighted four rebel scouts. One of our Nicaraguan scouts said he knew them as men who worked with Sandino's brother, Socrates. We were hot on the trail at this point, and I gave the order to capture the four scouts, but by the time the order to capture the four scouts was out of my mouth they turned tail and disappeared up the wash into the rocks and shrubs. We followed their spoor thirty days, thirty days up that wilderness. Every town we came to they'd tell us thataway, and thataway we'd go until we realized we had lost the trail. Back to the town and somebody'd say maybe the first guy was a little loco or made a mistake. Oh my God, what a radio would have done.

"We did find them finally on a small hill southeast of San Francisco del Norte. They were about a thousand yards up the hill from us, and the brush was too thick for a quick advance. We found a side trail and that was cut and I told everybody to double-time up that hill. The rebels were on a hill and had a BAR, which surprised us. They weren't supposed to have Browning Automatics. We took some heavy fire as soon as they spotted us, and it was very, very accurate. Our rifle grenades couldn't reach to the top of the hill, so I told Slattery to take one squad and do a half-flank of the hill while I took the other squad straight up. The rebels started throwing what seemed like an unlimited supply of dynamite bombs down the hill, but we peppered them pretty good, too. They made their own bombs by soaking cowhide in water, then wrapping it around a collection of nails, rocks and sand. They'd fill it with powder and attach a fuse, then tie the whole business with the rawhide strings, which tightened as they dried. When they lit it and threw it, that baby would go off.

"We couldn't get far up the hill, and I took my senior corporal, José Alemán, and told him to charge with me so we could knock out whoever was throwing the bombs down the hill at us. Corporal Alemán refused to charge, the s.o.b., so I took a private, Silvio Rocha. We went hard and our troops provided us good cover. Rocha was brave, he'd shout and fire, shout and fire, and run hard up the hill. We were going from rock to rock, sometimes only a shrub, firing as we went at the spot near the top where the dynamite bombs were coming from. They stopped coming. I waved my squad on up and shouted for Slattery to bring his up too. We'd had the hill under siege now for a little over three hours. Private Rocha reached the hilltop first and found a plateau, flat, a perfect position. It was empty. They'd just disappeared. The rear of the hill was like the back of an armadillo; it thinned out into a tail that sloped gradually and went off into a ravine that led to some other hills. We weren't hurt, but we didn't find any of their bodies either. We ate lunch. This kept up for thirty days."

In his written reports on his last patrol, Stanley Atha pictures the frustration of trying to find an enemy—whom he was ordered to refer to as "bandits"—that always keeps a hill or town or river ahead of him. He crisscrosses northwestern Nicaragua on poor roads and often no roads at all. At times the villagers' greeting would be a potshot at the Marines and the Nicaraguan National Guard soldiers whom Lieutenant Atha was commanding. "Segundo Velásquez ran from house armed with shotgun, point fired on him and wounded him in his right hip. Condition considered serious." Other times villagers were friendly but offered little help. "Lost trail of bandits" is a frequent entry. "Arrived Sebaco; no further information" is another.

Five entries for March 12, 1932, when the thirty-day patrol was almost over, are graphic for what they do not contain, which is any fixed location or sighting of the enemy itself.

"0830: Passed Monte Grande. Told that bandit group was at Embolsada at 0700.

"1200: Passed Embolsada. Bandits passed here at 0600.

"1300: Passed Tamarindo. Bandits passed here 0700. Here lost trail of bandits.

"1700: Arrived San Lorenzo. No information.

"2000: Small boy arrived from La Mesa and stated that Sandino group passed La Mesa at 1200 and went in the general direction of Colón."

When the patrol was over Lieutenant Atha was glad to get back to his regular command at Matagalpa, where he learned that the Marines would leave Nicaragua in a matter of months. He had not only trained the indigenous National Guardsmen, he had given them combat experience. Gracious to his noncommissioned officers, Lieutenant Atha was optimistic about the service they would perform for their country. In the conclusion to his report on the patrol, he puts the best face possible on the thirty days of hit-and-run frustration. "I wish to commend the entire patrol for the excellent spirit and gallantry before and during the contacts, and to especially commend Lt. Slattery, Sgts. Gutiérrez, Cabo Picado, Rasos Guido, Castro, and Urrutia for their coolness under fire." He accompanied his report with his own sketches of the scenes of combat with the enemy.

"But of course we assumed the National Guard would be a neutral force outside of politics," he remembered half a century later. "We thought they'd be just the way we were, servants of a national policy, right or wrong, not of a single political party or dictator, right or wrong. Before we left Matagalpa, there was some business to finish. I had José Alemán, the corporal who wouldn't charge, court-martialed. You just had to make an example of him so others wouldn't think they could get away with disobeying an order. Then I made Private Silvio Rocha a corporal in the new National Guard. It seemed the right thing to do."

When the Marines finally did leave in 1933, they placed the

National Guard under the leadership of the first Somoza. Stanley Atha got his honorable discharge, married a Nicaraguan and went on training the National Guard. He liked his wife's family and wanted to settle in her country. Later he was briefly the Associated Press reporter in Nicaragua. He also grew cotton and exported various other local products, such as alligator skin, that companies in the United States wanted to buy. Over the years, he became the representative in Nicaragua for Parker Pen, Empire State Brass and Jameco Industries, among other American companies. Though his finances were never more than middling, he was happy in Nicaragua. He was elected president of the Rotary Club of Managua. His wife and he had two daughters and three sons, one of whom became a doctor practicing in Mexico. His favorite authors were Conrad, Graham Greene and Louis L'Amour, and he saw me to the door with a paperback of *Lord Jim* in his hand. The last Marine in Nicaragua drew neither social security nor a military pension from the United States. But in one of the revolution's routine ironies, Stanley Atha did receive a Nicaraguan government pension from the Sandinistas for having trained the National Guard for the Somozas.

Though the Marines failed, one American who came to Nicaragua did find Sandino. Carleton Beals, sent by *The Nation* magazine to Nicaragua in 1928, finally reached the rebel general after several weeks on horseback through what he described as "driving storm" and "humid, reeking" jungle. He tried to get to El Chipote, but Stanley Atha and the Marines had already taken it, so he headed south and was at length led by a scout to meet Sandino in San Rafael del Norte.

After his long journey, Beals indulged in some romanticism but was hardly less graphic for having done so. The image of the intrepid American reporter being received by the dauntless revolutionary at four in the morning "by the light of a lantern" can hang in the mind like a picture on a wall. "When I saw him," Beals wrote, "he was dressed in a uniform of dark brown with almost black puttees, immaculately polished; a silk red-and-black handkerchief knotted about his throat; and a broad-brimmed

Texas Stetson hat, pulled low over his forehead and pinched shovel-shaped.'' Beals was impressed to find a commanding general so short, ''not more than five feet five.''

Sandino's conditions for disbanding his army were similar to the Contadora proposals of the 1980s. He told Beals he had three conditions: one, the Marine evacuation of Nicaragua (i.e., demilitarize the region); two, appointment of an interim civilian president; three, elections for a full-term president supervised by representatives of Latin American countries. He refused ever to become a candidate himself and said he would never fight again except ''in case of a new foreign invasion,'' which he thought would not occur if he could continue to elude the Marines. ''We have taken up arms from the love of our country,'' he told Beals, ''because all other leaders have betrayed it and have sold themselves out to the foreigner or have bent the neck in cowardice. We, in our own house, are fighting for our inalienable rights. What right have foreign troops to call us outlaws and bandits and to say that we are the aggressors? I repeat that we are in our own house. We declare that we will never live in cowardly peace under a government installed by a foreign power. Is this patriotism or is it not?''

The exasperation Stanley Atha felt at El Chipote and afterward chasing Sandino's forces around northern Nicaragua is reflected in Sandino's own version. ''I waited in El Chipote,'' he said to Beals. ''The Marines concentrated, shipped up supplies, laid month-long plans to oust me, crept gradually up and around my position. They are still there. I am here . . . halfway into the heart of the country. I shall go further into the heart of the country. When they have remobilized here and shipped in troops and more troops and get all set to come out and catch me, I shall be north again—or somewhere else.''

Sandino gave a lesson on the modern guerrilla-warfare tactic of taking military supplies from the regular army while living off the land, swimming in the sea of the peasantry, as Mao Tse-tung later put it. ''We owe all to our enemy,'' Sandino said. ''If he had never attacked us, then, indeed, our condition would be miserable. From him we have taken everything we possess. If we had not been attacked, we would have no clothing and no ammunition and we would have perished, for we are incapable of living by banditry. We have taken nothing from the peasants save that which has been tendered to us voluntarily. In El Chipote the entire countryside used to toil up to the heights with food and animals for our soldiers, laying what we needed at our feet . . . the countryside is with us almost to a man. Do you think we could have existed in one fortified place for half a year with all the might of the United States against us, if we had been merely bandits? If we were bandits every man's hand would be against us; every man would be a secret enemy. Instead, every home harbors a friend." Carleton Beals was transcribing a primer for insurgency, passing it along to his readers in *The Nation* and the New York *Herald Tribune.*

In his vision of history, Sandino contracted the distance between the American and Nicaraguan revolutions. Other rebels had used 1776 and would again. In 1928, Augusto César Sandino was making a judgment and a prophecy. "We are no more bandits than was Washington," he told Beals. "If the American public had not become calloused to justice and to the elemental rights of mankind, it would not so easily forget its own past when a handful of ragged soldiers marched through the snow leaving blood tracks behind them to win liberty and independence. If their consciences had not become dulled by their scramble for wealth, Americans would not so easily forget the lesson that, sooner or later, every nation, however weak, achieves freedom, and that every abuse of power hastens the destruction of the one who wields it. We march to the clear light of the sun or to death. But if we die, the *patria* lives on, indestructible. Others will succeed us."

Meanwhile, First Lieutenant Stanley Atha was giving on-the-job training to Nicaraguans to take over their own constabulary in obedience to the first Somoza, who was consolidating his strength as head of the new National Guard. Although Sandino continued to evade the Marines until they gave up and went home, Somoza got him on the first try. Early in 1934, Somoza had the National Guard pick up Sandino as he left a dinner party with Nicaragua's President Juan Bautista Sacasa. While Somoza himself went to a poetry reading, the Guard took Sandino to the Managua airfield and executed him. The party at the presidential palace had been held to celebrate peace among the country's hostile factions.

VI MANAGUA

WE TELL OURSELVES STORIES for guidance in a foreign land, to forget and remember. In the next block beyond the school destroyed by the earthquake dwells a nurse who used to work in the plasmapheresis center and now raises lilies of the valley. At the meeting in the church tonight someone will break through the wall of rhetoric, exciting envy. Our delegation from Denver could find peace in that *barrio* if allowed two hot showers a week, and they could use our devoted savvy. The *compañero* argues with his daughter, the old woman hugs her tearful icon, gunfire cackles in the distance, and from the tin shack next door come the zealous noises of pleasure well under way. The landscape plays with all shapes and echoes.

"No *necesario* to like my goberment, señor," a man said to me as I stared up at a movie marquee one blazing afternoon in Managua, "to hate what the Yankee goberment does to us. Joo don' know how bad until joo look around and give consideration to the historical."

I said I had been to Corinto.

"That's okay." It was unclear whether he was consoling or approving. He was taller than most Nicaraguans, teetering a little as though he could not bear the height, standing in line to get in the theater, where it would be, if not cool, at least dark. The man said he had been drinking *Flor de Caña,* the rich Nicaraguan rum, since early morning. He wore a soiled white shirt with a black armband, and he was alone. Earlier in the week, his son, a health worker in northern Zelaya, had been killed while he gave vaccinations in a farm village. "They come in a truck, *la contra,* they go in the tent where my son and the nurse give injections, they shoot my son and take the nurse. After they rape her, they cut off her breasts, dump her back in the village still alive. My son was lucky." He disappeared, taking refuge in the theater where Sam Wanamaker had directed *Sinbad and the Eye of the Tiger,* starring the children of John Wayne and Tyrone Power.

Since the Somozas never rebuilt the city after the 1972 earthquake, siphoning off approximately $100 million in international relief aid, and since the Sandinistas have been unable to afford much construction, many parts of Managua give the impression of having had a variant of the neutron bomb dropped on them. Buildings themselves are destroyed, but not people or vegetation. It is hard, on many streets, to find two adjacent commercial establishments still standing. Three blocks from the Intercontinental a veterinarian and a casketmaker have shops next door to each other, a juxtaposition that stands out not because of any professional incongruity but because of its structural rarity.

Managua could have been dreamed by Gertrude Stein. With no center and a destroyed past, the city does not seem to be *there* at all; it can be found in desultory forms. Block after block of wasteland and brick piles will be followed by three movie theaters, two vacant lots, a marketplace choked with people buying and selling. More vacant lots and rubble-strewn blocks are succeeded by a contemporary shopping center with airline offices, real estate firms, a government bureau, jewelry stores. Then a hill with nothing on it, an army base, a few blocks of one-story middle-class homes, a gaping ravine, and a working-class *barrio* pieced together from beaverboard, tin, flattened beer cans, an occasional prized plywood door.

The Marine commandant and the chief of the U.S. Southern Command will find difficulties in taking and holding positions in such a city. If the Marines were confused by Beirut, they will be likely to become unhinged in Managua. In a city where nothing seems to lead anywhere, what plaza and which wide avenues would lend themselves to meaningful roadblocks and barbed-wire barricades? Where bearings are uncheckable, how do you set up checkpoints? The Nicaraguans have dug trenches and thrown up sandbags all over town, but it is not clear who these defenses would best serve. Trenches and sandbags might help local militia at the outset, but they would at least give an invading force a sense of what to aim for, what to capture, after which these initial obstacles would become a means of controlling occupied neighborhoods. In the prevailing absence of street signs and distance markers, people give directions in Managua by describing how many blocks a particular spot is from where the generating plant used to be before the earthquake destroyed it, or they will say a man's house is three and a half blocks in the direction of Lake Managua from where the little tree used to be before the truck knocked it down. When he comes up from his SOCOM HQ in Panama, where will the commanding general tell his platoons from New Jersey and Oklahoma and Seattle to fan out in order to secure defensible positions against the Nicaraguans? Except for the trenches and sandbags, there simply is not much to go for, and once you've squeezed into the trenches, you're a sitting gringo for every *barrio* kid with a popgun or Coke bottle filled with kerosene.

Despite its vulnerability to counterattack, our generals will find the Hotel Intercontinental does have aspects of a command post. As its pyramid rises, windows are staggered from floor to floor in a modular arrangement so that no balcony or window is directly on top of the one below. The architectural effect is one of a series of pillboxes dug into an ancient monument. If the pyramid itself does not propitiate the gods, its inhabitants can at least hold them off temporarily from the pillbox balconies. Howard Hughes, modern master of the fortified residence, said he felt snugly bunkered living at the Intercontinental. When Hughes stayed there in

1972, he looked out over a Managua that was still there to be overlooked, testing the business climate of his host, Anastasio Somoza, though never actually permitting the dictator into his presence. Somoza wanted only to buy a plane or two, while Hughes had plans to put up a casino that could become his own Vegas SOCOM.

The trouble was, Hughes stayed too long. Two days before Christmas in 1972, a series of earthquakes destroyed or damaged approximately 80 percent of the buildings in Managua. Thirteen thousand Managuans were killed almost immediately, swallowed or crushed or burned up when the earth opened and the city collapsed. Over 200,000 people lost their homes. Inevitably, the poor suffered and lost the most, but much of the middle class was wiped out economically, which helped eventually in the forging of an anti-Somoza alliance with the more dedicated revolutionaries of the left. But the oligarchy itself lost factories and department stores, and a number of businessmen threw open their warehouses to the poor and homeless afterward. Even the American embassy was destroyed, with one employee killed. Relief agencies throughout the Americas went to work promptly, but Somoza and his National Guard effectively hoarded the donated commodities. They sold off the beans and rice, rented the tents and shovels, leased the construction materials back to their own government (which never used them), kept the trucks, banked the money. "Can't you see plainly," Somoza asked a reporter impatiently, "I'm just a businessman trying to do a little business?"

Holed up in the reinforced concrete of the Intercontinental, Howard Hughes was safe enough but apparently not happy. Several times on the night of the earthquake he was heard shrieking at the Mormons who guarded him. The way the old paranoid could have seen it, a jealous God might be punishing him for leaving his encampment in benighted Las Vegas and escaping to the beguiling town on the shores of lovely Lake Managua. As soon as he was sure the tremors had died down, Hughes had himself taken to the airport, where he flew from the ruined city and never looked back at Nicaragua.

In the 1980s, Managuans, as well as most Americans in Nicaragua, were convinced of the imminence of another visitation in the way ancient tribes living within the throw of a volcano were certain of their early doom when they could smell lava. The American invasion of Grenada was regarded as a preliminary eruption, a *petit mal* seizure, to be followed inevitably by the *grand mal* that would engulf Nicaragua. But once they had dug their trenches, formed their fire brigades and block committees and sent their sons off for training, Managuans still had to get through each day. There is always music in Nicaragua—salsa, samba, mournful Spanish ballads, American rock, tango, rumba, skippy Latin rhythms recalling the Cugats, who have been vanished for decades from Northern consciousness. There are also the movies.

Spanish westerns and Latin American romances were plentiful in Managua, but the products of Anglo culture enjoyed special favor. It was possible to wander around Managua on the torpid afternoons of December bumping into movie houses spaced like oases. Archaeologists would have to decide whether the artifacts they contained were prerevolutionary seepage from the North or just fun for poor people escaping for a couple of hours from wartime tension and their own underdevelopment.

By four o'clock, groups were milling on the steps outside the theaters, fighting the heat with Ziploc bags filled with crushed ice and artificial fruit flavors, waiting for the first show to start. General support for the revolution among the movie fans was combined with unconcern for ideological purity in what they looked at. At the Cinemateca de Nicaragua there was much less interest in *Pan Oro* from Sovexportfilm than for *Summer Lovers* from Twentieth Century–Fox.

Alsino y el Cóndor, coproduced by Nicaraguans and featuring a number of Latin actors along with Dean Stockwell, was a big local favorite, while *Under Fire,* though hostile to Somoza and sympathetic to the revolution, had not played in Nicaragua when I was there. The Sandinistas felt the script exploited rather than clarified their cause. They had not allowed the film to be shot in Nicaragua, an act of sacrifice possibly against their own interests, since they desperately needed the foreign currency a big movie production would spend in a small country. *Under Fire* also offended the Sandinistas because Gene Hackman and Nick Nolte, playing American journalists, inevitably seemed to be the stars of the revolution itself rather than the Nicaraguans.

These movies and their stars played in Managua in December 1983: *Death Wish II* with Charles Bronson ("Bronson's loose again," said the poster); *The Archer and the Sorceress* with George Kennedy and Victor Campos; *Warriors of a Lost Martial Art* ("Hired Assassins—Human Killing Machines," said the poster flanking a gentle statue of Venus de Milo, unarmed as always, at the Margot Theater); Clint Eastwood in *Any Which Way You Can;* Tom Selleck and Bess Armstrong in *Gran Aventura en China; Evil Under the Sun* with Peter Ustinov, James Mason, Roddy McDowall, Diana Rigg and Maggie Smith (*El Demonio Bajo el Sol,* the Nicaraguans called the Agatha Christie story); Miles O'Keeffe in *Ator the Fighting Eagle*; and Susan Sarandon and David Steinberg in *Tan Cerca del Paraíso,* which was originally *Something Short of Paradise.* A member of a Sandinista youth brigade looked at the poster for the last and nodded his head.

The movies furnished Managuans with something for every mood. If things were not bad enough, you could find something worse; if they were not good enough, you could escape to something better. Vicariousness reached an apex in a picture called *Shocking Asia,* which offered displays of surgery, torture and animal sex, a coproduction of someone in Munich and someone else in Hong Kong. The poster promised the skinning of live animals, cremation along the Ganges, transvestites and hermaphrodites, a "sinsational" sex-transformation operation, a Japanese sex festival, tattooing as an erotic art, "a gruesome S&M show," an amusing elephant festival, "the famous sex museum of Toba" and female and midget wrestlers. While he drank and prepared for his concubines, the first Somoza was said to favor exhibitions of midget wrestling. As they do everywhere, the movies provided Nicaraguans with fantasies of their own history, attractive and repellent.

Next to *Shocking Asia* in the Cabrera Theater was one of the
ubiquitous signs: *Todas las Armas al Pueblo.* "You know what
that means, *compa?*" A young woman in uniform, a *miliciana,*
asked me on her way from her job in a textile factory to do
evening guard duty. Her rhetoric, lined with the revolution's own
logic, does not dissolve easily in the acid of skepticism. "That
sign means we all really do have weapons. The government gives
them out to everyone—to defend Nicaragua. If the government
of El Salvador, Honduras or Guatemala did that, it would fall
tomorrow. They are there, those governments, to control their
people, to keep them in the past. But those are the governments
your government prefers in Central America. *Por qué?* Can you
tell me?"

From a distance, Managua's cathedral looks intact. The feudal
grandeur of the eighteenth century seems to have withstood the
twentieth-century earthquake. It is merely one of Managua's il-
lusions of wholeness. Across the renamed Plaza of the Revolution from the National Palace, which did survive not only the
earthquake but a dramatic capture by the Sandinistas a year before they overthrew Somoza, the cathedral is in fact only a skel-
eton of itself. Its roof is gone, its crumbled walls open out to the
plaza, and in the aisles and floor of the nave, where once the
pews were ranged, the grass grows thick and short. In paintings
flanking what used to be the altar, saints still command ships at
sea and horses in battle; sculptures of Christ and an idealized
Mary, a figure of cult worship in Nicaragua, sit over the doorways. But the principal object of devotion is outside, where a
gigantic full-length portrait of the revolution's patron saint, General Augusto César Sandino, hangs on canvas, obscuring much
of the front of the cathedral. Sandino is dressed like old tintypes
of Pancho Villa—tall cowboy hat, ammunition bandolier, high
boots with spurs. Above the picture is a sign: *Venceremos al
imperialismo.*

The cathedral in its present state, still in ruins a decade and a
half after the earthquake, with an armed revolutionary draped
over it, embodies the conflict between church and state. Many
priests in Nicaragua have embraced the revolution. "Liberation

theology,'' the doctrine that the poor can be helped through their faith and by the church itself in a form of consciousness-raising, has thousands of adherents. The revolution is compatible with the kind of social progress and reform envisioned by the social activists in the church. Sandino's portrait on the face of the cathedral is a natural expression of their revolutionary enthusiasm. The activists trace their immediate lineage to Pope John XXIII; his encyclicals on poverty stirred their hopes and have animated the efforts of a generation of priests and nuns throughout Latin America.

But the older, more conservative priests and, most particularly, the church hierarchy find themselves colliding with the revolution. Priests thought to be insufficiently enthusiastic about the Sandinistas have been set upon by the *turbas divinas,* "divine mobs" of young men and women who see themselves as the revolution's guardians. Foreign priests working in Nicaragua have been banished from the country for counseling draft resistance in the same manner clergy in the United States did during the Vietnam War. The church accuses the state of abridging its freedom of worship. The state accuses the church of disloyalty to Nicaragua. The church complains the state puts its own rigid dogma even into Catholic schoolrooms. The state complains that church works with *las fuerzas capitalistas traidoras* and never once has objected to the mining of Nicaragua's harbors or any other attacks on the country by the counterrevolutionaries and the CIA. The church replies it must remain above politics.

Large as it is, the Managua Cathedral is a microcosm. The FSLN wants to keep it the way it is, a ruined monument to an oppressive past that no longer exists. The state has offered the church money for a new cathedral elsewhere in the city. Cardinal Obando y Bravo insists the old cathedral should be restored and rebuilt right where it is. The cardinal's faith is strong; the old cathedral sits directly on top of a fault in the terrestrial crust, which was why the earthquake destroyed it in the first place.

The earthquake sheared structures away until they became cross sections of themselves.

Near the cathedral is an empty arcade lined with the husks of many old shops. The mezzanine, which appears to have contained the smarter boutiques, looks vacantly down on the barren ground floor, vacantly up to rooflessness. Two more blocks of rubble lead to the indoor municipal pool, still intact with its pretty colored tiles, two feet of liquefied green slime in the deep end. One hundred yards away a destroyed office building, vestigial beams still extending upward for seven stories, has on its facade the ghosts of block letters demarking the prerevolutionary period: "First National City Bank of New York." Where it bustles, Managua could be Hong Kong; where it is deserted, Pompeii.

With no discernible "skyline," the sky itself becomes one of Managua's distinguishing features. When it is saturated, almost ready to rain, the sky is a clam-belly gray. To be underneath it is to smother, like being underneath a mattress. But in December there were often no clouds at all and the sky would become a light blue parasol. Then clouds would form up gradually, changing their shapes and colors with the time of day and weight of the air. The clouds could be thin, heavy, wispy, serrated like the scales of a mackerel, pink, dark, a smoky industrial brown, then purple in a final efflorescence at the end of a hot, vivid day fragrant with hibiscus, oleander and jasmine all fighting the reality of a vanished city.

In the newer parts of town, where the revolution has not only triumphed but built, reality is perceived as both opportunity and message. Close to the military headquarters is a large mural a block long and ten feet high on a wall of reinforced concrete. The figures—people and animals—are portrayed at the moment of highest passion or anguish. The artists (it was a group effort) were clearly aiming at Picasso but their model was only the Picasso of *Guernica.* Every shape is distorted by its own intensity at the moment of pain, victory or death. Grave priests, passionate women, rearing horses, men at war all struggle with an ultimate truth about themselves. Unlike *Guernica,* the mural is in the brilliant colors—flaming reds, Caribbean blues, jungle greens —that give life in Central America its sunny look no matter what happens to be taking place in the tropical brightness.

In front of the mural, Managuans passed each other in the late afternoon, revolutionary ardor nodding politely to bourgeois doubt. A few stray beggars cadged, as they do in large cities everywhere. Their presence has a special poignance in a country where a socialist dream intends the dignity of labor for everyone. It is possible to meet a dozen or so children begging on a given corner, though their entreaties are not harsh or persevering; generally they give a passerby one good shot and then go back to their play. More serious, for themselves and their society, were the several able-bodied and sober men who were begging near the mural. In an American city you know who you're dealing with, careless hoboes blowing in the wind or the detritus of post-industrial prosperity stewing in self-contempt, dependent on the occasional pity of a fellow citizen not yet calloused to a point beyond indifference. In Managua it is harder to know whether begging is a sign the revolution has not gotten itself together enough to provide jobs for everyone or merely an inevitable reminder of the human condition. Since a political system tends either to widen or narrow the gap between those who have and those who do not, begging becomes a confirmation or a denial depending on which socioeconomic aim the state has in mind. However much the Sandinista government would like to see the beggars occupied gainfully, they have so far resisted disappearing into productivity. In Nicaragua, underdevelopment reaches down into the animal kingdom. There are dogs, too, who trot the streets of Managua, not starved packs wild with hunger, only bony little families unable to scratch enough to put more than a thin layer of flesh over their ribs.

When scarcity is the rule, shopping becomes an art form. At the *supermercado* in the Plaza España, which looks superficially like a Safeway, there are aisles with wooden shelves forty to fifty feet long that are completely empty. Above one naked shelf hovered the familiar slogan *Todas las Armas al Pueblo*; it is never easy in Nicaragua to know whether this is the work of a patriot or an ironist. Other counters were about a third filled, sometimes with a single row of mayonnaise jars or tomato juice cans in front and vacant space behind them. The day I was in the market there was a limit of two quarts of milk per person. The red-meat rack was almost empty, but fish were plentiful, as were pastas, rice, vinegar, soap and hundreds of cans of a Shell Oil product that seals leaky radiators. This radiator sealant is a sign of how difficult it is to get replacements or even spare parts for the aging cars that lurch around Managua. Mosquito coils were abundant, along with poisons for rats, scorpions, roaches and ants. In the produce department were dozens of kinds of fresh fruits and vegetables, including some not seen even in North American specialty stores. *Guisantes* and *habichuelas* did not look precisely like any peas and beans I had seen, and the Spanish names for other vegetables carried them toward the exotic: *granadillas, espinaca, rábanos, remolachas, pipianos, perejil, zanahorias.* Ropes of chiles and green peppers hung from the ceiling.

"In the old days," the assistant manager said to me, "we had more products, but only the rich could buy them. Now we have fewer things on the shelves, but everyone can come. This market is partly owned by the government. Some of the private ones are better stocked."

Were the empty shelves due to the economic and military squeeze from the United States, or were they the result of Sandinista mismanagement?

"We have our problems," he said. "Many of the better men in management and distribution left after 1979, and that hurts. But that's not the reason for the big shortages. Let me put it this way. Every time you give twenty million dollars to the contras, we have to send more people to fight them, spend more money to import weapons, go deeper in debt to Communist countries—is that what Reagan wants us to do?—and so we have fewer people to milk the cows, we have smaller crops, we can import less medicine and almost no tractors. Who wins in that cycle?"

We were standing in the book and magazine section. *Vogue Patterns* featuring "Summer Surprises" were available for those who made their own clothes, and so was "Detective Dragnet." Dostoevsky's *Crimen y Castigo* led the shelf from Russia, followed by several hundred copies of various books on Communist theory that the assistant manager said were not selling well. "We get the books from Cuba and Russia free. People look at them more than they buy them.'' Curiously, there were several dozen copies of *The Iliad* but none of *The Odyssey*. ''No one bought *The Odyssey*, so we took it off. We are the loose cannon on the deck of the American empire,'' the assistant manager said. He smiled through his mustache. ''You have us under siege. *The Iliad* is our book for now. We have not yet started the voyage home.''

It was almost sunset. The wind came up and hurried a few clouds toward the horizon. A pink plume rose in the west as though something nice were ascending from a city that was not even quite there. The Bank of America Building, the Intercontinental and a few more surviving pillars of the extinguished skyline loomed over the municipal rubble.

At the hotel, several new Cherokee Chiefs and Volkswagen microbuses had arrived, with ''TV'' spread across their windows in gaffer's tape. These initials were supposed to protect the occupants in combat, the theory being that no side in any conflict was cankered beyond the sensible aspiration of seeing itself on the evening news. The Chiefs and microbuses were fighting for parking spaces nearest the door.

Pushed into the lobby by the dusk, people said and heard and saw what they needed to. ''The Israelis won't talk about what they do in Guatemala.'' ''D'Aubuisson is still pissed about the visa.'' ''The Sandinistas will lift all censorship next month.'' ''Only until the election, then they'll clamp down again.'' ''Our gunboats in the Gulf of Fonseca''—this last was uttered without a verb, becoming just a caption for whatever emotion was meant to be evoked. Perhaps the gunboats were patrolling, attacking, firing, repelling attack, hunting, being sunk; the listener would believe his hope or his fear, whichever was stronger at twilight. A net of guillibility dropped over the lobby each day when the sun went down. The voices in the lobby became antiphonal, chanting at each other until they were inside one's own head, charged with articulating one's own conflicts, playing the district attorney and the devil's advocate.

The scale of lobby sophistication, depending on what the day had brought, might register anywhere along a fixed number of points. Point: Ah, if we could only save this struggling revolution. Counterpoint: First, save it from Washington, you mean; second, from itself.

A fixer for one of the networks was sizing up a correspondent for another network. Fixers were Nicaraguans—usually women —who translated, guided, made contacts and literally fixed things for the television crews. This particular fixer was known for waving slices of herself at each new correspondent coming down on the invasion watch but for proving, in the clinch, to have an airtight pass defense. She would plead she was a Leo and Leos don't mix with Virgos or whatever. When I asked another fixer what this form of flirtation was called here, she answered, "The word in Managua for this kind of woman is 'cock-tease.' What do you call them?"

The chairman of a socialist splinter group in Seattle was issuing a policy declaration that placed the Sandinistas in a continuum of virtue between the Wobblies and the Castro government in Havana. A Santa Barbara massage therapist was collecting signatures of American citizens in Nicaragua willing to condemn his occasional neighbor, Ronald Reagan.

A photographer in from Honduras where he had been on patrol with the contras said they were not burning crops anymore because they were so close to winning they did not want to destroy the economy they were about to take over. Who analyzes their dreams for them? asked a stringer, adding that the government was never stronger, too strong in fact. The photographer said some of the contras were people he didn't want to see date his sister.

The waitress who served the drinks was crying. Two days earlier, her neighbor's grandson had been killed in the mountains. His grandmother—the waitress's neighbor—died when she heard the news. The waitress was not going to let her own son go north either to fight or to pick coffee. But she was not sure it made any difference. She said, "They'll kill us all soon."

A Swedish businessman had just checked in, hoping to sell

machinery to the Sandinistas, prepared to extend definite, but limited, credit. Like everyone else, he was preoccupied, invigorated, by what Nicaraguans called *la situación*. "My dear you," he said, waiting for the elevator, "it is imperative to realize that the geographical and historical and political fact is that the United States, for better, which is now and then, or worse, which is the rest of the time, is the hemispheric power and guarantor. In a just world you wouldn't have to be this, but this is not a just world. You can no more evade that responsibility than you can lop off Florida if you decide you don't like old people and Disney World. So you square your shoulders, which no American government seems able to do without either apology or ignorance, and you say, 'All right, bravo to your little revolution, but here are the limits of what we will put up with. Keep your Marxism to yourselves, and if you want our help, which you desperately need, you'll encourage your opposition and while you're at it steal their better ideas.' "

But the revolution may spread anyway. Isn't that what's threatening to a hemispheric power?

"How threatening? This is a country so poor it can scarcely blow its own nose. Central America is ripe for change and you should be leading it instead of trying to stop it, later on accepting it only when you fail to stop it. The rebels are angry at you. All the more reason for the United States to take the lead, use your prosperity to the rebels' advantage, push your disgusting bourgeois values for all they're worth."

Isn't that what we're trying in El Salvador?

"You haven't tried anything in El Salvador except keeping the lid on when it wants to blow off. The dirty little secret about building on change instead of destroying it is that it would be good for business. The United States doesn't understand that."

The Swedish blueprint was, however, remote from the reality of the elevator. The elevator, when it arrived, was packed with flak jackets and filming equipment. The NBC cameraman said his crew was on its way to the Honduran border.

I asked what they were going for.

"New York wants footage of the Americans up there on a

peace vigil. They're willing to be shot at so we have to shoot them."

Have you been to the border before?

"Twice. The guns have real bullets in them."

How dangerous is it?

"It can be quiet. Nothing. It can be dangerous dangerous."

VII AMERICAN EMBASSY—I

IT WAS NO SURPRISE that the best place to find a cluster of opinionated Americans in Nicaragua was at the American embassy. They were not necessarily, however, *inside* the embassy. Every Thursday morning at seven-thirty, American residents opposed to American policy held what they called a vigil outside the embassy gates. According to the Committee of U.S. Citizens in Nicaragua, six to seven hundred Americans were working in the country, most of them helping the revolution. The vigil often turned into a spirited demonstration attracting several dozen Americans, including clergy and churchworkers, employees from the Nicaraguan ministries of labor, education or culture, workers in agrarian reform, and visiting delegations from all over the United States. They would warm themselves up with a chant that came out like a football cheer at a pep rally: "DOWN WITH THE CONTRAS/DOWN WITH THE MARINES/STOP THE REAGAN WAR MACHINE."

Vigil regulars led the chants and the declarations of conscience, but visitors were often ready with testimony of their own or even a brief performance. One Thursday morning early in December, with forty to fifty Americans in attendance, the Bread

91

and Puppet Theater from Vermont did a short skit called "The Foot." It was a simple piece of street theater in which two actors pantomimed working, eating, sleeping, singing and making love. This, it was implied, was what life is supposed to consist of. A villain, in the form of the Big Foot, arrived to try to do away with all this. The Big Foot embodied bullying, imperialism and war. In case the moral about what country the Big Foot represented was not clear enough, the piece ended with a chant for the rest of the demonstrators to join: "USA, CIA/OUT OF NICARAGUA/ RIGHT AWAY."

"Okay, well-meaning people can get a little extreme at times," said Doug Murray, a thirty-eight-year-old specialist in pesticides who worked for the Nicaraguan ministry of labor and stopped at the vigil on his way to work. "But everyone feels so surrounded, so vulnerable to the threats and power of the United States. You let off a little steam here, and you can last out another week."

A cream-colored car driven by a chauffeur pulled up across the street from the embassy and the demonstration. A young man in a dark suit with a striped shirt and tie got out of the front seat of the car to look at the demonstration. He had the fresh good looks of an actor just getting his first continuing role on a television series that had some chance of survival beyond thirteen weeks. "He's a Marine in civvies doing a recon on the invasion," said a man who had earlier read a statement comparing the U.S. government's current menacing posture toward Nicaragua with the overthrow of Salvador Allende Gossens in Chile ten years earlier.

"Some senators are coming down this week," a woman said as she held up her baby so he could see the Bread and Puppet Theater's peace placard. "I'll bet he works for one of them."

"CIA all the way," said a thin, balding man with a delegation from the midwest.

A black man among the demonstrators, announcing himself as an actor and dancer from New York, gave a brief speech in which he equated U.S. policy toward the Sandinistas with most of what he did not like about America. "Who crushes Nicaragua," he proclaimed, "also crushes women, gays, lesbians, blacks,

Hispanics, Native Americans and other people of color in the United States, as well as the poor and the hungry, and also freedom-seeking peoples throughout the world." Some of those clapping for the actor seemed to do so out of politeness, but he had caught exactly the mood of a couple of dozen demonstrators, who cheered him enthusiastically.

Perhaps the angriest demonstrator was Jim Goff, coordinator for the Committee of U.S. Citizens in Nicaragua. After his wife read a statement condemning the aggression of the Reagan Administration against Nicaragua, Jim Goff remarked to me that the press had been relentlessly unappreciative of the Sandinistas. Thin and ascetic, Goff had observed American policy from the vantage point of thirty-five years in Latin America as a Presbyterian minister. Another American in Nicaragua had described him as more Sandinista than the Sandinistas. The fire in Jim Goff could serve as a reminder that American Protestants are descended from the righteous wrath of Cotton Mather. "The common people here were treated like dust before, deprived of all human rights, trampled by the aristocrats," Jim Goff said. "Everything was for the benefit of a small upper class. This regime works the opposite way, gears itself to the rights and needs of the vast majority. Without a doubt this revolution incorporates the values of the gospel, Christian values. But Reagan wants to make this economy scream the way Nixon did Chile. It takes a Machiavellian to understand how vicious Washington policy can be toward a people and revolution over which it has lost control." Jim Goff was close to spitting out his words. "My major criticism of the Sandinista leaders is that they are too nice, too human, to comprehend the depth of evil that can come from the White House. They are too good to understand the absolute corruption of absolute power in Washington." Those breathing such apocalyptic air could be certain every day was the day before the end, every night was opening night.

A forestry teacher from Massachusetts was passionately *para el proceso,* in favor of the "process," as the revolution is often called. "Here we are getting ready to crush this beautiful country," she said, "without understanding the first thing about it.

Our government keeps accusing them of not having democracy, yet they participate daily, often every minute, in determining the course of their lives. They vote in their block organizations, they vote in their unions, they vote in their professional committees, and they vote on who to send to the Council of State. Whenever a law is proposed it is debated by everyone and ripped to shreds if that's what they feel like doing. Gasoline is rationed and the rich can't get it to go to the beach every weekend the way they used to. But most of the people, way over ninety percent, don't even know what you're talking about if you tell them gas is rationed because they've never been close to owning a car."

The young man watching from across the street came over to talk to a few of the demonstrators. His suit and tie were enough to separate him from everyone else. Some demonstrators were suspicious and moved away from him. Inside the embassy gates the Marine detailed to observe the vigil spoke into his walkie-talkie. He was in civvies—no sense in giving the demonstrators a uniformed target—but his haircut suggested he was not long removed from Parris Island. When the Marine tried to listen to the walkie-talkie, it spewed static so rudely he jerked it away from his ear and shook it for its disobedience. A few demonstrators laughed at him. The young man from across the street went back to his car, got into the front seat next to the driver and had himself driven around to the back of the embassy, where there was another entrance. He apparently did not want to challenge the demonstrators by trying to go through the front gate, which they were blocking.

Where the young man's car had been, a black man in a gray T-shirt came and stood. He looked American, and the block lettering on his T-shirt said "Property of UCLA." He did not cross the street to the demonstrators but watched them carefully.

The demonstration wound down, becoming a coffee klatch without the coffee. Politics were mingled with references to home, exchanges of information on where to get fresh beef or flashlight batteries. The United States seemed much farther away than a four- or-five-hour plane ride, much closer than the phone calls that sounded as though they were connecting two extremities of the solar system.

"I haven't felt this way about our country since we bombed Hanoi for Christmas in '72," a middle-aged man on the fringe of the demonstration said to his wife.

"I'm glad we won't be here for Christmas," she said.

The black man in the UCLA T-shirt crossed the street as the middle-aged man began to argue with a young member of his delegation. The younger man seemed to be searching earnestly for a policy he could hang on to. The middle-aged man, whose wife stood next to him trying to get him to stop talking and board the delegation bus, wore a dark blue artist's beret. "No, but really, where do you think freedom's frontier should be?" the young man asked. He appeared to be still in college.

"Not here, I guess. What are we calling freedom this week? You going to the briefing at the ag ministry?" the man in the beret asked.

"If we're going, let's get aboard," said his wife.

"But why shouldn't the moon be freedom's frontier? Shouldn't every place we can reach be free?" the young man asked. "It's so much better for everyone. I'm not saying Nicaragua *isn't* free in some respects, but *if* it isn't, wouldn't it be better off if we helped it get that way? I don't like what our government is doing here, but if we did it right . . ."

"That's what they said about Vietnam. Tell him, Irma."

"Leave me out of your Vietnam powwows and let's get on the bus."

"But if freedom is indivisible, theoretically we should extend it everywhere. In ethics class we learned that if you have something you believe in, it could even be a sin not to make it available to other people."

"Do you know anything about wines?" the older man in the beret asked.

"I like Chianti. You're trying to wiggle out of this," the student said.

"Some of the better wines, in fact a couple of the very finest wines I've ever tasted in France, are not available on this side of the Atlantic. They are indivisible, too, but they don't travel well, they taste lousy after a boat ride. We exported a load of freedom down here, and it was called Somoza. By the time it got where we were sending it, it was no longer freedom. Good luck with your Chianti."

"Freedom's not as delicate as your wines. I'm saying we have to keep our options open."

"Your option is to nuke us," said the black man in the UCLA T-shirt. "I come from Puerto Cabezas on the East Coast. We never liked de Sponeesh over there, but you boys keep out of it. You come down here and don't nuke us, you gonna think Vietnam was a picnic, mon."

The vigil ended with a chant of *"No pasarán,"* echoing the Loyalists in the Spanish Civil War. Literally, they shall not pass, the Marines, the contras, anybody we don't want here.

The black man, clearly unfamiliar with these weekly demonstrations, saw he was dealing with Americans who were mostly, from his point of view, sympathetic. He smiled as he walked away. "My daddy used to go up to Tampa on a banana freighter," he said.

VIII   <u>AMERICAN EMBASSY—II</u>

THEN THERE WAS WHAT WENT ON inside the gates. Where in all this December fever stood the branch office of the foreign policy and armed might of the United States, the American embassy? The place looked sleepy. When the embassy gates rolled back to let in a taxi, what they revealed was only the stillness of a tropical coma. There was the usual attention to security, and the grounds were fenced with dignified vertical bars reaching a bit higher than a basketball hoop. Electronic devices were noticeable here and there, but the word "transponder" would have seemed overwrought. The compound itself appeared to house the working division of a multinational corporate entity, communicating normally with its world headquarters at the State Department and the leaders of the local competitor whom it was delegated to watch and occasionally take a trick from.

It was not hard to get an appointment with the ambassador. Stringers less than a year out of Columbia Journalism School were marching in loaded with questions about American intentions, Sandinista signals and the famous Contadora process that was praised by all sides as the key to peace in the entire region, meaning Central America. Completing the actual penetration to the ambassador's office could be a little more difficult than getting the appointment. The morning I was at the embassy a report was circulating that there was a shakeup in the Sandinista foreign ministry. Another had it that all Cubans were being sent home by the frightened Nicaraguan junta. The ambassador was busy chasing down these rumors for Washington and could not see anybody until he had established their definite falsity. State needed to know right away, last night if possible.

QUAINTON, ANTHONY CECIL EDEN, Ambassador; b. Seattle, Apr. 4, 1934; s. Cecil Eden and Marjorie Josephine (Oates) Q; B.A., Princeton, 1955; B. Litt., Oxford (Eng.) U., 1958; m. Susan Long, Aug. 7, 1958; children—Katherine, Eden, Elizabeth. Research fellow St. Anthony's Coll., Oxford, 1958–59; with Fgn. Service, State Dept., 1959—: Vice consul, Sydney, Australia, 1960–62; Urdu lang. trainee, 1962–63; 2d sec., econ. officer Am. embassy, Karachi, Pakistan, 1963–64, Rawalpindi, Pakistan, 1964–66; 2d sec., polit. officer mem sr. polit officer for India 1969–72; 1st sec. Am. embassy, Paris, 1972–73; counselor dep., chief mission Am. embassy, Kathmandu, Nepal, 1973–77; ambassador to Central African Empire, Bangui, 1977–78; dir. Office for Combatting Terrorism, Dept. State, Washington, 1978–81; ambassador to Nicaragua, Managua, 1982—. English Speaking Union fellow, 1951–52; Marshall scholar, 1955–58. Recipient Rivkin award, 1972.

—WHO'S WHO IN AMERICA

"Tony Quainton can't be too hard-line or else no sane president will ever give him another embassy," a former U.S. government official said of the ambassador to Nicaragua, "and he can't be too soft or the Reagans will fire him."

When the American community put on Agatha Christie's *Ten Little Indians,* he played the judge. Good-looking in the straight-arrow way favored by the State Department, he liked to play tennis or jog, but he could never be thought of as easygoing. He was too devoted to his work for anyone to call him casual. The night before I saw him, I heard an American at the Intercontinental complain, "Quainton is a preppy State Department dope." "I found him sympathetic, knowledgeable, a nice guy," a second American said. "So why doesn't he quit?" the first American asked. "Then he couldn't do any good at all," the second American said. "They just want him here to find out what the FSLN is thinking," the first American said. "Isn't that what an ambassador is for?" the second American asked.

In person, Tony Quainton's formal diplomatic loyalty to his employers was combined with his willingness to express himself directly and informally about the Sandinistas. The mixture suggested that he was not trying to be a hero to anyone, not to powerful conservatives nor out-of-power liberals. He was doing what Americans at the Intercontinental accused him of, finding out what the Sandinistas were up to, evaluating it in terms of his own experience and passing it along to Washington. When he talked to journalists, as he frequently had to, the ground rules were that he was not to be quoted directly. He was to be referred to in the vague-person singular, *always* the "Western diplomat."

As ambassador, Quainton got around to a good deal of the country but wished he could see more. He maintained wide contacts throughout the government and the business community, which meant the Sandinista *comandantes* and their principal opposition. When he was asked on Managua television why the United States was encouraging the contras, he replied there would be no counterrevolution if the country was truly democratic. The contras, he said, would disappear in a week if Nicaragua had a free and open political system in which everyone could participate. In the televised debate, which could never have occurred in Havana or Moscow, Tony Quainton and his opponents kept at each other for almost an hour. There was some rhetoric on both sides, and there were disagreements over how to bring peace to Central America, but the mood was respectful and serious. Both sides agreed that the key to peace was acceptance of the Contadora proposals for disarmament and democracy in Central America. These proposals, essentially creating a demilitarized zone, were formulated initially on the Panamanian resort island of Contadora by the foreign ministers of Mexico, Panama, Venezuela and Colombia.

In private, Quainton felt it was possible to talk to the Sandinistas if you did not take their lectures too seriously. Henry Kissinger and his Bipartisan Commission on Central America, appointed by President Reagan in the summer of 1983 to arrive at a policy consensus, had recently been studying the Sandinistas and Quainton's performance. The commission heard earnest lectures in Nicaragua and took them earnestly. As his commission prepared its final report, Kissinger had remarked that if the United States cannot "manage" our own region, we will be disregarded around the world as a credible ally. If we cannot control a strictly local affair in what we have properly regarded as our backyard, our word will be seen everywhere to have been uttered from a toothless mouth. "Managing" in Nicaragua meant facing down the Sandinistas. Accordingly, by the end of 1983 the Kissinger commission was preparing proposals on Central America that were military and confrontational, the opposite of Contadora. Silence, with an averted glance, was the way Tony Quainton answered a question dealing with the wisdom of going for military solutions in a crescent of countries already unstable, wracked by poverty and prone to idiosyncratic local conflicts.

Quainton saw the Sandinistas faced with still another problem, the historical sense of inferiority among their countrymen. Since the nineteenth century there had been the conviction that when there were conflicts in Nicaragua, only the United States could resolve them. It was an attitude that surfaced more among the Nicaraguan aristocrats than the peasants. The same effect had prevailed for generations among Indian Brahmans, helping to keep their homeland in the British Empire until after the Second World War. Many upper-class Nicaraguans had been sent north to school—a few had gone, like Tony Quainton, to Andover and Princeton—and they tended to believe in the country that had educated them. When Quainton was told at parties and receptions that he had better get the Green Berets in here soon, he was not hearing mere opposition to the Sandinistas. It was the traditional outlook among wealthy Nicaraguans that when confusion and difficulties beset the country, the time had come once again for the United States to come to the rescue.

Despite a recent loosening of censorship in Managua, Quainton was not particularly impressed with the concessions the *coman-*

dantes were making to their opponents. These, in his view, were not substantial and would not result in changing the revolution's relatively monolithic leadership. When I asked if there were not real differences of opinion among the *comandantes* themselves, he answered that he had found some differences, in philosophy as well as style, but that the leadership had so far managed to mute these behind a fixed party line. The embassy had been trying to get the exiled counterrevolutionary leadership into the active political system but was not making progress. Quainton wanted the Sandinistas to deal with internal and external problems simultaneously; the Sandinistas were claiming that the United States was the cause of both.

In the ambassador's expressed view, the invasion of Grenada accelerated a process of getting the Sandinistas to think carefully about conditions in the region that would be acceptable to the United States. If you were a "Western diplomat" in Nicaragua, Grenada made your job easier, no question about that. You might not have liked it when it started, it might have worried you badly, but it made your job easier. They knew in Managua you were willing to play hardball. From another perspective, Grenada was now our baby; what were we planning to do with it? That was one of the limits on a great power.

Most of the local business community was hostile to the Nicaraguan government and vice versa. The big companies remembered the old days and did not want to let go of the perks they had always enjoyed. But Nicaragua's chief trading partner (before the 1985 embargo) was still the United States. General Mills had a plant. The Esso refinery was there, now run mostly by Panamanians. Texaco hid in the middle of a genuine old-style imperialist compound. When the ambassador went out to the countryside, he visited the big coffee growers and cattlemen at their *fincas*. He had been recently to Matagalpa, Chinandega, León. The kind of people he saw—yes, they were upper-class, but they had all hated Somoza—did not like the government. They would admit, though, over their Nica libres, that they were doing all right financially. It was possible to do business with the Sandinistas. The Nica libres, which were rum and Coke (whatever else Nicaraguans may get from Cuba, they refuse to concede their national drink originated in Havana), were part of the problem for an American ambassador roaming the countryside. You had to avoid getting pickled in the *Flor de Caña* rum before lunch. *Finca* life in the Nicaraguan outback. The ranchers were used to it; ambassadors were not.

What *about* the Cubans?

A couple of thousand of them did go home, but they'll probably be back. Some go out, some come in. It was hard to tell for certain which way the flow was heaviest. Cubana Airlines landed at Sandino Airport every day, and people were still getting off the planes.

On the question of the inconsistency in telling the Sandinistas to stop helping the insurgents in El Salvador while the United States continued to help the Nicaraguan insurgents, the Western diplomat was all State Department: We'll stop if they do.

Encountered at a reception, Tony Quainton made a good conversationalist, a still-boyish and cheerful representative of his government who knew just when a topic was heading toward diplomatic thin ice. Gracefully, he would steer toward the safety of mutual concern. He opened his eyes when he spoke, unlike other officials, who often narrowed them suspiciously or confidentially. With the other kind of official, you could never know which look was aimed at you until the squint turned into a joke only he got (it was confidential, at least he wanted you to think so), or into an ossified reaffirmation of policy (it was suspicious and you were regarded as a hostile questioner; please go). That was a proconsul, and the United States was said to have one as its ambassador right next door in Honduras, but it was not the case anymore in Nicaragua. Tony Quainton knew he was in a country that had welcomed its last proconsul.

Henry Kissinger did not have Tony Quainton fired from the embassy in Managua until early 1984. Kissinger and his Commission on Central America had arrived in Managua in October 1983, five days after the CIA attack on the oil storage tanks in the port of Corinto. The papers in Managua were full of the Corinto raid—

as, more briefly, were American papers—and the whole country Quainton was assigned to was up in arms. Quainton, according to his associates, had not known the attack was coming, and now right after it here came Kissinger. Daniel Ortega read the Kissinger commission a Central American riot act about the misdeeds, past and present, of the United States. Quainton, when it was his turn to brief the commission, allowed that the Sandinistas might have some grounds for offense. Beyond that, he felt negotiations were possible, even though the commission had been offended by Ortega.

"Tony Quainton was fired from Managua for telling the truth," said a State Department colleague who was himself a former ambassador to a Soviet ally. "He was fired for telling Kissinger exactly what he did not want to hear, that we should listen to the Sandinistas and explore their intentions. Quainton advised the commission that the Nicaraguan government was not a dogmatic Soviet puppet. The Sandinistas could be tough, nasty, unpleasant, but we could work with them, and we should take their olive branches seriously. When they let opponents out of jail, lifted censorship, pursued Contadora, we ought to encourage all that. Kissinger had disliked Ortega personally and was in no mood for this kind of conciliatory talk from Quainton. He told Reagan and Shultz to get rid of Tony as soon as he got back. What he wanted to hear, what he would have paid attention to, was: 'The Sandinistas are making overtures but are, as usual, insincere like all Marxists.' "

Quainton's colleague, with over twenty years in the foreign service, perceived Latin America as a diplomatic dumping ground. "If you really want to see our country at its worst, go to Latin America as a foreign service officer. You'll see us in the most shameful guises—as bullies, racists, arrogant elitists, dirty tricksters. That's why the good ones in the foreign service don't go there, or they'll volunteer once, like Tony Quainton, and never again. Tony is one of the excellent ones. For the diplomatic service, Latin America is exactly what it is for American business, the last stop for a failure. If you can't make it in Europe, go to Asia. If you fail in Asia, they'll try you in the Middle East.

If you can't cut it in the Middle East, they'll send you to Latin America. Tony himself wanted to go because it's a very sensitive spot and they needed him badly. Never again, you can be sure. The sad part is what happens when he does get a new embassy. Will his spirit be broken? Has Tony learned the lesson that if they don't like the message they kill the messenger?''

Before he left Managua, Ambassador Quainton sent a secret cable to the State Department that was leaked in Washington to the International Press Service, a news agency specializing in the Third World. "Recent events have accelerated the polarization process, and compromise appears increasingly remote," Quainton's cable read. "The mining of the ports and the escalation in contra activities convinced FSLN leaders that a soft-line policy is hopeless, as the U.S. is determined to destroy the revolution." Quainton came as close as he could in the cable to opposing the Administration policy of mining harbors and supporting the contras. Attributing to the Sandinistas the conclusion that the United States was "determined to destroy the revolution" was a diplomat's way of telling the Administration that if it had wanted to make an enemy in Central America, it had succeeded in doing so.

Extremists on both sides were helping each other. Each time the United States raised the military ante by means of CIA or contra activity, the Nicaraguans asked for help from the place most willing to give it, the Soviet Union, fulfilling President Reagan's prophecy that the "evil empire" was spreading into the Western Hemisphere. Each time the *comandantes* exiled a priest or spoke of solidarity with their brothers who were trying to "liberate" El Salvador (regardless of whether they sent arms), someone in the Reagan Administration would call Nicaragua "an infected piece of meat" and liken the Sandinistas to the Nazis, as did Curtin Winsor, Jr., the U.S. Ambassador to Costa Rica. Curtin Winsor had been a member of the Reagan transition team at the State Department, much closer to Administration tone and policy than Tony Quainton.

When the CIA would put out a manual instructing the contras to assassinate their fellow Nicaraguans and hire criminals to create martyrs for their cause, it would chiefly strengthen the hand of those in Managua who were convinced that the United States was interested only in its own empire and not in freedom. The more the hardliners took over on both sides—opposites in one way, quite similar in another—the less room there was for a diplomat like Tony Quainton. Since his cable emphasized the remoteness of compromise, which after all is a principal goal of diplomacy, he was in effect saying he could no longer be useful. If his fellow ambassador next door in Costa Rica regarded as Nazis the government to which Quainton was accredited, how effective could Quainton be in discussing conditions of coexistence with the Sandinistas?

"Between Daniel Ortega's claim that the United States was responsible for the Sandinista revolution in the first place," a Western diplomat said, showing a touch of ennui with both interviews and diplomacy, "and the American claim that the Soviets are more responsible for the Sandinistas every day, an ambassador here has limited maneuverability."

Affirmation of policy, not trade-offs that might bring peace, had become the duty of an American ambassador in Managua. If there was one posture ideologues of any stripe could not abide, it was sitting still for facts unsupportive of their theses. This gave them lumbago. It was why Tony Quainton had to be fired. He had lost his influence in the government he worked for and, as a consequence, in the one he was trying to maintain relations with.

Given instant communication around the world, ambassadors no longer have the power to formulate policy, but often they have considerable influence. This was true of Winsor in Costa Rica and John Negroponte on the other side of Nicaragua in Honduras. Negroponte was a political officer in Saigon when the Vietnam War was at its height and later worked for the National Security Council under Kissinger. When American hostility to the Nicaraguans was growing and the Reagan Administration wanted someone to keep the Hondurans in line while running the covert contra war against the Sandinistas, Negroponte was sent to Honduras. He could occasionally be contradicted by the Hondurans, as when they fired a corrupt general who had become too embarrassingly groveling a servant of the United States, but Negroponte came as close to a proconsul as any American ambassador in the world.

With Winsor and Negroponte on either side of him, by December 1983 Tony Quainton was, like the country where he was serving, isolated in his own region. Quainton possessed little influence, not much confidence from his own government and in all likelihood very few secrets. All he knew was the facts of Nicaragua as he perceived them, and no one in power in Washington wanted to hear those. The hard-liners were in control wherever he turned. Quainton was all alone with his limited maneuverability.

It remained to be seen whether Tony Quainton had learned to be a messenger, as his State Department colleague was afraid he might, who would carry only messages his superiors wanted to receive. If he proved nothing else while in Managua, he had showed he could handle turbulence, hostility from the home office and an ambivalent relationship with the host country. The further adventures of Tony Quainton might test him again with all three of these confusions. After a brief period in diplomatic limbo, Quainton was given the embassy in Kuwait.

IX PURÍSIMA

THE ROCKETS FINALLY EXPLODED over Managua on the night of December 7, but not to commemorate Pearl Harbor. The sky was so brightened with flares it would have been possible to read a book outside long after sundown, except that no one was standing still. People ran in all directions, forming lines at certain pre-arranged spots around the city. The sounds resembled those of what in Vietnam was called "incoming," which meant shells headed in the direction of whoever was describing them. Everyone in Managua seemed at first to be deafened by the noise of the explosions, and then everyone adjusted. Everyone was also laughing and dancing in the streets.

This was a celebration combining aspects of Christmas, New Year's Eve, July Fourth, and Halloween. It was the Festival of Purísima. Colored lights were strung over all the principal boulevards. Children who did not carry ratchets and horns made noise with whatever they could get their hands on or blow into. Purísima, short for María Purísima, Mary most pure, is the feast celebrating the Immaculate Conception. Though this is often confused by non-Catholics with the doctrine of Jesus' virgin birth, the Immaculate Conception has nothing to do with the Annunciation (the angel Gabriel's announcement to Mary that she would bear the son of God) or with Jesus Christ himself but only with his mother. The Immaculate Conception, as promulgated by the church in the nineteenth century, holds that Mary herself was conceived without sin. As the Roman Catholic Church puts it, the Virgin Mary, "in the first instant of her conception by a singular privilege and grace granted by God, was preserved free from all stain of original sin."

The reverence in Nicaragua for Mary amounts to a cult. ("Bourgeois Mariolatry" it is called by those few who hold themselves aloof from the cult, though its roots are far more peasant than bourgeois.) In the representations found around the country, Christ himself is a pale and stoic figure. His mother is not only holy but also earthly. In Mary repose the tears for yesterday and hopes for tomorrow. Devout Nicaraguans believe she shares all joy, for she bore the son of God himself, and she understands all pain, for she endured the loss of that son. (The son himself, it is understood, had the higher goal of salvation of the world and could not preoccupy himself with mere sorrow or delight.) Such piety, inevitably, has its obverse. Worshiping one woman so devoutly casts all others in her shadow and makes it easier for men to assume superiority over women. Even mothers are on pedestals that only imitate Mary's; wives and mistresses contend for places below her in the female pantheon. It is a hierarchy the Sandinistas try to weaken without confronting directly.

But one night a year is set aside purely for the celebration of Mary.

"Madre de Heroes y Martires Ruega por Nosotros," the banner above one of Mary's shrines implored: Mother of heroes and martyrs pray for us. Children lined up with their parents beneath the banner to be given small presents when they reached the shrine itself. There was an element of waiting to see Santa Claus at Macy's. Away from the big shrines, in the neighborhoods it was more like Halloween, with costumed children going door to door to collect little gifts of candy and party favors. In a country as poor as Nicaragua, inventiveness was almost as noticeable as the celebration itself. One little girl received a necklace made of

clear plastic drinking straws that had been cut up and strung together; separating the two-inch straw segments were tiny pieces of colored cardboard rolled to look like beads. *"Gracias a María Purísima,"* the little girl said as she put the necklace on. Some of the Managuans had splurged on spangled costumes, while others wore only sport shirts with a splash of color. A number of stray Americans, wandering off from their delegations for the evening, were part of the throng enjoying themselves. When they were not taking pictures, they were expressing solidarity with the Nicaraguan revolution. It was soon clear that if people were wearing T-shirts that read *Viva Sandino* or *Todas Armas al Pueblo* they were likely to be Americans. If their T-shirts said Santa Monica, University of North Carolina, or Detroit Tigers, they were surely Nicaraguans dropping politics for Purísima.

Not that politics were absent on the Nicaraguan side. The sight of the *comandantes* parading down the Avenida de Simón Bolívar was the first sure sign there would be an election campaign in Nicaragua before too many more White House communiqués condemning Sandinista totalitarianism. Daniel Ortega's appearance was a high point for the crowd. They cheered the Coordinator of the Junta as he swept in with several of his own children. He stood next to a priest at one of the shrines and gave out presents. The crowd cheered more; in the angry split between the church hierarchy and the Sandinista leadership, they did not often see their padres standing next to their politicians. Ortega finally held several babies and was cheered as if he had just brought Nicaragua an international soccer championship. The earnest Coordinator could not quite bring himself to kiss these babies, but he was getting closer. He gave a brief, winsome smile. Campaign '84, which had not yet been announced or even agreed upon, was underway.

Beneath his dark mustache and intense brown eyes, Ortega is generally unsmiling in both public and private. Though his demeanor lightened somewhat as the Sandinistas consolidated their power, he was criticized in the early days of the revolution for lacking a sense of humor or even of fun. He has lived for ten years with a beautiful woman, Rosario Murillo, who leads the Sandinista Association of Culture workers. Together they make a handsome couple, but they are not charismatic and have made no attempt to place themselves before the public as embodiments of the national will. This requires some restraint in a country whose peasantry, under the influence of religious iconography and the traditional self-promotion of *caudillos* who seize power, is given readily to hero worship. Normally, Ortega is solemn, resolute, even dour.

There is a famous photograph in Nicaragua of Daniel Ortega being taken to prison by a member of Somoza's National Guard after his arrest during a bank robbery in 1967. He was twenty-two. Ahead of Ortega were seven years in prison, and ahead of his country were twelve more years of Somoza, including forty to fifty thousand deaths in the insurrection that finally drove Somoza out and brought the Sandinistas to power in 1979. The bank robbery had been to get money that could finance the Sandinistas, and it was not Ortega's first. He had been organizing, fighting as an urban guerrilla, and taking to the hills since he was fifteen. He was the oldest of three sons of a middle-class merchant who wrote pamphlets extolling liberty and criticizing the Somozas. When he was finally captured, Ortega was beaten so badly in prison by the National Guard that he almost went blind in his right eye; he still has a prominent scar on his temple. The only time he is known to have allowed himself a wistful moment was when he wrote a poem from prison in which he said he was sad never to have seen Managua when miniskirts were in fashion.

The future president was ransomed from prison when Sandinista commandos stormed an elegant Managua Christmas party in 1974 and exchanged their hostages for Ortega and two dozen comrades. For five more years Ortega continued to fight while most of his guerrilla superiors fell, one by one, in combat with the National Guard. When they at last achieved victory in 1979, so much of the Sandinista leadership had been killed that except for Tomás Borge the entire nine-man Directorate was under forty. But even in the early photograph with the National Guardsmen leading him away, before the beatings and torture, before the seven prison years and the five years of guerrilla warfare, Daniel Ortega looks to have one subject alone on his mind: Nicaragua.

It is boring to be this way. It is tedious for friends, at times unbearable for colleagues who would like to talk of something else, impossible for strangers who, on a first meeting, would like to hear about anything other than a small country somewhere along the umbilical cord connecting two of the world's great landmasses whose continental imaginations harbor the conceit of universal significance. It cannot be easy to be in such a man's family. It cannot always be easy to be the man himself, since so often he has to pretend to be interested in other problems or pleasures. But Daniel Ortega at twenty-two on his way to prison was what he remained at thirty-eight in the crowd celebrating Purísima, a man obsessed with his nation. I had been told at the State Department before going to Nicaragua that its leaders were "a pretty third-rate bunch." Whatever his rating on the scale of international political acumen, Ortega seemed to have a formidable attention span.

So it was natural for the Junta Coordinator and president-to-be, in the midst of a cheering crowd at a great religious and national festival, to remain almost somber. The turn of events that had brought him to Purísima could hardly be said to have stopped revolving. He would do what he could to influence them in his country's favor, and his eyes shone inward and outward at the same time, as they always had, while he calculated the chances of Nicaragua against both the gravitational pull of its own underdevelopment and the momentum of the national engine coursing toward it from the north.

He held his children up to see the crowd better. He waved to people he knew or who knew him. He never winced when the rockets went off. He threw a glance at an American who stood watching the surge, perhaps twenty feet away. Raising his eyebrows and nodding past the admirers directly in front of him, Ortega raised his arm in a half-wave that might be saying he would see the other man later. Did Ortega know him from somewhere? It was the kind of gesture that, when photographed during an assassination, allows police and caption writers to say the victim seemed to recognize his assailant. Ortega was only giving a quick look to the young man who, a day earlier, had commanded his chauffeur to stop the car so he could observe a demonstration at the American embassy. The demonstrators had wondered suspiciously who he was. He had worn a suit at the embassy; now the American was dressed more appropriately for the tropics, though his blue button-down shirt and pleatless slacks could not constitute a complete liberation from the Ivy League. The man moved off. Ortega pressed more flesh.

Wanting a picture of Ortega that would show him in the midst of an admiring crowd, an American photographer named Maria Morrison, a stringer for United Press International, looked for something to climb or stand on. A network producer at the Intercontinental, wanting to ask her to dinner, had said that with her rangy good looks she reminded him more of a model than a photographer. It did not get him the date, and her height, which put her above most Nicaraguan men, did not now get her high enough for a good photograph of Daniel Ortega. She spotted a rickety fence and started to climb it. She broke her flash attachment but got to the top of the fence anyway. It was unstable. There was no post, nothing to lean against, while she took the picture. Two young Nicaraguan men spotted Maria Morrison and offered to help. She asked them to steady the fence. They grasped her ankles and held them firmly. She took two pictures but wanted more. Then Maria Morrison realized that a traditional Nicaraguan law of diminishing returns was in operation, and she jumped down from the fence just before her helpers' hands reached her thighs.

In the next block a man stood in line for a late movie with his young daughter. He had had enough Purísima and she was glutted with candy, but they were not ready to go home. An older man, also in line for the movie, began an argument. It developed that the younger man was a bus driver and an official of the transport union. The older man was a retired customs inspector. Both had apparently irrigated themselves for Purísima with *Flor de Caña,* but neither was drunk.

"Look at these Sandinistas," said the older man, "so cozy with the church on Purísima. Tomorrow they'll send some more priests out of the country and call the bishop names."

"I think perhaps you do not understand," said the younger man with the daughter. "The priests who had to leave were foreigners telling the young *muchachos* to stay out of the army. We have to defend ourselves against the contras and the Yankees, and we need an army to do that." The revolution was still at a point at which its converts generally try to reason politely with its dissenters. Instead of calling them reactionary swine or imperialist lackeys, they begin as the bus driver did, imputing a lack of understanding or education, not an evil motive. They condescend to those who have not seen the light, but they seldom abuse on an individual basis. (In large groups it can be very different and confrontational.) "We are menaced everywhere. Our survival is at stake. Under the circumstances, don't you think draft evasion is treason?"

The older man looked a little suspiciously at the younger man. He had made his complaint casually and seemed to have expected a little grunt of agreement, or possibly a slightly different grunt of disagreement, not a speech. Now he noticed the FSLN pin on the younger man's pocket. "A man should be free to fight or stay home. Even Somoza let us alone that way."

"Somoza did not have the Yankees threatening to invade."

"The Yankees can call their leaders stupid fools, and the leaders can't touch them. If you try it here they don't let you print it or they shut you up fast."

"No one goes to prison who's not a *somocista.*"

"I didn't say prison, I said they just don't let you speak freely. They vex the holy church and her priests."

"I respect the church, I respect the bishops," the younger man said. "But sometimes I think they are working with the Yankees."

"They obey the Holy Father," the older man said, "and the *norteamericanos* want to be our friends, but your *comandantes* spit in their faces."

"The *norteamericanos* are attacking, trying to crush the revolution, which is trying to live, to breathe. Why don't the bishops speak out, just one time, against the destruction of our homes and schools by the contras, the rape of women, the kidnapping of young men? Why don't they say one word against the CIA which attacks us every day?''

"The church is not political.''

"The church is Nicaraguan. Do the Yankee priests not speak out against their enemies in war? What do you think the Yankee churches would say if they were attacked on all their borders by a country so much bigger than they are? They would say every Yankee with red blood should serve his God by defending his *patria.*''

"Why don't your Sandinistas talk to the rebels. They're Nicaraguans, too.''

"They kill our babies. Tigers! Four times during Somoza the Guardia beat my wife. You know they lead the contras now, you know it. Letting the contras back would be a betrayal of everything we fight and die for. *Nunca!*'' The younger man's daughter looked at the older man, then back to her father. At the age of eight or nine, she was probably familiar with his political opinions, but she did not seem to be at ease with this much heat coming from him.

"My young friend, your revolution also lives in the real world. There are pressures and limits on what a small, poor country can do in a world where the giants fight.''

"Why make concessions? The enemy is determined to destroy us.''

They were buying their tickets now, and they noticed me watching them.

"*Norteamericano?*''

Sí.

"I like U.S.,'' the older man said. When he spoke English he was a different person, no longer an elder but now suddenly ready to be subservient. "U.S. got de fockin' life, mon. U.S. trying to help Nicaragua, right?''

"Tell this to the mothers of the U.S. Marines, *por favor,*'' the younger man said in Spanish. "We will do anything to preserve our revolution. Stop your sons from coming here to defend foreign interests and bad policies. Your sons will come home in plastic bags. Fifty thousand of us died to get what we have. We can lose a few more. It will be hard, but we'll win. *Adelante! Forge ahead!*''

The younger man handed a ticket to his daughter. The older man scratched his head. Not quite together, and not separately, they walked into the theater to see *The Secret of NIMH,* an MGM/United Artists animated feature with the voice-overs of Hermione Baddeley, John Carradine, and Dom De Luise. One more rocket, brighter than all the rest, opened its technicolor umbrella over Managua, and then María Purísima's own starring role ended for the evening, regardless of whether she smiled or wept at the proceedings held in her sacred honor.

X FOREIGN MINISTRY

MOST VISITORS TO NICARAGUA, whether they are journalists, tourists, or members of delegations, find themselves at various ministries and bureaus for briefings that can last for hours. The briefings are given not only by progovernment sources but by the political opposition and the anti-Sandinista Catholic hierarchy as well. At times, they leave visitors dizzy with the world view of whomever they were last harangued by. I saw a man from Milwaukee run out of the union of agricultural workers one afternoon screaming that he had been briefed to within an inch of his sanity and would have to go home immediately.

The morning after Purísima I went to the foreign ministry for a briefing that actually turned out to be brief and to the point. The ministry is a former shopping mall, built rectangularly around a tiled courtyard. The windows onto the courtyard are all floor-to-ceiling, now curtained but originally for the display of hardware, travel posters, shoes, cosmetics. The courtyard features azaleas, ferns, a jacaranda tree, and the smells of Southern California suburbs.

While waiting for the secretary-general, whom I had come to see, I was introduced to Saul Arana, a young, eager official in charge of the North American section. He was excited. The revolution obviously worked for him as he worked for it. He could not stop smiling even when reciting the usual Sandinista litany of American misdeeds. "Look at us," he said. "In the face of political, economic, and military aggression from the United States, with hostile armies funded by the CIA on both borders, cut off from most international credits, still the revolution is able to fill between seventy-five and eighty percent of its promises to the Nicaraguan people. Literacy, health care, housing. We're doing it, we're succeeding." Saul Arana personified the pride and enthusiasm of Nicaragua, a David using the slingshot of the revolution against the northern Goliath. But he also saw Goliath in double vision, like so many Nicaraguans. "If we could only get our truth to the American people, we know you'd be our friends. We have to get past the U.S. government—and beyond that the CIA."

It may have been triple vision; for Saul Arana there were the American people, their government, and then the CIA. The immense popularity of the American president did not faze him. The fact that the American people elect their government, of which the CIA is an instrument, did not stop Saul Arana from having the impression that he was dealing with three separate entities. The people were friendly; their government was harsh; the CIA, uncontrollable and off in its own bellicose corner, was impossible.

A young woman who worked for Saul Arana, Sophia Clark, reinforced her boss. "We're doing everything we said we would. The triumph has revolutionized every aspect of Nicaraguan life," she said. Sophia Clark's mother is Nicaraguan. Her father is American, and she was raised primarily in the United States. She and her sister came down to work for the revolution and have renounced their American citizenship. "Whether we lift censorship, give amnesty to the Miskitos, or announce elections, Reagan's only response is to keep on helping the contras and to plan intervention."

Saul Arana trimmed a little, tacking toward history. "Perhaps we tried to solve our long-standing problems too quickly," he said. "We've learned you can't do it all overnight, especially if you're as poor as we are. It takes time to construct a workable democratic political system. Historically we had only two parties —Somoza's so-called Liberals and the Conservatives. In practice this meant there was really only one party, so we have no tradition of democracy to draw on. This will take time. Excuse us, please. We have to go to meet a very important visitor from the North."

"The United States is in a slump," Sophia Clark said. "All the cards are in Nicaragua's hands."

They were gone before I could ask how so many of the cards could be in the hands of a country my country could wipe out in ten minutes, and I was left in the foreign ministry waiting room staring at a poster of Augusto César Sandino with a rifle across one knee while his foot rested on a sign that read *"Muerte al Imperialismo."* The foreign ministries in Washington and Managua might have more to discuss with each other than they suspected. Like Arana and Clark, Washington had also put virtue on one side of the United States–Nicaragua dispute, sin on the other; one State Department official had told me Nicaragua was "the proximate cause of all the trouble in the region," while another saw nothing but "asphyxiating oppression and corruption" among the Sandinistas. There was always myopia, an engaging subject for those intrigued by the mysteries of vanishing depth perception. Why didn't the foreign ministries conduct an exchange program?

The secretary-general of the foreign ministry was Alejandro Bendana, a former instructor in Latin American graduate studies at Harvard. Young, overworked, and tired, Bendana seemed harassed in the universal manner of foreign-office diplomats, with reports descending on him from around the world, war and peace seeming to hang in the balance on every major decision. Bendana had to repeat himself endlessly to visitors from abroad. If it was my twenty-fifth briefing, it may have been Bendana's twenty-five hundredth. The air conditioner in his office oscillated between a hum and a roar, fighting a losing battle with the climate, at times a winning one with conversation. Yet Bendana became less weary the more he talked. Though five years is young for a revolution in terms of social transformation, surely it is old in terms of rhetoric. But Bendana curiously did not seem to be repeating himself, not parroting a line long ago memorized. He was still fresh, groping for new insights, considerably less myopic than many of his colleagues.

Like so many Sandinista officials, Bendana is in his thirties. He was actively helping the revolution while still teaching at Harvard, and he came home before the final victory over Somoza. His parents live in Nicaragua, but he has relatives in the United States, he said, "like every upper-class Nicaraguan." Not all his relatives, he acknowledged, were in favor of the revolution. "I believe in live and let live—for myself, my family, my country."

The only American promise Alejandro Bendana believed was the one conveyed by military superiority. "The threat of force should not be allowed to characterize relations between states," he said. "We don't think the United States accepts that as a working premise. Everything President Reagan says and does indicates that as long as the Sandinistas are around there is not going to be peace in Central America. That attitude denies to Nicaraguans the right to choose our own future."

As for his own working premises, the secretary-general thought Cuba had been mistaken to allow itself to be used as a Soviet base. Salvador Allende in Chile had gone wrong by failing to raise the social consciousness of the middle class. Nicaragua was imitating neither, identifying itself within a broad anti-imperialist framework. Private enterprise was an important part of this framework and would be retained as part of the mixed economy Nicaragua needed. Against this the contras fought not with an ideal of their own but simply to complete a homework assignment from President Reagan, an assignment they proved every day they were incapable of accomplishing.

I asked Bendana if the military freeze the Sandinistas wanted would not leave Nicaragua with the largest army in Central America. He said it would, just as Honduras would be left with the largest and by far the most potent air force. Negotiations could then take place to reduce both the Nicaraguan army and the Honduran air force. "Most of our army is a popular militia anyway," he said. "It is not highly trained. Our 'crime' is that we can trust our own people to be armed and to remain citizen-soldiers in defense of their country. No other government in Central America could arm its civilians without being overthrown by them."

Bendana claimed the reductions in tension and armed forces could begin as soon as the United States wanted them to. "We will do all this as soon as we have American guarantees for a general climate of security in the area. We might be flexible but we're not dumb. Our biggest achievement so far is survival, and we intend to maintain it."

The one issue on which Bendana was inflexible was the counterrevolutionaries. The soldiers in the ranks could return anytime, he said, but the leaders had forfeited all rights as Nicaraguans. "Give the counterrevolutionaries a share of power, the U.S. insists. It is out of the question for us ever to permit any members of Somoza's National Guard to come back. They committed genocide against their own people. Anyone now receiving funds from the CIA to destroy the revolution cannot come to Nicaragua. The poor *campesinos,* terrorized and brainwashed, yes, we welcome them. The leaders, never."

I asked Bendana if this attitude—the Sandinistas are all right, their opponents are all wrong—was not a good way to win a war against Somoza but a poor way to keep the peace or to govern.

"The *barrios* would never let us take the contra leaders back. They scream at us in neighborhood meetings—'Don't you dare let in the guy who killed my father, my brother, who raped my sister or my wife, kidnapped my babies!' The Thirteen Colonies were not very fond of monarchists in 1792, were they? The French were not terribly patient in 1945 with Nazi collaborators. Nicaragua needs reconciliation, yes, but the wound and the memories are still very fresh. Why can't the United States understand this?"

Bendana saw similarities and connections throughout Central America but drew a sharp line at comparing the insurgencies in

Nicaragua and El Salvador. "The rebels in El Salvador control significant parts of the country. They cannot be dislodged. This is not because they are a good army but because their roots are in the country itself, in a deeply unjust social structure and among the *campesinos* in the villages and on the farms. The insurgents are recognized internationally as a legitimate political force in El Salvador. In Nicaragua the counterrevolutionaries"—unlike most Americans and Nicaraguans, Bendana never said "contras"—"have no social base. They bully a few farmers into following them, and they deceive a number of Miskitos into thinking they have Miskito interests at heart, but there is no major bloc of Nicaraguans who want to support and feed and fight with the counterrevolutionaries. The insurgents in El Salvador are based entirely inside the country; the Nicaraguan counterrevolutionaries have no towns or even villages under their control and are forced to operate outside Nicaragua from bases in Honduras and Costa Rica. If the United States ever really suspended its aid to the counterrevolutionaries, they would not last three weeks."

Bendana said that despite differences between the countries of Central America, they shared many of the characteristics of a single nation. "There is a common language, a common recognition among Central Americans that economic disruption or war in one of our countries affects all the others," he said. "We have many historical, commercial, cultural, and personal ties between us. A high percentage of our commerce is with each other. We need to get on with regional economic development. When the United States wages war on us, this disrupts the economy of the region."

Bendana hardly seemed weary anymore. Neither was he indignant. He seemed to have enlisted himself, and his country, in a long struggle that he might well not live to see completed. Unlike some of his Sandinista companions, Bendana did not give the impression of being without second thoughts as to the course the revolution should take. There had been a time in his life, while he taught in America, that had been given to argument and contemplation, and this had now given way to the time for action.

But his determination was not won without his granting himself the occasional right to doubt. I asked Bendana what, in his view, was the United States' legitimate interest in Central America. "That there be no SS-9 missiles here pointing at Oklahoma is a reasonable request. That there be no foreign bases here, no breach of international conduct. That we live and let live, as we expect the United States to. We challenge the traditional view, now sustained by Henry Kissinger, that we are a backyard. We are not, and we are also no threat to anyone. Our revolution was in the first instance a creature of bad American policy toward Nicaragua. But that revolution has happened now, and we are better for it. Our independence is our own business. Will the United States recognize our right to live? This is what peace in Central America depends on. Even now, even in this moment of terror between our two countries, the contacts are strong between the United States and Nicaragua. We approach a fork. We are closer to war and closer to peace than we have ever been before."

Outside, on the steps of the former shopping center, guards and messengers milled in readiness. In the foreign ministry parking lot, where once upper-class Managuan ladies had their servants wheel shopping carts, a uniformed band stood at attention, prepared to break into anthem. A messenger wearing a Pittsburgh Pirates cap said two new ambassadors had arrived in Managua and were coming today to present their credentials. I asked what countries they were from. He said he thought one of them was from the United States.

The United States? I had not heard of Quainton's being replaced, but I remembered a conversation that morning in the hotel. In the coffee shop at the Intercontinental, over frijoles and rice, a network cameraman told his recently arrived soundman that it would be an easy day. The soundman asked how the cameraman knew that. "The whole country goes on vacation after Purísima. Sleeping it off. No action until tonight. Things pick up a little then. I got a senator coming in at six. Moynihan."

Possibly the senator from New York took an earlier flight and the rumor mill at the foreign ministry had him demoted—or in their eyes, promoted—to U.S. ambassador. But the name Moynihan caused no flicker of recognition in the eyes of the man in the Pittsburgh Pirates cap. "The ambassador's coming this morning from Kennedy," he said. That was the airport I had left from, too, I thought, and waited to see who would turn up.

A silver Mercedes pulled up to the entrance of the foreign ministry. An honor guard in chromed helmets in front of the ministry did not come to attention. The Mercedes contained only the advance men and security guards of the new envoy, whose siren could be heard a few blocks away. It was announced that we were awaiting the arrival of the newly appointed minister from the German Democratic Republic. The Mercedes, manufactured in Stuttgart, might be the very emblem of capitalism, but the East Germans were still German and they knew what they wanted to ride around in.

A half-dozen motorcycles peeled into the ministry parking lot, followed by another silver Mercedes, this one flying the flags of Nicaragua and East Germany on its front fenders. In a city where most people have no cars and those who do have them drive prerevolutionary Fords and Chevies or else small Datsuns and Renaults, a silver Mercedes cuts a figure comparable to the queen's coach in Victorian London. The honor guard snapped to attention, its helmets reflecting not one but two Mercedes and the disembarkation of the new East German ambassador. He, too, stood at attention while the band played his anthem and its own.

As the Nicaraguan anthem was finishing, a young man in an ice-cream suit, of the kind favored by patrons of J. Press, inched his way through the gathering on the steps of the ministry. He was not part of this ceremony and evidently wanted to get into the ministry before the ambassador from East Germany did. It was the same American who had watched the demonstration at the American embassy and then had been bestowed a glance of recognition by Daniel Ortega at the Purísima celebration. At the embassy he had been called, among other things, an obvious secret agent. No one wore suits in Managua—the East German ambassador was wearing a guayabera, the open-necked tropical shirt favored by the Nicaraguan upper class—but here was this American in his button-downs and Ivy League suits. As he was entering the ministry courtyard, I asked him what had brought him to Managua.

The man in the J. Press suit was indeed, as the messenger in the Pittsburgh Pirates cap had said, the ambassador from Kennedy.

He said he was going to start work soon as an aide to Senator Edward Kennedy and was in Nicaragua to test his perceptions of the Sandinistas and their revolution against the unfavorable press and political comment they had been getting in the United States. His name was Greg Craig, he was a lawyer, and he had recently finished working for Edward Bennett Williams's prominent Washington law firm. A couple of days before, Greg Craig had been met at the airport in Managua by the eager Saul Arana, chief greeter for important North Americans, who had hustled him right past customs into a waiting car. Saul Arana was again present to greet Greg Craig and whisk him into meetings at the foreign ministry, stealing a little march on the East Germans, who had to stand on ceremony before making their entrance. Two new ambassadors presenting their credentials, the East Germans providing economic help and military training, Senator Kennedy providing a hope—in Nicaraguan eyes—that the United States might permit the survival of their revolution.

Greg Craig ranked fairly high on the celebrity seismograph at the Intercontinental. Though most of the press did not know who he was at first, when they found out there was a "Kennedy aide" —in fact, he had not begun work for the senator yet—on the premises, a word with him became a small coup. Comings and goings were noted religiously on the seismograph that linked most of the Americans in the lobby of the Intercontinental. One night a former Peace Corps volunteer presently trying to become a stringer for anyone north of the Rio Grande told a friend she had heard that James Ridgeway and Alexander Cockburn, who were then both columnists for the *Village Voice,* had just arrived, were in the process of arriving, or would be arriving in the morning. This intelligence caused more interest among the Nica-libre drinkers in the lobby's rattan chairs than the advent of Senator John Chafee of Rhode Island and Senator Jeff Bingaman of New Mexico, but it registered lower on the seismograph than the prospect of Senator Daniel Patrick Moynihan, just as Moynihan caused a smaller squiggle on the Richter scale of arrivals than the future aide to Senator Kennedy.

Next door to the foreign ministry, at an upper-class restaurant called Los Ranchos, two journalists were interviewing one another. A television correspondent was telling a newspaper reporter why he did not like the Sandinistas. "They're a bunch of Marxists," he said.

"They don't know what Marxism means," the reporter said.

"They know. That's what they are."

"How do you know they know?"

"Everyone down here knows it except the Americans, who love them. The Sandinistas pretend they're not Marxists because the people up North don't want to hear that. But they see their society in terms of class conflict."

"You're getting caught in their rhetoric. They'd love to get some of the people back who know how to manage plants and sell sugar. Our government won't let that happen. We tell all those upper-middle-class Nicaraguans in Miami that if they'll just stay there a little longer, we'll hand the whole country back to them."

"The Sandinistas are just a bunch of pragmatists, then?"

"They have no choice. They have their ideologues, but they want to keep the revolution alive."

The waiter brought their lunches, and mixed them up. He gave the television man the fish, the stringy beef to the newspaperman. The television man got it straightened out with broken Spanish about *carne* and *pescado*.

"I hear Godoy will give up the labor ministry to run for president against Ortega," the newspaper reporter said to the television correspondent.

"If he does," the television correspondent said, "they'll be calling him a contra soon. New York says Alexis Argüello wants to come back to Nicaragua to fight with Pastora, but Pastora told him to stay in the United States and do propaganda against the Sandinistas.''

"Stupid of them to confiscate Argüello's property here. How many world boxing champions in three different divisions do the Nicaraguans have?''

At this time Edén Pastora, a revolutionary hero during the war against Somoza, had just enlisted the Nicaraguan boxer Alexis Argüello in his new fight against the Sandinistas. Pastora had become deputy defense minister for the Sandinistas after they took power. In disagreement with their policies and, reportedly, piqued at not getting a higher post, he resigned and went into exile in 1981. By 1982 he was fighting against the Sandinistas and was briefly promoted by Washington softliners as an alternative candidate to lead Nicaragua away from both the Somoza remnants and the Sandinista revolutionaries. Pastora was too independent, however, to make an alliance with the main force of counterrevolutionaries. When he refused to coordinate his efforts with those of Somoza's former National Guard officers who were commanding the contras, Pastora's aid was cut off by the CIA. He continued fighting until 1986, but with a much lower level of support.

"The AP guy told me Pastora is now back in the same camp in Costa Rica he was in five years ago when he was fighting against the Somozas," the television correspondent said. "That's got to piss him off—he risks his ass for a revolution, wins, can't stand not being top guy, so he leaves and finds himself back in the same place fighting one more guerrilla war against the government of his country."

"Our friend at the embassy tells me the U.S. wants him the way they wanted a third force in Vietnam," the newspaper reporter said. "Anybody who's not Communist and also not part of the reactionary right. But we promote these people and their *own* people don't want them. So Edén Pastora becomes the Big Minh of Nicaragua."

"What do you hear from the border?" the television correspondent asked.

"Lot of fighting up around Ocotal," the newspaper reporter said. "The Sandinistas don't want us in Jinotega now. They turned back *Newsweek* at San Rafael del Norte and *Time* up around Wiwilí."

"They took ABC's film and threw it away the other day. When our guys went up to Pantasma after the contra massacre there, we shot fast—the dead cows, burned school, kids' bodies. We changed film and put an empty roll in the camera, so when they confiscated it all they got was a free roll of unexposed film. You'd think they'd want the world to see what kind of tactics the contras are using."

"They're full of *machismo*. They don't want anyone to know they can't protect their own communities better."

"We went around a roadblock at Ocotal a couple of weeks ago. A sergeant was so pissed he radioed ahead to the next roadblock near San Fernando. We didn't know he'd done that, so we were barreling through and didn't expect to see a tank in the middle of the road. They told us there was no way we were going around this one, and they sent a scared young soldier to ride back with us to Ocotal, where the sergeant chewed our ass for getting around him the first time. Oh well."

"So did you file a story?"

The effects of pack journalism, the vulture qualities in circling a given event—though in Nicaragua it was never clear what was the given and which was the true event—were not limited to the coverage of Super Bowls and national political conventions. The invasion watch caused the pack to be almost everywhere in Nicaragua, at farming and factory cooperatives, in contra camps and on border patrols, siphoning leaks from the Sandinistas and the American embassy. Reduced at times to interviewing each other, journalists became part of the story themselves, worrying the same facts and rumors for significance. In this conspiracy of overreaction between the United States government and those paid to observe it, a little country became a big story. The revolution was like a stock to be gambled on. The press bulls bought the Sandinistas, the bears sold them short. Regardless of their feelings about Nicaragua, most journalists were against an invasion, not secretive about being motivated less by political or humanitarian concerns than selfish ones—if an invasion came, of course, they were not only the vultures, they were part of the prey.

XI MASAYA AND GRANADA

SICK OF THE REVOLUTION, I went one Sunday morning to a sprawling open-air bazaar called the Mercado Oriental, the Eastern Market. Managua neighborhoods have strange cycles unpredictable to foreigners. One *barrio* may burst with vitality by six in the morning as women do their washing, children play with broken tires, men haul produce or garbage in carts. The *barrio* next to it at the same hour will appear abandoned. An upper-middle-class section has cars and cyclos buzzing around all morning; another, apparently on the same economic level, is so quiet its residents seem to have caught planes to Miami, which in some cases is partly true. But the Mercado Oriental is always busy, especially on Sundays.

Vendors in different stalls hawked rat poison, toys for toddlers, sneakers, car batteries, television sets, transistors, and fertilizer. Among a spirited variety of regular and black-market goods was every conceivable piece of merchandise available in Nicaragua from cradles to coffins. Clothing was piled on tables in gaudy carnival colors. In the hot December sunshine one stand sold purple plastic Christmas trees, a reminder that, merely because we have elevated it to an art form, the northern part of the hemisphere has no monopoly on bad taste. The stall next door was exhibiting holographs of a pudgy Virgin Mary looking like Benjamin Franklin in drag. A man selling pants was arguing with a carpenter in the adjacent stall. The carpenter was fixing broken chairs while the pants seller drank coffee. He had evidently just come from Mass and was still wearing a pressed white shirt. "I didn't say no progress," he said to the carpenter. "I said no significant difference. We're getting along as we always did, by the will of God."

"What does a pants seller know about progress?" the carpenter asked. "If the zippers are there and you move the merchandise, that's all you care about. When you're a production worker like me, when you make something yourself, you know what the revolution is about. All a pants seller can do is complain about regulations and ration cards. Trade and commerce is all you know, and they are no measure of the revolution. The people who had nothing now have something, and beyond that, they have hope for more. This they never had before."

"I'm not against the revolution," the pants seller said, "and I know there are some improvements. But it isn't the revolution that makes things better, it's the grace of God. You forget that."

"Either way, it's a struggle," the carpenter said.

A loudspeaker truck bulled its way into the crowd before its sound system began to work. The announcement said the new shipment of refined sugar had arrived. A few people milled in the direction of the sugar stand; most went on with their shopping. Did those who moved toward the sugar stand echo the complaint I heard from the schoolteacher in León that white sugar was a commodity Nicaraguans craved? Or did their small numbers contradict the schoolteacher and enhance the credibility of the Sandinistas? The Mercado Oriental was not far enough from the revolution, so I headed out into the fresh air of the countryside.

A cab driver also eager to get out of town wanted only $10 for the whole day. We drove south toward Masaya, a farming center whose Indian name means "city of the flowers." I bounced along the country road in back of the driver, happy to be free of politics. When the driver identified himself as Adolfo Jiménez, a forty-nine-year-old widower living with his three daughters and mother-in-law, it was clear we were going to chat about family life in Nicaragua and the United States. Adolfo Jiménez suggested a side trip up a hill to the Santiago volcano. Better still: a natural wonder I had never seen before.

We hiked to the top of the crater bowl and stared down into the center. Sulfurous clouds of smoke and steam belched out of the crater. The hole appeared to be a lesion in the earth's crust like an orifice in a human body created by surgery or a wound, a navel that was not supposed to be there. But the crater also resembled an amphitheater the gods might have carved for themselves, and the smoke pouring from its center could be a signal from the earth's heart. Green parakeets dived and wheeled above the steam clouds, flirting with the erratic volcano, taunting it to erupt and end their lives of careless impulse. Some clayey quality in the lava caused an occasional billow in the steam to redden as it left the hole.

Adolfo Jiménez gave me a full minute or so to look, absorbing the unfamiliar, before he tenderly connected the Santiago volcano to recent history. "There was a patriot by the name of David Tejada who had once been a member of the Guardia," he began, and I knew there was no escape from the revolution, not anywhere. "He became a great oppositionist after resigning his lieutenancy. Tejada got information from the Guardia and passed it to the FSLN. He made important raids and embarrassed the Somozas by stealing some of their own cattle. Finally he led an attack on a Guardia post and killed a colonel who had been one of Somoza's worst butchers and torturers. The colonel's friend, a Major Oscar Morales, got an informer to tell him where Tejada was hiding. Morales, who was a friend of Mrs. Somoza, took a detachment of the Guardia to Tejada's room in the middle of the night. They woke up Tejada and his wife and took them outside. Morales went back inside and woke up David Tejada's little boy and brought him outside too, to make him watch. While the Guardia held Señora Tejada and her son, Major Morales beat David Tejada to death with his own hands. Then they brought his body up here and tossed it into the mouth of Santiago." As Adolfo

Jiménez gestured toward the volcano's noisy center the revolution's campy stage manager served up the next steam bubble in angry crimson.

We continued to Masaya, and Adolfo Jiménez admitted his life was more complicated since the revolution. He had driven a cab for a fleet owner before 1979, and it had been like working for the government. He got free gasoline and there were mechanics to repair his taxi, but he could keep less than half the fare money he collected, and he had to work when the owner told him to or else be fired. Since 1979, gas had been rationed, spare parts were almost impossible to get, and he had no idea where he would buy his next tires when the present ones wore out. But he owned his taxi and he kept what he made. When he was sick he stayed home, when he was well he drove, and when one of his daughters was in a school play he took the afternoon off. He loved the Sandinistas. The revolution made an independent capitalist of Adolfo Jiménez.

In the Monimbo district of Masaya, an uprising of the Indian population had sparked a general rebellion against Somoza in 1978. Camilo Ortega, the younger brother of the future Junta leader Daniel and defense minister Humberto, had gone to Monimbo to help the Indians and was killed by Somoza's troops. Masaya itself was a bastion of Sandinista support, and when the city of forty thousand exploded in September 1978, Somoza decided to bomb his own people. Following the air strikes, the Guardia launched rockets and mortars on the main squares from a hill just outside town. When the Guardia moved in on foot, the FSLN fought them with handmade *plastiques,* World War II rifles, and Coke bottles filled with a lethal mixture of kerosene and nitroglycerine. In one surrounded church, still pockmarked with shells, the FSLN held out for forty-eight hours against the National Guard, who finally killed the two dozen Sandinistas inside. In the neighborhood where the insurrection was most popular, rebels fought the Guardia machine guns with machetes and *plastiques* and drove Somoza's men away. The men playing cards in the plaza on this Sunday half a decade later were proud that their *barrio* had never fallen to Somoza, although the dictator's troops had managed to control most of Masaya after a week's siege. Many buildings in the town still lie in ruin, looking as though a selective hurricane had struck.

President Somoza had told American reporters the September 1978 uprising was his country's Tet offensive. He was drinking as much as three-quarters of a bottle of vodka at lunch while supposedly recovering from a heart attack, but he had said his Guardia would strike back and wipe out the rebels. According to Bernard Dietrich, who covered the Nicaraguan revolution for *Time* magazine before writing a biography of the Somoza family, Somoza was drunk at a party in his bunker one night when a musician sang a song that made Dinorah Sampson, his mistress, weep. The lyrics described a love affair similar to their own. Though Mrs. Somoza was living abroad by 1978, as a Catholic she would not divorce her husband. Somoza broke his toe when he tried to kick the musician to punish him for the sad song.

After Masaya was relatively quiet again, Somoza had announced that he would levy higher taxes to buy more munitions and planes. "The National Guard," he told a news conference, "has done nothing but defend itself. I don't think it's fair to call this repression." The Carter Administration, cutting military aid to Somoza, proposed mediation between him and his opponents. One of the rebels who had fought at Masaya and had escaped was indignant. "How can we sit down and negotiate with a man who has just this week slaughtered three thousand Nicaraguans?" he asked. "A river of blood separates us."

As hard as it is to avoid politics in Nicaragua, there are moments that transcend the political situation even while offering partial explanation for it. The sight of a peasant woman just outside Masaya, bent over and making her way across a dusty square, sticks in the present tense like a figure in a painting. She is walking toward a small church, except that as I see her she is immobile, the momentary vessel of her culture. As Adolfo Jiménez drives past, the woman is beneath the higher of the church's two crosses. The lower cross is in a niche above the arched double-doored entrance; the loftier one rests on a cupola above the church. The church is beige stucco, with yellow piping around its windows and doors. I am grateful there is no picture of Sandino visible, because the woman about to make her devotions is present before Somoza and beyond the revolution. The scene could be at a mission in the American southwest, in New Mexico or Texas or a hundred years ago at Santa Barbara. Despite the warm weather she wears a dark blue shawl over a russet skirt so long it hides her shoes and drags a little in the dust. She moves, but cannot be seen to move, into the church to pray, to confess or find a peaceful half hour, and she could be anywhere in greater Hispania from the end of the sixteenth century until we can no longer surmise.

The open-air crafts market in Masaya displays itself in a profusion of undifferentiated rarities and schlock. The Sunday I saw the market, an official from the American embassy was there showing two visiting European businessmen the sights. Embroidered tablecloths, hammocks, sculpture, baskets, and pottery were being sold by Indian artisans, who looked neither defeated nor defiant but simply blended into the culture. The Indians of Nicaragua were conquered as thoroughly as those of the United States, but they were not annihilated. Those who remain in the more populous western portion of the country are less segregated than they are in the United States. It is as though Chicago, New York, and Los Angeles all contained small but thriving Indian neighborhoods whose food, music and dress mingled rather comfortably with those of the majority.

Careful copies of pre-Columbian gods of fertility and war squatted next to stuffed iguanas that might have been fashioned by the same hands that produced Jabba the Hut. A lady sold T-shirts that said "Dodgers—World Champs 1981." Since Daniel Patrick Moynihan's arrival had caused the most recent squiggle on the celebrity seismograph at the Intercontinental, I asked the American embassy official how the briefing between Senator Moynihan and Ambassador Quainton had gone.

"They were, well, cordial," the embassy man said. "More than the proprieties demanded, less than warm buddies."

What did they say to each other, these two officials of the

United States government meeting in disputed territory, one the local representative of the Administration, the other a prominent member of the opposition?

"Quainton told the senator about what he told you. This is a tough post, but the Sandinistas will deal if we will. Moynihan asked the right questions about possible Sandinista flexibility and Soviet armaments. When the meeting was over he talked like he was getting ready to make a policy declaration at home. He told Tony that if Nicaragua posed the strategic threat to the United States that Cuba had during the missile crisis, then we must prevent this. Absent that threat—he uses phrases like that—we ought to leave Nicaragua alone."

As statesmen remembered Munich for a generation, were formed by it and used it to promote or oppose every issue that arose for the rest of their careers, the Cuban missile crisis had become the normative moment in foreign policy for the generation that followed. It did not matter whether the crisis of 1962 had been more a political maneuver than a real confrontation, had been accompanied by other, private deals with the Soviets that remained secret still, had been a personality clash peculiar to the characters of Kennedy and Khrushchev, or had genuine application to any other event. What mattered was that for the young American political scientists of the 1960s, the missiles of October became the childhood trauma against which all future disturbances would have to be measured.

"Now we're waiting for Chafee and Bingaman to drop by, our next senators," the embassy official said, steering his European guests through the bazaar away from two stuffed frogs made up to look like a matador and his bull, toward a pre-Columbian maiden whose oversized eyes, as large as her breasts, were frozen, with her mouth, in perpetual gape.

Adolfo Jiménez apologized for his ancient Ford, which refused to start until he applied a screwdriver to its private parts and threatened it with graver abuse. We headed south to Granada, the old capital of Nicaragua's landed aristocracy and of their political arm, the Conservative Party. Hoping to plunder or barter for the gold of the local Indian chief, Nicarao, after whom they named the country, Spaniards had founded Granada in 1524. It quickly became a center for the marketing of the blue dye indigo, sugar cane, and cacao. An early example of agribusiness in the New World, the city's character was formed by rich merchants and the owners of vast plantations.

The English grew fond of sacking Granada, first as pirates, afterward as the crown's authorized representatives. They would approach from the Atlantic coast by sailing northwest up the San Juan River, then across the largest lake in Central America, Lake Nicaragua, on whose far-western shore was Granada. In the sixteenth century, Francis Drake, before he was officially endorsed with knighthood by Elizabeth I, invaded Granada. Henry Morgan led his Barbados pirates to Granada in the seventeenth century before he himself was knighted and given the lieutenant governorship of Jamaica. In the eighteenth century, Horatio Nelson, while still a young British naval captain, was heading upriver for the lake approach to Granada when Spanish defenders attacked his ship. They not only drove Nelson away from Granada but also, according to Spanish accounts, shot him in the right eye. In the French version, Nelson lost his eye while fighting them at Corsica. Either way, this became the most expensive eye in history, or at least the one which, over the years, drew the highest rate of interest, when Nelson made both countries pay for it at Trafalgar.

After the adventurer William Walker offended the Nicaraguans by reinstituting slavery and provoked Commodore Vanderbilt by expropriating his property, Walker made his last stand at Granada. When he was on the point of being driven out, Walker raised a flag that read *Aquí Fue Granada*—"Here was Granada" —and then he lighted the old city on fire. Fortunately, Walker was not much better at arson than at ruling Nicaragua. Adolfo Jiménez and I found the substance of colonial Granada—Alhambran architecture, graceful plazas, Castilian churches, arched colonnades—intact. Oxcarts and fringed surreys drawn by horses gave sections of the town an atmosphere that at first beguiled me into the illusion that not only the Sandinistas but also the entire century had forgotten Granada.

A two-hundred-year-old church brought us back to the revolution. An elderly priest was chanting five-o'clock Mass to his Sunday-afternoon parishioners. When he completed the Mass he walked in front of his ornately carved altar and spoke a brief homily. "Put not the program of your temporal leaders before the will of God," he said, "but use your strength as His congregation to work for peace and reconciliation between all Nicaraguans while guarding always against the impurities of alien doctrine."

"He means for us to do things the old way," Adolfo Jiménez translated. "Listen to the Pope and the Americans. Sit down with the contras because they represent the wishes of Washington. Pay attention to your bishops because Rome wants nothing to do with the popular church or liberation theology. The Communists infest your homes like bedbugs."

A younger priest took the pulpit and led the congregation in a hymn. Noticing my scribbling, a middle-aged parishioner next to us tapped my shoulder and smiled. "They only let the young priest sing," he whispered. "They know he likes the revolution better than the old man. The young one was educated in Barcelona. He told my wife he likes the Sandinistas but he thinks they need more maturity. The old priest has been here so long he baptized me and he married me. I love him like my father. I am a ropemaker. This was a hard job under the Somozas, just as hard now. But no more bribes, so I keep what I earn." Between Adolfo Jiménez with his taxi business and this ropemaker, the Sandinistas were emerging, on this particular Sunday, as the promoters and defenders of private enterprise.

In his union headquarters, the local labor organizer for construction workers was not sanguine about gaining new membership. Or he may have been gloomy because someone told him he had to sit in the union hall on Sunday. "In this area we have so many conservatives and reactionaries," he said, caressing seven syllables out of *reaccionarios* as though he relished the word if not its designees, "it is very difficult to organize for the union. People here were so obedient for so long they don't come easily to *sandinismo*. The union itself has as many conservatives as revolutionaries. Six months ago we threatened a strike just to embarrass the government. The union head was a former *somocista* and we got rid of him. Now we have a new man who is more progressive but weaker. It's hard."

The construction union organizer also complained that Granada's equivalent of a landmark commission made problems for new buildings. As if money and materials were not scarce enough already, the local traditionalists still wanted arched doorways, painted ceilings and hand-carved banisters. Every time the union or a contractor proposed something new, it seemed as if several dozen Granadans had to give their approval before a shovelful of dirt could be turned. "We started work on a new school last month. *Un milagro.*" A miracle.

The organizer was discouraged, confused, an organizer not doing much organizing, a member of the construction industry doing very little he felt was constructive. The situation he found himself in was a reminder that even in the 1980s in a country whose governors extol labor's virtues, there is still some relevance to an old grumble of Rudyard Kipling:

> I tell this tale, which is strictly true,
> This by way of convincing you
> How very little, since things were made,
> Things have altered in the building trade.

Adolfo Jiménez' prerevolutionary Ford was flanked by two oxen whose burdensome humps almost drove their necks into the ground. He had to persuade them to move before we could drive away. "Come, my *muchachos*," he said, "and move your backpacks with the rest of your gear across the plaza to block the car of the old padre from the church. He moves at your pace anyway." A quick three minutes of hard rain fell as we left the vicinity, blistering the countryside around Granada into a silvery veld.

XII CENTRAL POST OFFICE

LA REVOLUCIÓN ES UNA CHAVALA DE CUATRO AÑOS, the sign said at the entrance to the Central Post Office in Managua. The revolution is a little girl four years old. The rest of the poster was filled with the features of a small child whose spirit and message were intended to sustain Nicaraguans through their troubles. Don't expect me to do everything yet. I cannot do calculus or ballet or heart surgery; I cannot produce enough meat for your tables or new bicycles or gasoline or even guns for your defense. I can walk and talk; for now that is enough.

The revolution makes its own myths. Next to the poster of the little girl were pictures of Sandino, Carlos Fonseca and Rigoberto López Pérez. Except during an election campaign, whenever actual photographs of revolutionary heroes are displayed, they are invariably dead. Sandino was, of course, killed on the orders of Somoza I. Fonseca, one of the founders of the Frente Sandinista de Liberación Nacional, was killed fighting against the soldiers of Somoza III. Rigoberto López Pérez assassinated Somoza I in León and was immediately killed by the dictator's guards. Somoza I lived long enough after López Pérez shot him to summon the American ambassador and tell him, in one of the dated movie colloquialisms the Somozas leaned on when they spoke English, "I'm a goner."

Every night after work, dozens of Managuans stream past these posters into the Central Post Office, but they are not buying stamps. Most Nicaraguans do not own a telephone, and thousands of them observe a monthly ritual of calling relatives outside the country. The cavernous post office has an alcove for foreign calls, where after a wait of two to three hours, a Managuan can talk to a daughter, a nephew, a widowed mother, a grandparent. This lifeline to relatives is so important to the callers that it is not uncommon for them to spend between 15 and 25 percent of their monthly income on a single call abroad. The post office is especially crowded late in the evenings when the phone rates go down.

Most of the calls are to the United States, but in addition to the phone books for Miami, San Francisco, Los Angeles, New York and Houston, the post office also stocks directories for Costa Rica, Honduras, Guatemala, El Salvador, Mexico City, and Madrid. According to my informal exit poll with citizens emerging from telephone booths, a significant majority of the relatives abroad had been there since long before the revolution. Some of them come back to Nicaragua every year or so to visit their relatives as long as they can afford to, then return north to their jobs in other countries.

The central operator would announce each call as it was put through. "Alicia Muñoz, Tampa a la cuatro." An old woman in a maroon shawl shuffled to booth number four, where she listened to distant, familiar tones from Tampa before she spoke. "Uncle Alberto is sick. It's the same thing. We don't know how long. . . . Teresa had a boy? *Gracias a Dios!* Name him after your grandfather. . . . Kiss the twins."

"Ernesto Vallecillos, Boston in booth number seven."

"Rosario Urbina, Tegucigalpa in booth number five."

People waited patiently, sitting or milling. Very few read, and if they talked it was only in murmurs. When they heard their names called, all but the very old leaped toward their assigned booths, suddenly animated and bursting with their news.

"How's everyone? I have a great surprise! I can't tell you anything except to go to the airport at five o'clock next Saturday and meet flight 743. If I can get her to take the plane you may see a short woman with a crazy scarf who can't keep a civil tongue in her head and it might be your mother coming to spend Christmas with you. Don't ask me how we're managing this."

"Madre, can you hear? Pablito walked yesterday!"

"The operation is next week. Pray for us."

"He what? The police are sure he did it? I told you last summer not to marry the *cabrón*. Make sure you get a lawyer who speaks Spanish. What does the judge say?"

"His whole unit was sent to the far north, near the Río Coco. I know, we're all praying."

"I'm calling from Nicaragua for my sister. Are you sure she's not there? She said to call tonight. Tell her I'll try tomorrow at eight. Make sure she waits. *Por favor, señor.*"

People went into the booths as fast as they could, left them slowly, still saying goodbye after they had hung up the receiver, not quite willing for anyone else to talk on the same phone that had just carried their father's voice to them. The central operator was, for the moment, destiny. An old man cursed her.

"Antenor Zavala, San Francisco in booth number four."

"Mercedes Castillo, Miami in booth number six."

"Cleotilde Ordóñez, Los Angeles in booth number two."

In some cases whole families had come to wish an older brother or a father happy birthday. As many as four people would wedge into a booth where, although they could barely breathe, they could easily laugh or cry. Then they would be tugged at by three more people from the same family who wanted their turn. Papa you come back; Reynaldo you're a scum; I start work next week in the textiles, the old plant where you used to work; the teacher said I was best in history; can you send a transistor radio; when will I see you, you scum Reynaldo. Everybody all at once, a tumble of declarations and demands, almost a commercial for the phone company if it were not nationalized. But when Reynaldo hung up at his end, did he turn to the cousin who had sponsored him in Fort Worth, to the neighbors who had allowed him to send their phone number back to Managua, to a boss who might lend him the money to go home for Christmas, to a woman just up from Guatemala as lost as he himself, or worst of all to a gringa with her gringa ways?

"Paulino Largaespada, Wichita in booth number eight."

"Don't send your money to them. They burned a school in Jinotega the other day. Of course it's hard, but we're making it. I don't care what you read up there. I've lost fifteen pounds, I'm almost back to where I was before María and Manolito. I miss everyone so much. *Un abrazo cariñoso a todos,* a warm hug for everyone. I miss you. *Nos vemos,* we'll see each other, *adiós.*"

An old woman wiped her eyes with her sleeve as she pulled herself out of a booth and made a little shamble toward the operator's desk. She groped in a small black cloth purse for the money to pay for her call. "I knew it," she said to herself in a deep sigh. "I can't believe I've lost her forever." She crossed herself just before she reached the cash register.

XIII TOMÁS BORGE

EARLY ONE MORNING I was paged and told to report to the government press office in the Intercontinental. The *cognoscenti* in the lobby had finished breakfast and were deciding where to find the crisis that day. Anything worth reporting in the Sandinistas' loosening up on the Miskitos or tightening up on the press? Who was the next fireman due in from Washington? Someone said the U.S. gunboats had formed into an attack mode in the Gulf of Fonseca, this generation's Tonkin, the bathtub inlet separating Nicaragua from El Salvador. Someone else said the Sandinistas would be getting Russian jets, the contras surface-to-air missiles to shoot them down. A beautiful photographer is just racing off to the Philippines; a recently divorced wire service man has been called to Lebanon; a Danish cameraman will leave this afternoon for Angola. No one claims to know what's really going on; everyone is merely conducting revolution as usual.

My contact in the press office was a stern Sandinista named Myrna Torres, whom I had so far found full of decorum and the party line in equal measures. For a change she was affable and chatty. I assumed I was about to be offered a junket to see captured contras or liberated Miskitos. Fidgeting during her warm-

143

up on land redistribution, I interrupted her as soon as I could find an opening to ask why she had sent for me. Oh yes, she was glad I had brought her back to the subject. What she had in mind today was officialdom. How would I like to interview a deputy foreign minister? I felt I would soon have been briefed into a robot, so I declined. "Well, then, I'll see you at three p.m.," she said, unstoppable, "and we will all go over to the speech by Tomás Borge."

That was different. Tomás Borge, the minister of the interior, a member of the nine-man ruling directorate, was the last surviving founder of the Sandinista movement itself. The rest had been killed fighting Somoza. He was the only current leader in his fifties, none of the others being out of their thirties. In the postrevolutionary hierarchy, he had become the second most powerful man in Nicaragua after Daniel Ortega. When Myrna Torres said I could interview Tomás Borge after his talk, that clinched the afternoon. Perhaps the offer of the deputy foreign minister had been only a test. The devious red plot was that I had to turn down the middle-level functionary if I wanted bigger game.

I had seen Tomás Borge once before. Across the street from the Intercontinental is the restaurant Los Antojitos. The most favored part of the restaurant in fine weather is the terrace in front, where on balmy December evenings, delegations from Milwaukee or San Francisco ordered *churrascos* (barbecued steak), *medio pollo asado* (half a grilled chicken) and *tostones* (fried bananas) while they compared notes on the day's briefings and tours. Middle-class Nicaraguans came to Los Antojitos for its international flavor and the prospect of beef on the menu. The first time I was there a waiter told me I should look inside, before taking a table on the terrace, if I wanted to see what Managua used to be. I assumed he meant to show me some touch of colonial grandeur that hung on from pre-Sandinista Nicaragua.

Instead, the waiter wanted to show me the wall-sized photographs of a city that exists only in memory. As relics the pictures have the sting of little wounds, bearing just enough resemblance to the destroyed present to make a traveler wistful for what he never saw. There is the undamaged cathedral, Sunday worshipers pouring out of it as though they would return every next Sunday until the end of their days. On a facing wall there are the department stores, restaurants next door to shops, a block crowded with contiguous buildings from one street to another. A twelve-story mate stands near the seventeen-story Bank of America, with two more large commercial buildings in the foreground, clothing stores and tenements in the front of the frame.

The city that remained outside Los Antojitos offered few blocks with adjacent door-to-door buildings. The buildings that stood stood alone, as though the earthquake had forgotten them or some capricious imagination had thrown them up the day before yesterday, either of which could be true. You can stand almost anywhere in Managua and think you are looking at the opposite of a city, not countryside but a sort of inverted metropolis in which most of the buildings must lie underground and if you could only go far enough beneath the surface you could say at last with relief, Ah, this is where the city is, it has been hiding down here all along.

"We have *guapote* tonight, fresh from the lake." The waiter wanted me to take a seat back outside on the terrace, but he wanted me to listen to him even more. He himself had never seen Managua before the earthquake, having grown up in Puerto Cabezas on the East Coast, a Caribbean black brought up in English schools to distrust and disdain "de Sponeesh" who ran the country from the west. His name was Wylie Howe, which he also wanted me to know, and he grew up during the relative prosperity of the East Coast while the American lumber companies were taking out the pine and mahogany. When the companies had taken all they could and gone home, leaving the workers with no work, Wylie Howe's father had gone north to Honduras to cut timber there. Wylie Howe himself could find nothing to do, so he migrated west to Managua.

"I had de big dream den," Wylie Howe said in the lilting Caribbean English of the East Coast. "I would become a psychologist. There was no opportunity to go to school and I had to go to any work so I could rub two cordobas together, mon. Dat's how I lost my first dream. But den I got another dream, I wanted to be independent. Make something myself and sell it, you see, something more fetching dan de other fellow is making. I'd like two kinds of independence—first, no boss, and second, nobody to wait on hand and foot like customers in de restaurant, no offense intended please.

"So de revolution come along and I help out. No joining de army, no fighting, but hiding people in my home, carrying ammunition and messages, just someone doing what needed doing. If it wasn't for de likes of us, de Sandinistas would still be in de mountains.

"I like de notion de land belong to de mon who works it. Where dey go wrong is on free enterprise. I might have more opportunity to fulfill my dream of independence under de old system. In de old days, you drive around and run a stoplight, de police stop you and you fumble around wid your wallet. You pull out fifty cordobas and hand it over to him, and you're on your way widout no ticket. Nowadays, if de Sandinistas arrest you for speeding, you go to court and pay three hundred and fifty cordobas. *Everybody* pays three hundred and fifty cordobas.

"Same thing if I wanted to start in business like selling shrimp. I don't have de money so I go to a banker and ask him for a loan to start my shrimp business. I can't qualify for de loan, but before de revolution he slips me de money anyway and we make a deal, de banker and I, to split de profits because he give me de money I need. What I'm saying is, mon, corruption works. A little corruption is what we need around here. It oils de wheels. Begging your pardon, mon, here comes someone."

The eight guards marched in first. Bristling with their Ahkas and bandoliers, they could have been advance men for Pancho Villa. Following them, paying no attention to his unsecret service, in animated conversation with a civilian friend almost a foot taller than he, Tomás Borge made his entrance onto the terrace of Los Antojitos. Wylie Howe receded, part of what Borge, or anyone who tries to govern Nicaragua, is up against.

"What is indisputable," a man from Milwaukee was telling a fellow member of his delegation after two days of briefing and touring that had included a cooperative farm, three Miskitos, a progovernment newspaper, an antigovernment newspaper, two foreign ministry officials, a union leader, two factories, a grammar school, and an anti-Sandinista bishop, the aggregate amounting almost to the Nicaraguan version of what true love gives on the twelfth day of Christmas, "is that the vast majority of Nicaraguans now feel they can express themselves through their institutions, which they couldn't do before."

"We say we support freedom, and the Marxists say they support liberation," a woman listening to him said. "Shouldn't there be someplace where freedom and liberation can coexist?"

At the sight of Tomás Borge, all earnestness vanished from the terrace, along with laughter, the trill of silverware and glasses, even the sound of chewing. The moment of recognition was followed by an instant of silence, followed by applause and cheers as Borge and his friend found a table near the center. They drank beer and talked, now animatedly, with gestures, now in what seemed intimacy, and Borge smoked cigars. It was a kind of silent movie, since no one could hear what they were saying, but still a, movie, the best show in town, and curiosity was greater simply *because* no one knew what they were discussing. There was nothing else but the revolution, but the revolution was everything.

Around Borge and his friend, talk resumed, at a higher pitch. People wanted each other to know they could go right on normally, it did not matter who had just walked in. But it became like a cocktail party already in full swing that has just been graced by Sinatra or Muhammad Ali. The wattage goes up enough so that people find it difficult to concentrate on conversations already in progress. Where are we going tomorrow? I already told you—UNAG at eight a.m. What's UNAG again? I already told you that, too, it's the union of medium-sized farmers. Oh, right, what time are we supposed to be there?

The sense in Los Antojitos was of relative identities shifting slightly during Tomás Borge's presence there, as they do after a minor earthquake that causes no real damage but moves everything in the room enough so that no single perspective is quite what it was a few minutes before. Fighting this change brought by the presence of celebrity, onlookers concentrate at first all the more intensely on what they were saying, denying in effect that the presence of Sinatra or Ali means anything to them, reassuring the person they are speaking to that this topic, this conversation, matters more than anything else. Shortly, their attention wanders to the real center of attention and they give themselves up to the new focus. As for the focus itself, Managua in December 1983 presented an opportunity to observe the dirty little secret of revolution—that revolutionaries on winning power become precisely what they claim to abhor, an elite class.

"His eyes are so intense," a woman said, a schoolteacher from St. Paul. "He looks straight ahead, never to the side, completely concentrated on that man he's talking to. His jaw is strong and decisive, yet his nose is soft. I'll bet he's gentle."

"He's so short," a wire-service stringer from California said, sipping her planter's punch, "and his arms are so long. He looks like a monkey."

To me, Borge looked like a perfect middleweight and just as ready to punch. He has a short neck, and his ears roll out a bit so that they, too, are facing whoever is in front of him. Even in his mid-fifties, if he could give up cigars for a week and do a little roadwork, he might swarm all over Marvelous Marvin Hagler, coming at him with what would look and feel like five or six arms, until Hagler dropped into retirement in about the seventh round. Like his country, Borge would display the alert left hook that could catch Hagler, like *his* country, unprepared.

But Borge's eyes were dark and serious, difficult to gauge, possibly never free from brooding on all they had seen. Lowered voices in Los Antojitos several times articulated themselves into a single word—"torture." Borge had first been arrested when he was a law student in León in the 1950s; he was charged with having consorted with Rigoberto López in the weeks before López assassinated Somoza I. Borge escaped and sneaked over the Honduran border disguised as a woman. After he founded the FSLN in the early 1960s, Borge stayed out of the Guardia's hands until 1977. Somoza's men killed Borge's first wife when they could not find Borge himself.

When they finally did catch him, the Guardia held Borge incommunicado for seven months. They kept him alive to try to learn the structure and composition of the Sandinistas. Borge's lawyer provided the court with a document describing the Guardia's refinements in the torture of his client. "For the first fifteen days of detention," the document charged, "he was beaten twenty-four hours a day, except for the times when he passed out, but the minute he regained consciousness the inhuman beating continued." The document proceeded with a description of Borge's being forced to stand for two entire months, with shifts of Guardia members by his side to keep him from changing position. He was handcuffed for seven months, kept with a hood over his head for nine months. When they took the hood off and he adjusted to the light, Borge was occasionally allowed to read. His jailers prevented Borge from receiving a book on psychic energy because they were afraid he would use it to teach himself to escape. They permitted a friend to give him a copy of Marx's *Kapital* because they thought it would instruct him in becoming a capitalist. Now Borge could dine, or simply entertain himself with beer and cigars, in Los Antojitos, formerly a rendezvous for Somoza cronies and the Guardia itself.

"Did you see him the other night at the circus?" an artist from Vermont asked a paralegal researcher from Oakland. "The actor with that New York group was way off base."

Borge had come to a Managua circus a few evenings earlier, accompanied as always by his bodyguards. No one had known what to do about the New York actor who was smoking pot in the row in back of the Borge party. On the one hand, the actor was a guest in Nicaragua and, needing all the support they can get, his hosts wanted to treat him politely. On the other hand, smoking marijuana is against Nicaraguan law, which the bodyguards are sworn to enforce. No one wanted a scene, and the clowns were in the middle of their act. (The circus had clowns, acrobats, dancing dogs, and chimpanzees—low-maintenance acts—but no bears, tigers, or elephants.) The actor was finally persuaded, with some difficulty, by a member of his own delegation that it was not a good idea to smoke pot in back of the man charged with public security in Nicaragua. As the clowns finished their act, they played a game of throwing buckets of water on each other. The climax came when one of them took a bucket over to the box where Borge sat. The audience held its breath, the bodyguards tensed—or was it an act? Borge put his hands over his face and prepared to be doused. The clown emptied the bucket, but what came out was feathers. The crowd laughed and, after a moment, so did Borge. The crowd was grateful to be able to cheer.

Borge is tailed, like a comet, by rumor—torture, obsession, sex—the way movie stars and rare politicians are. They become as famous for informing our dreams as for any positive or negative achievements. The talk at Los Antojitos circled Borge's table as if it had been a conga line formed only to celebrate him.

"He's the biggest swordsman in Managua, you know."

"With what he's been through, he deserves a little fun, doesn't he?"

"When the Sandinistas won, Borge captured the man in charge of all the torture done to him. The moment for revenge was at hand, his own torturer in his grasp. He let the guy go, a Guardia major who later joined the contras."

"He won't stand for brutality. He's put three hundred members of his own police and militia in jail because they mistreated enemy prisoners."

"What a man with the ladies, especially *las gringas.*"

"He scores all the time."

"He invited a woman from California to this little apartment he keeps. She was thrilled to go, and she said he was a great lover. He never took his pistol off, she said, the entire time they were together, and everyone in her delegation loved the story. But then she said how impressed she was with his humble dwelling, and their guide started to laugh. He told her the *comandante* really lives in a big house with his wife—'His wife!' she yelled; she didn't know he was remarried—and only kept the little apartment for women like her."

"He met a friend of mine at a party, she's down here stringing and translating for six, eight months. He said, 'We must have dinner.' She said, 'That would be nice, Comandante, but I won't be the dessert.' He said, 'You misjudge me, señorita, I am a married man.' ''

"When he tried to put the make on a *Life* reporter, she told him she only goes places with her photographer. He said that was fine, he would find someone for the photographer. The *Life* lady said no dice."

"You're too snide. He writes beautiful poems about his old friends before the revolution. He's devoted to his country and his family. He can be dignified, too. When Bianca Jagger came down to look over the revolution, she met Borge. There he was, sizing up the one really glamorous Nicaraguan celebrity who lives in the States. He finally said to her very gently, 'So, my dear, are you the envoy of charm from the enemy?' It was the right question from the right Sandinista to the right émigrée."

"He knew he couldn't get her, so he played it straight."

"You're such a cynic. The guy's a genius at love and war— what more do you want? My roommate's cousin came down for a week and he swept her off her feet. She went home saying if that's Marxism, sign me up."

It was time for the *comandante* to go. A midnight conference awaited him, or a tryst, or he was tired, who knew? He had exploded across the terrace of Los Antojitos like one of the sparklers at Purísima, but while he was there he had done nothing more than smoke two cigars, drink one beer, talk to his friend, and tip the waiter. When he got up to leave, smiling broadly, having said absolutely nothing to anyone else in the restaurant, Tomás Borge was applauded for a performance he never gave. He waved and let his guards escort him out. The show, in whatever quadrant of the audience's collective mind it had taken place, was over.

The attention to Tomás Borge's speech, in the converted dining room of a country club Somoza had owned, was approximately what it would have been if the interior minister had been expected to announce a cure for cancer. Japanese television required two interpreters, a tall American woman floating over her employers, who could get English into Japanese and back again, and a short Nicaraguan boy who was poised to render Borge into English for her so she could tell the Japanese what the message was. The wire services were there with their photographers, as were all three American networks and every newspaper with a man, woman or stringer in Managua. The presence of television crews from Australia and Europe—Sweden, France, West Germany, England—completed the media event. No one anticipated that the problems between the United States and Nicaragua would dissipate as the result of a speech. It was more that the invasion watch, bored at the Intercontinental, unenthusiastic about a dangerous trip to the combat zones on the Honduran border, did not know what else to do with itself.

Yet it was not really a media event, or not simply that. It was the same occasion, transplanted two thousand miles to the south, that had been scheduled to occur on campuses, in town halls and in a Congressional hearing room until the White House refused to grant Tomás Borge a visa to come to the United States that month. Elements of the American press felt cheated of Borge's presence. "In denying an entry visa to Tomás Borge, one of the Nicaraguan Revolution's top leaders," the Washington *Post* said in an editorial, "the Reagan Administration looks weak and foolish. The impression is that it believes its Nicaraguan policy is too flimsy to stand up against the questions and criticism that a qualified Nicaraguan might put to it." His speech was to be, in Borge's words, Nicaragua's petition to the United States. Every American in Managua who could squeeze into the room was on one of the folding chairs that pointed toward the Sandinista and Nicaraguan flags flanking the podium. Solidarity groups mingled with converts to liberation theology, coffee harvesters, peace workers, delegations from city and country, American employees of Nicaraguan government ministries, the assembled *internacionalistas*. Old friends embraced, ignorant of one another's presence in Nicaragua, not having seen each other since Chicago, Thailand, Berkeley. Borge was introduced by a striking brunette in military uniform, wearing a pistol with a webbed ammunition belt and one raised shoe to compensate, someone said, for a heel blown off in the revolution. The setting was effective enough, either as theater or reality; the trick in Nicaragua was to know the difference.

A rumor swept the room that the Sandinista air force had mistakenly bombed a Miskito village on the East Coast that morning. The counter-rumor was that the village had been obliterated by a five-hundred-pound bomb dropped from a helicopter first used in Vietnam but given recently to the contras by the CIA. Someone else said the U.S. Air Force was poised in Florida, accompanied by the 101st Airborne Division, to make a lightning strike against Managua and military targets around the country. There were still more than two weeks to go before Christmas. Except for mop-up operations that would continue in the mountains, Nicaragua could be securely American within ten days and most of the troops would be home for the holidays. A middle-aged man said authoritatively that there were too many blacks and Puerto Ricans in the 101st. They might not be enthusiastic about invading a poor, Hispanic Third World trouble spot, so Reagan would be sure to use the 82nd Airborne instead.

Tomás Borge was welcomed to the speaker's platform by prolonged applause. He went right to work as the cameras began to roll. The speech was called "Eight Mistaken Theses," a caption that might have been hung by a professor of English literature above a shelf where he kept rejected doctoral dissertations on Henry James. Alternatively, it could have been the headline for a *Pravda* editorial intended to correct a number of alarmingly deviationist tendencies that had sprung unbidden into Soviet custom.

With such a silly title, who would expect a good, even important, speech? The "theses" referred to a variety of American accusations: Nicaragua was a Communist satellite, had become totalitarian, was stimulating a regional arms race; the Sandinistas repressed Miskitos, Catholics, and dissidents. While Borge took pains to refute the charges, his chief concern was for the relationship between the United States and Nicaragua. This was the subject he had wanted to address if he had been permitted into the United States.

"We wish to speak to you from a country that is at war," Borge said, pausing to let the concept of war seep into the placid old Managua country club. The cameras zoomed in. "This is not only the single war we would wish to have waged, the war against underdevelopment, but also a war against military forces organized by the North American Administration. What does not seem to be much discussed is the right of one country to attack another, or the right of a powerful country like the United States to decide the destiny of a country that is nearly eighty times smaller in size and population."

Clarifying what he meant by destiny, the interior minister compared the high Central American infant mortality rates with the low ones in the United States. He related the dictatorships of the region to its poverty, convinced that the latter would last until the former were overthrown. "Hunger, dear friends, is not a conflict between East and West; hunger is a conflict between the dictatorial regimes and our peoples, who are hungry as well for justice. 'General Hunger' is the commander-in-chief of Central American peoples." As if he were throwing punches at an opponent who could not get out of the way, Borge recited the numbers of Central Americans who had died in the last three decades from starvation, assassinations and war. "Would it not be more logical if, rather than making and unmaking dictators, rather than arming and training oppressive armies, rather than supporting selfish oligarchies, rather than perpetuating underdevelopment by means of a profoundly unjust international economic order, the United States were to support profound social change, stop opposing popular revolution, stop arming oppressors? Would it not be more logical if the United States were to orient its gigantic technological proficiency toward the overcoming of poverty and misery?"

The audience was polite enough but hardly demonstrative. A few people clapped when Borge stopped for a gulp of water, but more were passing notes and whispering. Someone was just down from Estelí, someone else had flown in from Bluefields on the Atlantic Coast. "It is still fresh in the memory of Nicaraguans that the highest authority in our country during the times of Somoza," the interior minister continued, "was the ambassador of the United States. We are struggling, fundamentally, to be masters of our own decisions. This is an elementary principle of national pride. The affirmation that Nicaragua is dominated by the Cubans or the Soviets seems to be based on an ignorance of Nicaraguans."

His countrymen were overwhelmingly behind the revolution, Borge asserted, citing "levels of popular participation that have no precedents in our history." The new organizations of workers, farmers, women, artists, professionals, and businessmen—"yes, businessmen," he repeated—were not due to international alliances but to national self-confidence brought about by the war for independence. "The decisions of our revolutionary Directorate are as closely linked to the sentiments of our people as blood is to arteries. This, too, is democracy."

With no hesitation about admitting "errors, many errors," Borge said the "abuses" of the early days after the 1979 triumph had been corrected. The persecution of the Miskitos had long since ended, he claimed, along with cultural and religious prejudice against the other non-Spanish ethnic groups. The revolution's successes were there for all to see; its failures showed only how far it still had to travel. Borge denied that "nuclear missiles pointed at the United States" would ever come to Nicaragua. "Nobody has asked us to install missiles in Nicaragua, nor have we requested missiles of anyone."

Borge pleaded, finally, for a new level of information to flow between Nicaragua and the United States. Americans, he said, should have "real facts rather than lies or half-truths" to help them know Nicaragua better. "Nicaragua is never going to attack the United States. Nicaragua is being attacked by the United States." Borge made a gesture that was almost a shrug, as if he had stated a truth so obvious no one could doubt it. "Our revolution continues—despite pressures, despite economic boycotts, despite war," he said. The Sandinistas' determination to continue on an independent course was central to Borge's petition. Concluding, he saw the United States faced with two choices. "Either it continues along the belligerent path that presages an immense cost in lives, not only of Central Americans but also of North Americans, or else it decides to engage in dialogue, to understand our peoples, to collaborate with social change and with the possibility of development. Thank you."

Silence. Tomás Borge looked grave. The interpreters were still whispering their translations into the ears of listeners who spoke only English, French, German, Swedish, or Japanese. As the translations finished and the audience realized that Borge himself had finished, perhaps a dozen people clapped. Five or six more joined them, and a woman in the back shouted, *"Viva la revolución!"* She got a good hand. The Japanese completed their double translation of Spanish to English, English to Japanese, and, thorough as ever, filmed their reverses of the audience.

The bulk of the gathering paid virtually no attention to what they had heard, if they had heard it. The element of Managua's being an oasis in the leftist diaspora was present in the auditorium more strongly than anything Borge actually said. The event quickly metamorphosed back again from speech to class reunion. File and forget. Tomás Borge was a natural orator who had given a passionate speech, but what most of the audience was interested in was each other. Gossip resumed immediately. The revolution's supporters appeared, in this instance at least, to be attracted not so much to the specific cause of the Sandinistas as to the quality of life that attached to having causes in general, the ceaseless postgraduate quest for rejuvenating ideological football games that become the emotional equivalent of a packed stadium at four o'clock on a crisp Saturday afternoon in November. It's always third and long, two and a half minutes left in the fourth quarter, a field goal won't do it. Nicaragua was not so much a place or even an issue as it was an occasion.

One of the *internacionalistas* read a statement for the television crews that on behalf of the U.S. citizens living in Nicaragua he wanted the American public to know that he and his compatriots did not want to be rescued—a verbal inflection denoting that quotation marks surrounded the word "rescued," accompanied by ironic laughter—as their fellow citizens had been in Grenada. He got more cheers than Borge, and, as it turned out, more time on the nightly news back home. In Reagan's as in Victoria's empire, the anti-imperialists were able to command more attention than the targets of imperialism itself.

As soon as the *internacionalista* was finished, most of the journalists hurried out to make their feeds or phone calls or airplanes. A few of the press approached the podium, where the public-relations officer, Myrna Torres had taken brief charge of Borge. I looked at Myrna Torres for a sign indicating where I should wait for my interview; she made a beckoning gesture for me to stand near Borge along with the other reporters. Myrna Torres had promised me an interview and she was delivering a press conference. Well, she never said "exclusive."

Borge took care to stay elevated on the speaker's platform, where he was still shorter than Reuters, the Miami *Herald* and *Newsweek,* though taller than the Washington *Post,* UPI, and I. When he was making his speech, Borge had varied the pace. Now he was fast with us, the boxer he had resembled at Los Antojitos. He bit off his words as he might have snapped jabs at the cheeks of Marvin Hagler, or, preferably for Borge, at the Nicaraguan boxer Alexis Argüello, who had combined his contra support with staying in the United States to do beer commercials.

One of the reporters asked Borge why the Sandinistas were not allowing greater freedom of expression.

"We want critics, not liars. We're in a war for survival and we can't listen to repeaters of Hitlerian slogans."

Who decides what's a lie?

"All right, everyone has his own idea of what truth is. We took over a country in ruins, not only physical but institutional. We're building everything from the bottom up. Our critics criticize us and we criticize them. The people can listen to everyone and decide."

Aren't you interfering with freedom of religion when you expel priests and criticize the church hierarchy?

"When a priest tells his parishioners not to defend themselves or their country under attack, is this a religious or a political position? When the church raises a counterrevolutionary banner, when it criticizes the government but never the contras who murder their own people, this is not a religious position but a political one.''

But pacifism can also be deeply religious, servants can believe they are being religious by obeying their masters. Isn't the word of God open to many interpretations?

"God spoke many words. We believe Christ was crucified because He was an anti-imperialist who would not kneel before the Roman Empire. Today, we ourselves refuse to kneel before the empire. We will concede anything but our dignity.''

You accuse the counterrevolutionaries of crimes against humanity. In the war against the contras, haven't you violated human rights yourselves?

"Look, you're either for human rights or you're against them, and we are for them. The fact is, those we have arrested for trying to overthrow our government are treated humanely. They are not tortured or killed. Can you say that of dissidents in governments the United States has supported in Guatemala, Chile or El Salvador?''

What do you think about the situation for the Chicanos in the United States?

"I don't want to comment on the Chicanos or I'll *never* get a visa to come to the United States. *Nunca!''* The reporters laughed, but Borge did not smile.

Would you negotiate without conditions with the United States?

"We will do nothing behind our people's backs ever. That doesn't rule out having private talks, which we welcome. We want good relations but we won't be your slaves. We have many debates and disagreements among ourselves and we express them freely. What is not debatable is whether or not to continue the revolution.''

XIV THE OPPOSITION

WHAT NICARAGUA LACKS MOST in its political life is a tradition of comity, the sense of civility between those who disagree with each other, an opportunity for those out of power to gain it by a peaceful expression of the popular will rather than by shooting their way in. Nicaragua was born in the collective harshness of a militarized colonialism, the landed Spanish oligarchy and the Catholic hierarchy that emerged from the Inquisition. Anyone outside those small but omnipotent forces was barely entitled to live, much less have an opinion. While the country was being governed alternately by its old Liberal and Conservative parties, elections were frequently held but real power was traded at gunpoint.

"My country is quite used to elections and knows nothing of democracy," a thoughtful Nicaraguan told me, a woman who favored and criticized the Sandinistas. "The Somozas were big ones for elections, you know, always rigged." In the context of poverty, inequality and intolerance, the revolution became inevitable. It is as impossible to imagine the Sandinistas without the Somozas as it is the Soviets unpreceded by the czars.

Given the autocratic nature of Nicaraguan history, what was

surprising about the Sandinistas was how much tolerance they showed their opposition. With American liberals of the mid-1980s disoriented by their own failures as well as the popularity of Ronald Reagan, the anti-Sandinistas in Nicaragua were significantly more cogent and provided a wider range of opinions and options than the domestic opposition in the United States. Anti-Sandinistas were perhaps more vocal than numerous, but their representatives were all over the place. This did not mean they described their lives as a picnic. Some were former Sandinistas. Choosing friends, it turned out, might have been more dangerous than choosing enemies: When friends become enemies, they take with them the close knowledge of all your foibles.

First, as a matter of perspective, the headquarters for opposition to the Sandinistas was in Washington, D.C. Ronald Reagan announced his hostility to the new government in Managua within two weeks of its victory over Somoza in 1979, three and a half months before he declared his candidacy for president. In the years that followed it was always clear, as it had been for over a century, that survival of the government in Managua depended on the attitude of the government in Washington.

Second, there were the counterrevolutionaries. Creatures of Washington in one sense, the contras were also indigenous Nicaraguans for whom the revolution was hateful and war had become a profession. Their military leadership was descended from Somoza's National Guard. The contras were sustained by Washington's steady encouragement and sporadic funding, but they also had a constituency among those in the Nicaraguan peasantry who were unreached by Sandinista reforms, who were most loyal to the established Catholic Church and who were from remote northern communities that had traditionally supplied the membership of Somoza's Guardia units. When their lines were not being written by Washington public-relations coaches, the contra military commanders made no pretense of knowing anything about, or aspiring to, democracy. They were fighting an army that had beaten them badly and were anxious for revenge. "We have a lot of scores to settle," one of the contra commanders told a reporter from *Newsweek*. "There will be bodies from the border to Managua."

The contra political leaders often criticized the conduct of their military colleagues and promised a genuine democracy in Nicaragua once they liberated the country from the Sandinistas. It was not clear that contra success, if it came, would enable the political chiefs to control the military ones, but it was clear they wanted to. They had not only different agendas but also completely different roots than the military commanders had. Some of these political leaders were former Sandinistas, and virtually all of them had fought against the Somoza dictatorship.

Though his support inside Nicaragua was confined to a small minority, the most prominent of these leaders was Arturo Cruz, a banker who traveled the long road from early Sandinista supporter to counterrevolutionary convert. He had been a member of the revolutionary junta and had served the Sandinistas as ambassador to Washington. When the Sandinistas' policies toward business and the United States became too harsh for him, Cruz resigned from their government. He became a critic not only of the Sandinistas but of their international supporters. "Those who have the fortune to live in democratic countries," Cruz said, "but prescribe socialism without freedom for developing nations, might unintentionally be adopting postures as patronizing as those who are nostalgic for paternalistic exploitation. The greatest disservice to Nicaragua's revolution has been the 'blank-check' solidarity given to its leaders through thick and thin— regardless of their faults—by some governments abroad. Unconditional support, whether for reasons of idealism or partisanship, risks taking my country on a round trip: from the past to the past."

Sandinista supporters argued with Cruz that the revolution's severity was due to American pressure; they pleaded with him to stay in Nicaragua and help the revolution achieve its goals. The CIA was said to have offered Cruz financial and political support if he would leave the country. He refused to participate in the 1984 elections but remained part of the internal opposition until

1985, when he went into exile and shortly after that became one of the leaders of the counterrevolution.

For other contra political leaders, closeness to Washington could be measured by distance from the Sandinistas. Edén Pastora Gómez, the former revolutionary hero and deputy defense minister for the Sandinistas, led the Democratic Revolutionary Alliance, known as ARDE, based in Costa Rica. But Pastora refused to join any coalition that included former members of Somoza's National Guard. The CIA dropped him. Eventually, in 1986, lack of support from Washington forced Pastora to drop out of the fight altogether. Faced with ostracism from the counterrevolutionary cause, he had quarreled with ARDE's political director, Alfonso Robelo Callejas, a progressive businessman who had been an original member of the Sandinista ruling junta. Once a young radical, Robelo had gone to Havana to see Castro in 1959. Later, as a merchant in Nicaragua, he made over $20 million in cooking oil and cotton. American liberals found him congenial, but like Pastora, Robelo was uneasy with the prominence of National Guardsmen in the largest contra group, the Nicaraguan Democratic Force, called the FDN.

The CIA continued to insist on the National Guard officers as the most credible and experienced military leadership the contras had. The civilian most comfortable with CIA judgments was Adolfo Calero Portocarrero, the president of FDN's directorate and former head of the Conservative Party in Nicaragua. Before the revolution, Calero had run the local subsidiary of Coca-Cola in Nicaragua. Among American residents and former Nicaraguan colleagues, it was no secret in Managua that Calero's ties with the CIA went back to his Coca-Cola days. "Depend on Washington to pick the sleaziest guy among the opposition to both Somoza and the Sandinistas," an American who had known Calero in Managua said. "Shake hands with Adolfo Calero and count your fingers."

While I was in Managua, the Nicaraguan government announced that in three years of attacks, the contras had caused $1 billion worth of damage and displaced 200,000 people. In a single year there had been 620 air raids, 120 attacks by sea (including the successful assault on Corinto and the mining of half a dozen harbors), and ninety land incursions by the contras. The announcement could only have been received as good news in Washington. With less than $100 million spent on the contras through the end of 1983, the covert war had proved strikingly cost-effective.

Getting all the contras to work together was more difficult for the CIA. In mid-1985, the Agency finally succeeded in grafting several contra branches together to form the United Nicaraguan Opposition. UNO's three leaders were Adolfo Calero (who was by far the most powerful militarily), Alfonso Robelo, and Arturo Cruz. The CIA's graft was not a secure one. Calero, Robelo, and Cruz agreed on neither political objectives nor military tactics. This led to confusion among their subordinates and on the battle-field. "There is no sense among the military commanders of what the UNO stands for," a contra official told the New York *Times*. Near the end of 1985, Arturo Cruz said, "It's very difficult, but I'm not ready to quit." The counterrevolution remained deter-mined, if divided.

Into the margin between the unassailable verities of the San-dinistas and the unalterable vows of the contras trying to over-throw them, the domestic Nicaraguan opposition squeezed itself, hoping for a continued existence in the national consciousness.

As the third tier of antagonism to *Sandinismo* after the politi-cians in Washington and the contras on the Honduran and Costa Rican frontiers, the domestic opposition liked to proclaim its independence of the first two. These anti-Sandinista rivals for the public affection were plentiful in Managua and represented a wide spectrum of opinion. There were Communists who accused the Sandinistas of selling out the revolution to the bourgeoisie, a number of centrist parties that basically argued for a more busi-ness-oriented economy and accommodation with the church, and fundamentalist Christians who accused the Sandinistas of hand-ing the revolution over to the devil. Splinter groups became rig-idly hostile to the main parties they had broken away from; I heard a Managuan fond of American popular music say that every little meaning had a movement all its own.

Mauricio Díaz, general secretary of the Popular Social Christian Party, which was friendly to the Sandinistas, believed a "patriotic front" was the best means of governing Nicaragua. "We are part of the trustworthy opposition," he told me in Managua. "That means we believe in having a freer press and greater political liberties. These will demonstrate to the world exactly how strong the revolution is. I think we are on the path to full democracy. Fundamentally, my party agrees with the Sandinistas that nonalignment, a mixed economy and political pluralism are the three cornerstones of our society." Mauricio Díaz's differences with the Sandinistas were similar to those of a moderate with a liberal Democrat.

The tone among members of the Social Christian Party contrasted dramatically with Díaz's. Here was the real opposition, embattled and bitter. (Mauricio Díaz's Popular Social Christians had split from the Social Christians; the similarity in party names disguised the polarity in their attitudes.) In the Social Christians' headquarters, the blunt instrument of disinheritance was inescapable. The offices were in a state resembling the start of a nervous breakdown; both compulsive tidiness and utter collapse were visible. Broken windows went unrepaired, but the floor was swept. Party functionaries made desultory phone calls but let other phones ring unanswered. Papers on desks were neat but no one seemed to know what to do with them. Employees were suspicious of everyone who was not part of the party, but they politely served demitasses of coffee—which they threatened to refill every time the level sank half an inch—with a strength that tasted sufficient to blast the Sandinistas all the way to the Panama Canal. (Except, of course, that the Sandinistas themselves fired the same kind of coffee with the same nuclear potential.) The party leader applied her sense of disinheritance to the raw data of the revolution she felt disinherited by.

"The middle class exists, that's all, but we are not allowed to reproduce ourselves," said Azucena Ferrey, second vice-president of the Social Christians and acting president in the absence of the president himself, who was traveling in Europe. "They say they need us. Let them give us the security we need to keep our businesses and the guarantee to express ourselves in our politics as we must in a pluralistic society. If we mean so much to them, they should give us the freedom to make our proposals as widely known as they make theirs." The antecedents for "they" and "them" in Managua were always the Sandinistas.

Azucena Ferrey wore a cotton print dress that sported white bells on a field of basic black. Her husband owned a coffee *finca* and was general manager of a flour mill, and they had a nine-year-old son. Azucena Ferrey still kept her small diamond baguette engagement ring on her fourth finger. *La Solución Somos Todos*—"We are all part of the solution"—hung on a banner near the cracked window to her office, but the Social Christians had begun to think of their slogan with irony. Only those in partnership with the Sandinistas, Azucena Ferrey now believed, were permitted to be part of the solution, and it was not a solution she agreed with. She sat beneath portraits of Sandino and Pope John Paul II, with a prominent wooden cross above the Pope. The delicate gold cross on her neck bumped against her collarbone when she shook her shoulders to emphasize her disdain for the Sandinistas. For the Sandinistas, not for Sandino. Like dissidents in any religion, she claimed descent from the founder himself.

"We are the true heirs of Sandino," Azucena Ferrey said. "In 1957 we recognized Augusto César Sandino as a true nationalist and antimaterialist. The FSLN did not discover Sandino until 1961. But he was against the Marxist-Leninist systems they are trying to implement now. When Sandino met Farabundo Martí, who led the revolt in El Salvador and was a Marxist, Sandino said, 'I accept your cooperation but not your ideology.' These so-called Sandinistas are trying to force us to accept what Sandino the man hated."

Azucena Ferrey said her party was reluctant to put forth its own program at a moment of such crisis in the very existence of Nicaragua. "When national reconciliation has been achieved, you will see us present a program like that of the Christian Democrats of Europe. We favor the private sector over nationalization, but first we must have peace and democracy. We don't want the government to interfere in business, but we do support the direct participation of workers in the businesses they work for. This will bring about a more equal balance of resources than you find in a capitalist country. We are against the exploitation of man by the state, as in socialism, and we are against the exploitation of man by man, as in capitalism.

"Everyone is losing here, *including* the state. The role of the state should be as a regulator of commerce, not its administrator. The state is the worst administrator, because it has no idea how to order cows around or how to sell dresses. A coffee producer like my husband who sold freely before now has to sell at state-decreed prices, and he has to sell his coffee to the state itself. The state may turn around and sell at a higher price on the international market, which is unfair to the producer, or it may have to sell at a lower price, which means it loses. In either case, the state is the middleman, which is a role it fills very poorly. It just isn't working, and incentive is reduced for everyone from the *campesino* to the owner."

What happens when you tell this to the government?

"Marxism is too hard to reason with. Nicaragua is not now Marxist, but it is heading in that direction. The Sandinistas talk out of both sides of their mouths. First they said, 'Let's all get together and defeat Somoza.' We did that, we made a united front, and it worked. Then they said, 'The alliance to defeat *somocismo* was only a tactic. Now we are going to take away all the property of the enemy.' At first this meant expropriating the holdings of the Somoza family and a few prominent *somocistas*. Then they said they're going to take the property of those who obtained it illegally. We were a little suspicious already of that— who's going to decide what was legal under the old system?— but we said okay. Then they started expropriating property of a person just because someone denounced him, or maybe the owner once sent a birthday card to Somoza. One day they proclaim their devotion to a thriving private sector as the only way to build the new Nicaragua. The next day they tell you, 'Excuse me, I'm off to Moscow to get more help to build the perfect socialist state.' Which one of those builders should we believe? Contradictions! We live on them, but we can't eat them.''

The Social Christians' headquarters showed several scars from vandalism. Mrs. Ferrey complained that the police were less than zealous when the Sandinista *turbas*—mobs—harassed the Social Christians and attacked their offices. ''The police are supposed to protect us; instead they protect the *turbas*,'' she said.

Feeling that some of the damage might have been left alone to prove a point, I asked if Mrs. Ferrey kept her window unrepaired so everyone could see that a Sandinista kid had put a brick through it.

''Do you know how hard it is to get a new pane of glass in Managua?''

Is it possible for you to live with the Sandinistas?

''If they change, if they allow all points of view to circulate.''

If not, should the United States invade Nicaragua?

''All invasions hurt the invaded country. A Marxist government never abandons power willingly, but we have always opposed invasion. What we need is peace. Principally, we wish the United States would support disarmament throughout Central America. The main trouble with the revolution right now is that the FSLN is not treating us all as Nicaraguans but as members of separate classes that have to be taught to hate each other. This is where the Social Christians are needed: first for reconciliation, second for the liberties that will make democracy possible in Nicaragua.''

On the walls outside the headquarters of the Social Christians, Sandinista supporters had spray-painted graffiti. The two most prominent splashes were *Viva el FSLN* and *Muerto a los Vendepatria*—''Death to those who sell out their country.'' The Sandinistas have a law forbidding the defacement of a political party's offices by an opponent; clearly, it was not being enforced. The Social Christians' own sign proclaiming their identity had been broken in half, and the half that remained hung down off its hinges. The rest of the wall was scratched and battered.

If the building had been a person, it would be said to have been mugged. I realized I had been unfair to Azucena Ferrey in implying that she was showing off by leaving her window broken. The Social Christians were only presenting proof of what the Sandinistas permit and possibly encourage. In the absence of a regularly accessible uncensored opposition press, letting the window go unrepaired was a form of free speech. Providing an insight into the virtues of pluralism, William Blake said that opposition is true friendship. The Sandinistas had yet to learn that lesson.

The antipathy between the Sandinistas and a segment of the business community is almost total. Yet they need each other. If it were not for the Sandinistas, the businessmen would still be paying a big cut to Somoza, and if it were not for the businessmen, the Sandinistas would be faced with an economic disaster even more acute than the one they have already. Sick economies, dependent on fluctuating international markets in a few export products, become epidemics in Central America. Nicaragua's foreign debt stood at almost $5 billion in 1986, approximately the same as that of its widely praised capitalist and democratic neighbor, Costa Rica. In an unpublished paper analyzing the fate of commercial interests in the Sandinista revolution, Professor Dennis Gilbert of Hamilton College evokes the image of an unhappy couple who cannot separate. "For the conceivable future," Professor Gilbert writes, "*comandantes* and capitalists will continue as they are today: locked together in an embrace which neither wants and neither is able to escape."

The principal business representatives who would like to think about divorce are in the Supreme Council of Private Enterprise, an umbrella federation that includes organizations from industry, agriculture and commerce. The council, known as COSEP, has opposed the Sandinistas almost since they took power. In the COSEP office in an upper-class Managua neighborhood, the day of the Nicaraguan tycoon did not appear to be entirely over. On the desk of Enrique Bolanos Geyer, COSEP's president, was a letter from David Rockefeller promoting a Reagan Administration economic plan called the Caribbean Basin Initiative. The letter, which contained references to its having been sent to commercial leaders throughout the Caribbean and Central America, called for partnership between American and Latin American businessmen. The partnership would be mutually beneficial, Rockefeller wrote, since the Caribbean countries need access to U.S. capital and customers to foster economic development just as the United States needs political stability in the region, less illegal immigration, a halt to narcotics smuggling and expanded markets for its goods and services. It was a classic job of brokering, something for everyone. If Ronald Reagan's view was that Nicaragua did its business exclusively with the Communists, the letter on Enrique Bolanos' desk was an indication that David Rockefeller had reached a different conclusion.

"In Cuba they left," Enrique Bolanos said, jangling a large set of keys against each other and their chain while he spoke, "and it didn't work. We stay. Maybe it will work. I only know that we are trying to do the opposite of what the Cuban businessmen did."

In Enrique Bolanos there was more rancor toward the Sandinistas than there had been in Azucena Ferrey. Bolanos, virtually the same age and a world apart from Tomás Borge, was a prosperous cotton processor, rancher and farmer from Masaya. He was volatile, by turns amused, irritable and ebullient. Bolanos and his COSEP associate Ramiro Gurdian chuckled over a story on the front page of the opposition paper, *La Prensa,* which said that Dennis Martínez, one of the few Nicaraguans currently playing major-league baseball, had been arrested for drunk driving in the United States. "Resisted arrest, too," Bolanos said to Gurdian. "He may be pitching for Sing Sing next year," Gurdian said, and Bolanos laughed. Both men were burly, but Ramiro Gurdian was younger—in his forties—and more muscular. He was vice-president of COSEP and a prominent opposition leader from León who described himself as an "agribusinessman" in cotton, bananas, cattle and eucalyptus.

"These people are Marxist-Leninists without any question," Gurdian said. "They talk about a mixed economy, but they don't mean it."

"On July 19, 1979," Bolanos said, "for all practical purposes

we lost everything we had here." He quickly added that Somoza
was a greedy monster but that at least under the old regime a
man knew what he owned. Bolanos' main business at present, he
said, was "trying to rescue Nicaragua for the West and trying to
help my workers by keeping them employed." He shook his keys
the way an indignant peacock would ruffle his feathers.

Bolanos handed me a photocopy of a letter he and other
COSEP leaders had sent to the ruling junta in 1981. It contained
accusations of everything from "a seemingly endless debt spiral"
to "a new genocide in Nicaragua" to "transforming the revolution into a Marxist-Leninist adventure that must bring only blood
and tears to our people." Four of the letter's authors had been
immediately imprisoned. The Sandinistas I spoke to were quick
to admit an "excess" which they claimed could not have occurred after 1981.

"The letter talked about oppression," Bolanos said, "and the
Sandinistas proved its accuracy by throwing us in jail. They
wanted to show they were evenhanded, so they threw some local
Communists who had been criticizing them in jail at the same
time. I had not actually put my signature on the letter, and I was
released after six days. The other COSEP leaders stayed in
prison four months."

What happened to the Communists?

"Who cares?" An office boy, who had come in to deliver the
mail, laughed. He wore a cap that advertised Ray-O-Vac batteries. Enrique Bolanos brandished his keys and the office boy disappeared.

"They have betrayed not only their own principles as they
proclaimed them in 1979," Bolanos said, "but also the dreams
we all shared for a new Nicaragua. They deserve whatever they
get. Excuse me, I have an appointment with Chafee and Bingaman." Enrique Bolanos gave a final furious shake of his keys and
hurried off. I had, I supposed, seen a dress rehearsal for the
senators from Rhode Island and New Mexico. The Sandinistas'
best chance for survival at that moment may have been Enrique
Bolanos' keys; if he kept on jangling them, the senators might be
annoyed enough not to back the invasion.

"We get mad, and sometimes we're not so mad," Ramiro Gurdian continued, softening the atmosphere while making sure that his criticisms themselves remained as sharp. "The main problem is that private enterprise is not private anymore. We can't make our own decisions. The government moves deeper all the time into private areas. They own factories, plantations, mines, discotheques, restaurants, motels. What does a government know about discotheques, barber shops or dollmaking? Where will this end? I want to help my own workers, pay them more, get them better jobs, see them produce more. But my hands are tied."

Would you like to see the Marines come in?

Gurdian stared out his window at the walled estate next door. "I don't agree with the contras, but I don't condemn them. Some of their leaders, Robelo and Calero, are good friends of mine. Robelo and I fought Somoza together. No one can tell me he's a *somocista*. These guys call anyone against them a *somocista*. Daniel Ortega says that neither bullets nor ballots will get him out of power. I say we should believe him."

Should we send in the Marines then?

Gurdian looked at his fingernails, which were glossy. I could not recall ever having met a farmer with buffed nails. The office boy in the Ray-O-Vac battery cap came back in and reminded him that it was time for him to meet Senators Chafee and Bingaman for lunch.

"There is Sandinista rhetoric, there is Reagan's rhetoric, and then there is reality," Gurdian said. "The game here is far from over."

Ramiro Gurdian was driven off in a butterscotch Mercedes by the boy in the Ray-O-Vac cap. The COSEP office provided another in Nicaragua's seemingly endless supply of archetypes: the rich man who complains he is powerless to help the poor. The opposing archetype was equally available. Revolutionaries are forever making people like Ramiro Gurdian feel strangers in their own countries, reducing the human condition to a terminal case of class antagonism, shouting power to the people while making sure that the people singularizes itself into whoever is doing the shouting. It may be hopeful for their constituency that the Sandinistas admit making "mistakes" with Miskito Indians, businessmen or opposing politicians, but surely behavior itself defines individuals and governments at least as accurately as apologies do.

Looking for a viewpoint on the private sector and the Sandinistas less filled with personal animus, I went to see a foreign businessman with lengthy experience in Nicaragua. Inside his company compound, parrots screamed among the flaming hibiscus. It was a dry month, but a whole tropical garden bloomed unseasonally behind the high cyclone fence topped with barbed wire. At the center of the compound was the low-slung colonial outpost of an international conglomerate. Ruling over what was left of his domain, the foreign businessman agreed to speak only on the condition that neither his name, his company nor his nationality be revealed. "I still have to live here," he said, "and someday I hope to go home. I could do neither comfortably if any part of my identity were disclosed."

After such a melodramatic opening, I expected an immature multinational cog afraid of his own shadow. He was hardly, however, in hiding. "I don't want to criticize the Sandinistas," he said softly. "I want to eradicate them—like weeds."

He let the remark sit for a moment.

"With them it's always five minutes to midnight, everything is an emergency, this is government by crisis. The economy is in hell already and it's winding itself farther down every day. A car is on the fritz and needs a bearing; you can't get a bearing. Someone brings one in clandestinely and you pay ten times its real value. My friends in cotton and coffee say it's not worth their while to plant their crops anymore, since the Sandinistas control every seed and bag of fertilizer."

Where's the private sector?

"*We* are the private sector, but *they* control everything we do. Their foreign exchange is so scarce they won't let our cordobas out of the country no matter what they're worth, which isn't much. It's obscene. If you have dollars here you can still buy most things. If not, not. No tickee, no washee." He hissed when he said "Sandinistas" or "scarce" or "obscene."

I asked him why he stayed.

"In the hope that the fyootcha will be bettah—that's all that keeps any of us here. That and the will to survive in a hostile environment. The Sandinistas are experts in constructing that." Though he was a thin, fastidious man who restrained himself even in fury, this multinational executive appeared to take a perverse pleasure at his own affliction, and the severity of his judgments made him smile repeatedly. His voice rose. "Nobody, but *nobody,* here trusts them. They do things with a garrote. Nothing you do or say means anything to them, no ideas but their own are worth even discussing. They're impossible!"

He reined himself in, pressing a buzzer on his desk. When a maid appeared, his sarcasm was at my expense rather than hers. *"Que traiga café a nuestro invitado honorado, María."* Some coffee for our honored guest. *"Muy distinguido,* heh, heh."

I asked why he said nobody trusts the Sandinistas, who were obviously popular among major segments of the population.

"In-doc-tri-nation. That's all their popularity amounts to. All day long, everywhere. Everyone is indoctrinated—children, women's groups, neighborhood committees—and then everyone in turn becomes an indoctrinator. Though they won't permit a truly free election because it's not the Commie way, I'm willing to believe the Sandinistas could win a free election here. Besides the indoctrination, you have many people who have gained advantages under the Sandinistas. The problems are never the Sandinistas' fault. The government *always* says more people are consuming more now, and that causes some of the scarcity, while Americans cause the rest. My maid and I find there are shortages of almost everything, and the biggest shortage is liberty. But for Nicaraguans it's impossible to think in terms of liberties they've never had anyway. The issue for them is food on the table. They'll go to war over sugar, even over processed sugar. They think brown sugar is a crime against nature. Liberty they don't miss. They've had generations of domination and exploitation;

now they've exchanged one form of domination and exploitation for another.''

When I asked how the revolution had affected him, the corporate executive described "hotheads" who tried to bring "a Commie union" into his business. He had fought them and made concessions, but nothing would satisfy them. Finally, the union organizers occupied the plant for nine days. "Damn them!" he yelled, pounding his desk, still furious almost four years later. The union won but, according to the executive, did little for the workers, who soon lost interest. At the next election, the union could not muster a quorum for a meeting, and the company threw the union out. That led to pickets and a mob outside the plant gates, but this time the Nicaraguans were not the only nationality.

"A busload of American tourists was there," the businessman said. "This wretched delegation of idiots, goddam them, joined the pickets and they put my name on a sign. 'Mr. So-and-So Go Home,' it said, next to a big placard saying 'Reagan out of the White House.' First time I ever wanted to be identified with *that* ignorant creep. My daughter was here for a visit, and I was glad she saw the mobs. Well, we finally got a new union that started right in with a lot of demands, but we beat them in an arbitration with a Sandinista magistrate from the ministry of labor. We've had no bother since."

Since he won the arbitration, I asked if the businessman had not at least been satisfied that judgments for his side were possible. His victory left him unimpressed, a mere Sandinista gambit to lull the private sector into relaxation. "Give 'em time," he said, "the Gulag's on its way." He had not liked Somoza either, he added, mostly because of his greed. "But money and power were enough for Somoza. This groups insists on faith and truth, blind faith that theirs is the only truth. Somoza didn't care if people hated him as long as they left him alone. This group makes you love them *all the way*. The arrogance of the revolutionary is astonishing."

I asked if his family was in Nicaragua.

"My wife is out of the country, teaching. My kids are lefties.

They're away, too, in college. One of them is taking a course on how companies like mine destroy the environment. Great, eh?''

The foreign businessman shook his head; his own children didn't seem to know the 1960s were over a long time ago. He himself had watched revolution here in its oven, was still watching what he considered to be the inevitable doom as it approached. "Revolutions destroy all you have and leave you with nothing. *Nothing.* You know what nature abhors most. Into the vacuum seeps arrogance. Add the Sandinistas' prescription for centralization to their arrogance, and lust emerges, the lust for power. In a Communist regime there is more power concentrated in the government—less check on that power—and this is a Communist regime. The Gulag is *coming.* This place is a disaster!"

What do you think the United States should do?

He was silent. His face blazed; it could have lighted a cavern. He was beyond choler. For a moment I thought it was possible he had graduated into mineral form.

I asked if he had nothing to recommend.

"Oh, but I do." He lit a cigarette and watched it glow before he continued. "Drop an atom bomb on this place, but let me go on vacation first." He was reanimated, I thought, more by the force of his own arguments welling in him and demanding expression than by what I had asked. He seemed aroused as well by the memory of all revolution, and a hatred for it. "Nothing short of war will get this group out and turn back what they are doing. *Drop the bomb!"*

Now I was silent, his punch leaving me with nothing further to ask. The revolution was a whore, then, eating its own and everything else in its path. Invasion would be medical, the necessary step toward salvation. The businessman inhaled deeply on his cigarette.

"That stopped you, didn't it?"

XV RAMIRO LACAYO

THE OPPOSITION TO THE SANDINISTAS was that strong, that unyielding. It was not disagreement with the Sandinistas that was so striking, it was the wish, as the foreign businessman said, "to eradicate them—like weeds." Did the Sandinistas, in their hearts, in their *Marxist* hearts, also wish to eradicate the business community? Surely this would continue the Nicaraguan tradition of noncomity, of solving problems by not granting your opponents the right to exist. It would also conform to the Western stereotype of Communists.

As good politicians, the Sandinistas naturally denied they harbored any such wish. "We need them," one could hear in any government ministry. "All you have to do is look at the tin shacks and barefoot kids and empty shelves, the queues for milk in stores even in the countryside where the cows are. We need the managerial and commercial experience of every Nicaraguan." It was the party line. But were they making conditions hospitable for business to proceed, or was activity in the private sector becoming, as the COSEP officials and the implacable foreigner maintained, impossible?

Like every other group in Nicaragua, business itself was di-

176

vided. In the comfortable though not extravagant ease of his home in an upper-class residential section of Managua, a semi-retired industrialist had no doubts about living with the Sandinistas. "Business now is better than it was last year, and it was better last year than it was the year before," said Ramiro Lacayo, former head of the Nicaraguan subsidiary of Pennwalt, the giant chemical manufacturer. "The government helps the private sector and encourages us as much as possible. When there are problems with the workers, the government helps settle them, but it does not impose settlements."

Ramiro Lacayo was sixty-nine, retired from Pennwalt but still an active investor in that company as well as others. His son-in-law was the current general manager of Pennwalt and was also finding it possible to do business with and under the Sandinista government. One of Ramiro Lacayo's brothers was a coffee producer; another raised sugar cane; a third had a sugar-cane-processing plant. The four brothers had owned a sugar refinery together before the revolution. After the Sandinista victory, they donated half the refinery to the community and sold the other half to the government. All the brothers remained in Nicaragua. Four of Ramiro Lacayo's nephews, however, had moved to Miami. "Not really for political reasons, more for business opportunities," he said, but when I looked doubtful he added, "Though in Nicaragua today, who can say what is or is not political?" Indeed.

An article in *Life* magazine had featured Ramiro Lacayo as one of "the nervous rich of Nicaragua." By Nicaraguan standards he was certainly rich. His one-story California ranch-style house curved around an open tiled patio, and he had a long glass case filled with a collection of small silver spoons from around the world. He showed the spoons proudly, mementoes not only of pleasurable travels but of distinctly bourgeois acquisitiveness. He was nervous, however, only about the United States, not about the Sandinistas. "We wait to see what Reagan will do," he said, "and we pray for him not to do it to us." Nothing could blunt the force of the tirade from Enrique Bolanos and Ramiro Gurdian at COSEP nor turn down the furnace of hostility from

the foreign businessman. But Ramiro Lacayo added another
color besides red to the Nicaraguan economic picture. I asked
him how his response to the Sandinistas could be so different
from that of COSEP.

"Bolanos and Gurdian are no longer even trying to do business. They are now only doing politics. They don't know cotton
and bananas anymore, they know only political maneuvering.
You know what happened when we had private financial control?
The banks would lend huge amounts to their favorite customers
at eight percent; later on it went up to about fourteen percent.
They wouldn't lend anything to the people who only needed to
borrow a little. But the big borrowers, meanwhile, would turn
around and lend their borrowed money to the small farmers and
tradesmen at sixty percent interest. That's right, sixty. The end
result was that the tradespeople and smaller landowners would
lose their property and become vassals to the big landowners.
Was that capitalism or was it feudalism? Perhaps it was capitalism in a sense, but the form capitalism took in Nicaragua was a
feudal form. Do Reagan and Shultz understand what we had here
under Somoza? All systems have some corruption, but this one
ran on corruption. Corruption was the oil that made all the parts
move."

I asked whether private enterprise had guarantees that it could
survive under the Sandinistas.

"Ah, you have to know how to live with this government.
Some of the businessmen don't even want to try. Government
controls drive them crazy. But look at the Pellas family, the
second-richest family in Nicaragua after Somoza. They were in
banks, rum, cattle, beer, sugar, coffee, automobile distribution.
The revolution came, and some of them left for Miami. But others stayed. Carlos Pellas decided to do business with the Sandinistas even after they nationalized his banks. He still has the
largest sugar refinery in Central America, and he is now expand-
ing it. All business is inhibited by the lack of foreign currency,
but we're still in business.

"Guarantees? I don't know. What is *garantizado* when the
bombas can fall on Managua tonight? I think the private sector

will keep on as long as the Sandinistas need it, and I can't imagine a time when they won't need it. North American pressure makes it harder to do business and encourages Marxism. Is that what you want? Who knows what the Americans will do?"

Ramiro Lacayo did not like the law permitting the government to confiscate property if an owner remained out of the country six months. It was an unjust law, he said, but it was also a law with a purpose. "If people are not here to help build up this country from its awful poverty, the government wants to put their resources to work." What Lacayo hoped to see the Sandinistas do was to pass a law attracting foreign investors by making it possible for limited profits to leave the country. He was not worried that some of the Sandinista leaders were what he called "theoretical Marxists." They still had to live with the reality of their country. "The Sandinistas understand," he said, "that classic Marxism is not applicable to Nicaragua. They are constantly offending the real Communists here by *not* nationalizing industries the Nicaraguan Communists have always wanted collectivized. The worst thing about the economy now is that in a country of three million people, one hundred thousand of them are bearing arms, which means they are not producing. This is no way for the economy to become healthy, but as long as the contra war keeps on, that's the way it has to be."

I asked if he thought the government should negotiate with the contras. Theoretically, he said, any two parties at war should negotiate. The contras made this difficult in the context of the war against Somoza, a context all Nicaraguans still lived within. "They keep on committing crimes against humanity," Lacayo said, "the kind of crimes the Guardia was known for. They are not making war so much as making murder, attacking farmers and teachers who have nothing to do with any war. The government would lose support if it negotiated with such people. My second daughter's first husband was tortured to death by the Guardia in 1972. Almost every family in Nicaragua has a story like that somewhere. These are difficult things to forget, especially when it is the same Guardia members leading the contras."

Has the revolution been hard on you personally?

"Personally, no. Economically, *absolutamente*. I used to go to Europe every year, and every year I bought two new cars. I have no new cars since 1979, and I have been to Europe only once."

How do you support a government that forces you to give all that up?

"The government didn't force me to give that up. My country has very hard times, and I am part of my country."

What does Nicaragua need most?

"Peace, of course. Accommodation with the United States. Economically, we need an agreement on loans, credits, investments, we need again to be attractive to the North American businessman—oh, we always end up in the same place, how to make an agreement with the United States."

Waiting for Washington—doesn't that maintain Nicaragua's age-old dependency?

"No. We have made our independence. Don't be our protector, but don't be an enemy. Neither one. Be an *amigo*. That's all."

Ramiro Lacayo led me into his backyard, which was bordered by a low hedge. In the center of his lawn was a hole big enough to walk into. *"Refugio de bomba,"* he said. He led me down the stairs into it. As shelters go, it was roomy, with tinned foods and a single electric light bulb. When we came back out he pointed past his hedge to the house next door. His second daughter lived there, remarried now, and *her* backyard had a swimming pool. Ramiro Lacayo looked from his daughter's pool to his own shelter. He smiled. "I don't know which one I'm going to jump into tomorrow," he said.

XVI THE BORDER—I

IT WAS TIME TO GO to the border.

When everything is relative, confusing, ambiguous, when he cannot find any ground to stand on that does not shortly become quicksand, an American in Nicaragua always has a last resort. See the revolution at its most challenged point and moment; go to its frontier. Where the challenge was strongest, feelings would be least covered, behavior most honest, party lines most stripped away, motivation clearest. In the laboratory Nicaragua had become for the study of both freedom and compulsion, a trip to the border was a kind of litmus test.

It was also, for Americans in Nicaragua, an initiation ritual that fell somewhere between a fraternity hazing and a scarification ceremony. "The border" indicated not only a geographical but an emotional destination. Along with the obvious *machismo* element, never far from the surface among visitors, there was the opportunity to check every other impression Nicaragua had made on one. Occasionally, journalists had been wounded at the border. Earlier in the year two had been killed. More recently, several had gone north with the Sandinista commander in charge of public affairs, Roberto Sánchez. They had come to a roadblock and been told to go back. The journalists insisted on going farther toward Honduras. The government soldiers at the roadblock insisted on giving the journalists an armed escort. They were ambushed by the contras. The journalists escaped unhurt, but Roberto Sánchez was wounded and two of the soldiers in the escort were killed. "I wouldn't want that on my conscience the rest of my life," an American journalist said to me. (Like everything else that went on in Nicaragua, that particular event had spawned a small rumor mill so industrious it soon became impossible to divide fact from fantasy.) "The Sandinistas were killed," she added, "only because they tried to protect citizens from the country that is attacking them." "The point is," said the man she lived with, also a journalist, "keep your city wits about you."

Recovered from his wounds and still running public affairs, Roberto Sánchez gave the briefing for the American group I decided to accompany to the border. Several delegations were given a sort of basic training for the border one night at the defense ministry, which had formerly been Somoza's military compound. We were to leave early the next morning. For members of the American delegations, who had been living in close quarters in Managua for the last week, anticipation of the border trip brought the kind of excitement that comes before a class outing. Delegations were free to wander wherever they liked (outside military areas) and talk to anyone they wanted to; *but* they had also been subjected (or treated, depending on the occasion) to large doses of propaganda from the Sandinistas and the opposition. Now, at last, they were about to experience the North American threat at first hand.

"You don't photocopy a revolution," Roberto Sánchez said. "We're not Cuba, we're Nicaragua." Roberto Sánchez, a poet, journalist and former priest, delivered his theme enthusiastically. Six years earlier, in what now must have seemed another life to him, Roberto Sánchez had written the original investigative reports for *La Prensa* on the Managua plasmapheresis center. The blood plasma stories had helped bring about the assassination of his editor, Pedro Joaquín Chamorro, but also the downfall of his dictator, Anastasio Somoza. Now Roberto Sánchez was urging everyone to be calm at the border. "One of your senators who was here recently asked me if I could guarantee his safety at the border. 'No, Senator,' I told him, 'your presence will guarantee mine.' "

Beneath his rhetoric, Roberto Sánchez seemed quite eager to be liked. His face, in early middle age, had puffed a bit under his gray hair, and he had the florid complexion that comes to those who have not turned down every drink they have been offered. If he had been an actor, Roberto Sánchez would now be getting parts for the Latin roué who likes younger women but whom the heroine easily resists by converting him into her uncle. "We remain small, poor, weak, as always," he said, "but when we discovered the dignity in ourselves through our revolt against injustice and fight for justice, we gained a real moral force and overcame our traditional inferiority complex."

Roberto Sánchez was assisted in the briefing by a much younger man, Noel Corea, who was a kind of cultural ambassador-at-large for Nicaragua. He had studied engineering at San Francisco State and marched in the San Francisco victory parade when the Sandinistas won. Afterward, he became the Nicaraguan consul in New York until the Reagan Administration closed down all consular offices in reprisal for Nicaragua's expulsion of three U.S. embassy employees in Managua who were accused of a CIA plot to assassinate several Sandinista officials. Noel Corea was small, quick, dark, a sharp contrast with Roberto Sánchez. The next day he was to accompany the group I had temporarily joined. "We will leave at five-thirty," he said, "because the roads are bad and I want to be out of the border region and heading back toward Managua well before dark. North of Estelí, we never know what we can count on."

"Will it be safe in the hills past Ocotal?" asked an American who knew where the recent fighting was and had been looking at a map.

"We'll call Washington tonight for you," Noel Corea said rapidly, but with a smile. "The Pentagon should be able to give us an answer."

"Seriously," a woman from California asked, "what do we do if we are ambushed?"

"We do not plan to take you anyplace where we feel in danger of ambush," Noel Corea said, "but if we are wrong—and sometimes we are—you will find out what it is like to be a Nicaraguan these days."

"As a military man," a minister from Milwaukee said to Roberto Sánchez, "you have to be aware that if our country decides to invade, you don't stand a chance. What can you do then?"

"Well, they can come, the Marines and the bombers," Roberto Sánchez said, "but they can never kill us all. They'll occupy us, but someday they'll also leave. They'll have to. And many of them will leave in body bags." There appeared to be no distinction, in either Roberto Sánchez or Noel Corea, between their rhetoric and their feelings. They were making a presentation they had made before, answering questions they had heard before, yet in a curious way they did not seem to be repeating themselves. If they were actors, their teacher was Stanislavsky.

A short, thickset woman from New York arose for a final question. As she began to speak she looked down at a piece of paper. "On behalf of my delegation . . ." she began.

"Por parte de esta delegación . . ." the simultaneous translator began for the benefit of the members of the defense ministry who did not understand English.

"Uh oh," said a man from Kansas City to his wife.

"Shhh, give her a chance," said his wife.

"I'd like to offer my humble apologies . . ."

"Quisiera disculparme humildemente . . ."

". . . for the crimes of my ignorant countrymen . . ."

"What did I tell you?" said the man from Kansas City.

". . . por los crimenes de mis compatriotas ignorantes . . ."

". . . and affirm that I respect, honor and share your anger at the brutish behavior . . ."

"We're under attack from the know-nothing left," said the woman from Kansas City.

". . . y a la vez me gustaría afirmar que respeto, honro y comparto su rabia al comportamiento bestial . . ."

". . . of the animal-trainer in the White House . . ."

"It's the counterinaugural," said the woman from Kansas City.

"Sometimes I'm ashamed to be a progressive," said her husband, "when I look at the company I keep."

". . . *del entrenador de animales en la casa blanca . . .*"

". . . who treats all of us like animals and has lost the respect of the civilized world."

". . . *quien trata a todo el mundo como unos animales y quien ha perdido el respeto del mundo civilizado.*"

"It's our responsibility in the U.S. for electing such a monster, since so many of our fellow citizens are illiterate politically, spiritually, and culturally . . ."

"*Es nuestra responsibilidad . . .*"

"Bring on the contras," said the man from Kansas City.

We would not be going to Ocotal, Noel Corea announced in the dawn on the small bus that was taking fourteen of us north. Neither the lady from New York nor the Kansas City couple were on our bus. The situation around Ocotal was uncertain, Noel Corea said; there had been *actividad* just outside the town last night. (In the context of the Sandinistas versus the *contrarrevolucionarios,* "activity" was not a sign of life but of death.) The contras were trying to take a town, almost any town, so they could announce to the world that they had a piece of Nicaraguan territory as their new, liberated capital. As a consequence of the activity, Noel Corea said, we would head for a different, quieter section of the border between Nicaragua and Honduras. We stopped at the foreign ministry to pick up two Cubans before heading north out of Managua.

No one spoke as the bus climbed into the hills. In the long stretches of empty countryside, the revolution faded into the stream of Nicaraguan history, whose direction was as concealed as its end. Four centuries upstream, the aboriginal Chief Nicarao had made the mistake of showing off his gold to the Spaniards who came north from Panama, a display that cost him his sovereignty and his future, allowing him to bequeath nothing but his

name to the territory. The Sandinistas had inherited the stream
from Chief Nicarao, whose gold attracted the Spaniards, whose
colonialism produced the Central Americans, whose dissension
produced the Nicaraguans, whose location and resources enticed
the North Americans, whose power produced its antidote, the
Sandinistas. Now who polluted the stream least, and where was
it heading?

The bus stopped momentarily in Ciudad Darío, birthplace of
the Nicaraguan national poet, Rubén Darío. Writers as different
as Federico García Lorca, Octavio Paz and Pablo Neruda have
given Darío credit for virtually lifting the Spanish language from
a medieval to a modern idiom. Though he was born in 1867, died
in 1916 and spent most of his working life in South America and
Paris, Darío is a saint in Nicaragua.

He shortened his life by drinking, and his love affairs were
often unhappy, but the fact that he was regarded as a prisoner of
both—love and alcohol—serves only to pump up the romance of
his image. Almost any Nicaraguan, from Daniel Ortega to a high
school student to a bus driver, is happy to talk all night about
Rubén Darío. They quote him on subjects as diverse as sex and
politics, arguing whether his lyricism, irony, anti-imperialism or
precociously psychedelic imagery was his strongest point.

> First, a look:
> then the burning touch
> of hands; and then
> the racing blood
> and the kiss that triumphs.

next a pause:

> She wept in my arms. She was dressed
> all in black.

and then the sensual bombardment:

> When the serpent whistled
> and the hawk sang songs,
> when the flowers groaned

and a planet sighed,
when the diamond sparkled
and the coral bled,
When Satan's eyes
were silver dollars,
that was when
she lost her virginity.

The tumble of nature reflects an aesthetic Darío formulated after his association with the French Symbolists: "Words should paint the color of a sound, the aroma of a star; they should capture the very soul of things." Coins in this denomination have been so cheapened it is easy to forget that in the nineteenth century rhetorical flourishes were far commoner than direct, simple perception. Darío could kiss off a line or a lover with equal dispatch:

Our love is forever and ever.
Our marriage—never.

With all his years in Europe, Darío never affected Frenchness, never forgot what nourished his poetry:

My pick is working deep in the soil of this unknown America, turning up gold and opals and precious stones, an altar, a broken statue. And the Muse divines the meaning of the hieroglyphics. The strange life of a vanished people emerges from the mists of time. . . .

The United States intrigued Darío. He admired the vitality and the zealous enterprise of nineteenth-century North Americans, and he loved Walt Whitman, regarding himself as the Whitman of Latin America. He was also scared of the United States. When he considered Theodore Roosevelt, Darío was hopeful and terrified at the same time. In a poem called "To Roosevelt," he wrote:

You are primitive and modern, simple and complex;
You are one part George Washington and one part
    Nimrod.

You are the United States,
future invader of our naive America
with its Indian blood, an America
that still
   prays to Christ and speaks Spanish. . . .
You think that life is a fire,
that progress is an irruption,
that the future is wherever
your bullet strikes.
   No.
The United States is grand and powerful.
Whenever it trembles, a profound shudder
runs down the enormous backbone of the Andes. . . .
   . . . a wealthy country,
joining the cult of Mammon to the cult of Hercules;
while Liberty, lighting the path
to easy conquest, raises her torch in New York.
   . . . Be careful.
Long live Spanish America!
A thousand cubs of the Spanish lion are roaming free.
Roosevelt, you must become, by God's own will,
the deadly Rifleman and the dreadful Hunter
before you can clutch us in your iron claws.

One cannot leave Rubén Darío angry and afraid, with his prophecies regarding the future invader. Too many other concerns, too much passion, animated Darío to justify running away from him on a note of what in contemporary terms becomes social protest. Though his chief translator, Lysander Kemp, is modest about rendering the beauties of Darío's rhythm and meter into English, the fierceness of Darío and his clarity of voice are preserved in Kemp's own translation.

Noon is burning the whole island.
The reef is in flames,
the blue sky pours down fire.
   . . . Far off,
rough with antiquity, solemn with myth,
stands the stone tribe of old volcanos
which, like all else, await their instant of infinity.

Darío's own instant of infinity was upon him in this late poem. His wandering life in Buenos Aires, Paris, Mallorca and elsewhere was almost over. At the onset of the First World War, Darío came home to Nicaragua to die.

> The sunset hour is nearing,
> and there is a touch of coolness now
> on this sun-stricken tropic-coast.
> There is a breath of ocean air
> and the west pretends to be a forest
> lit with purple flame.
>
> The crabs are marking the sand
> with the illegible scrawl of their claws,
> and seashells, color of roses, of gold
> reflections, and little snails, and bits
> of starfish, are a singing carpet
> when you walk these harmonious shores.
> And when Venus shines,
> imperial love of the godlike evening,
> you can hear in the waves the sound
> of a lyre or the song of a siren.
> And a star like that of Venus glows in my soul.

The mottled shells weave into the singing carpet of Darío's poems. Like the shells, he is almost empty, but also like them, he can still be heard by anyone who listens. The shells reveal the world of Rubén Darío and hide it, speak that world and fall silent.

"I can imagine what my parents would say if they knew I was on this bus heading for a combat zone," a cheerful passenger named Nancy Cooke said as we got closer to the region where contras had penetrated. It was a war—similar to Vietnam in this respect —where front lines did not exist. Most of the time government soldiers would have border towns themselves fairly secure. But once the contras had crossed the border in deserted areas, they ranged southward in forces of three to four hundred that could remain almost invisible in the sparsely populated northern mountains, the same mountains where Sandino had successfully hidden from the United States Marines. The contras maintained close radio contact with their headquarters in Honduras, which sent out American planes to airdrop supplies to them. Though they burned crops when they came to a farm, tortured doctors and teachers (among others) when they came to a village, the contras frequently had large supplies of money and could temporarily cause a small economic boom in a sympathetic village. They remained without the broad popular base the Sandinistas had had when they were insurgents.

"After I told them I was coming down," Nancy Cooke continued, "my parents thought I'd probably be shot right in Managua and they weren't sure which side would be shooting me. The fact is, I've never felt safer in my life than in Managua. Up here I don't know."

Noel Corea sat at the front of the bus next to a beautiful Nicaraguan woman with long dark hair. Both wore army uniforms. Near the back of the bus the two Cubans sat alone, in civilian clothes. We were told they were from the Havana literary magazine *La Bohemia,* that they understood no English and preferred to keep to themselves. They answered briefly and politely when spoken to in Spanish but did not initiate any conversation.

"If you go about two hundred kilometers that way," Noel Corea said, pointing northeast as we passed through a small town called Sebaco, "you will come to Siuna, a Nicaraguan treasure in more ways than one, with a great history." The bus driver, who had made virtually no sound since we left Managua, suddenly asserted himself. "If you know Siuna," he said, "you can know something about the heart of Nicaragua." He was quiet again. For the United States, Siuna had been a key hallucination in the stories we told ourselves about Nicaragua. It was a town that had once been the subject of a newsreel.

On their most accessible level, American newsreels of Nicaragua had presented history as press release. The Nicaragua that Americans saw over the years was first an unruly mess, then a pacified colony under the calming influence of U.S. troops, later an obedient client state with the Somozas holding court. In its unblinking way, the camera did not lie about the Somozas, ultimately charting the family's greed, artifice and downfall. But that view has the advantage of retrospective judgment and irony. What had been clear in the film footage I had watched before going to Nicaragua was that the Somozas in their prime were essentially identified with order and the imprimatur of Washington. Until the family's final defeat was inevitable, almost no Nicaraguans were accorded film crews other than the Somozas themselves, and almost no places in Nicaragua were shown outside Managua. On the rare occasions when there was an exception to the exclusion of everything but the dictator and his capital, the result was likely to resemble the story of Siuna, the town Noel Corea had pointed toward from the bus. Siuna stands alone, crowning American newsreel coverage of Nicaragua.

Gold mines at Siuna have been in operation for over a century. Sandino once worked in the machine shop at the mines and is said to have made some of the first weapons there that he used in his revolt. Adolfo Díaz was a manager for the main Siuna mining company, which was owned by Americans. When Díaz was made president of Nicaragua in the 1920s by Henry Stimson, he was therefore working for the United States in more than one way. The information about Sandino and Díaz was not what got into the newsreel coverage. When a Paramount Pictures team came to Siuna in 1948, its purpose was to observe American technology at work.

Entitled *A Town Survives—By Jet Plane*, the newsreel opens with an aerial shot of the tops of trees, followed by scenes of a country village. The narrator barks every phrase with an exclamatory Wow! just beneath his words. "Deep in the heart of Nicaragua's dense mountainous interior! the gold mining town of Siuna—a town that keeps going, amazingly enough! thanks to jet-equipped planes! Hemmed in by mountains, Siuna is the site of the largest gold mine in Latin America! and is entirely dependent on airplanes! for its existence! Every piece of machinery here! was brought in by air transport!" We now see excavating and rolling equipment. Miners' shacks are nearby. "Today more and more jet-assisted planes are being used in Nicaragua!"—we see peasants wearing machetes and loading sacks aboard a cargo plane, guarded as they work by an armed man on horseback—"for safer takeoffs from hazardous jungle-rimmed airstrips!"

Three men on mules, joined by a little boy on a donkey, peer curiously into the camera; the newsreel cuts to a shot of an airplane taxiing on a runway, then back to the tableau of the four Nicaraguans. The men wear wide *sombreros*; the boy, who has delicate features, wears a white shirt, white pants and white shoes. One of the men removes his *sombrero* and scratches his head while another calms his mule, which the movie camera or the plane has made nervous. The boy pokes his donkey in one of its ears and it gives a little start, which makes the boy smile. He has embarrassed himself and tilts his head down. "Ranch hands look on as the DC-3s take off for Siuna! The chief value of jets here is a positive safety factor in case of motor failure! even with heavy loads!" Music, especially violins and French horns and kettledrums, swells here as we fly over the mountains and finally spot a small settlement below.

"Arrival at Siuna! and the first and largest airborne line in the world! carries on!" The plane taxis to a stop on a smaller airstrip than it took off from. Tractors and heavier machinery are wheeled off the plane by workers. One of them smiles and seems unhindered by the fact that he has only a left arm. A man in a pith helmet pushes a mechanical digger down a ramp as if it were a slow mule, and we see mountains in the background. "In one of the strangest! phenomena of the air age! a community of six thousand persons owes its existence to the beat of engines! and the roar of jet propulsion!" The plane takes off, music crescendos. The camera has not had enough interest in the Nicaraguans it has pictured for them to have acquired individuality, but they become, in the accumulation of shots, a conglomerate vision of underdevelopment. They ride mules, their saviors ride airplanes. We are left with a jet's contrail streaming into the lagoon of our consciousness as the plane heads back toward a world we know.

Three decades after the newsreel was made, with Somoza III still in power, there was running water at Siuna one hour a day. It was piped up from the mines, filled with chemicals. Penny

Lernoux, an American journalist specializing in Latin America, saw water in Siuna hot enough to boil an egg. Children got a variety of diseases from it, adults got diarrhea. Down in the shaft where the miners worked, temperatures exceeded 110°F., and no safety precautions were in effect. Silicosis was common. The company took x-rays of its employees every six months but did not show them the results. "We don't know how sick we are," a shriveled miner told Penny Lernoux. The miners were paid fifteen cents an hour in 1978. They referred to the mine as *el infierno*.

Noel Corea told all of us in the bus that we were approaching Estelí and would stop for a briefing and clearance to go farther. He repeated the announcement in Spanish for the two Cubans, who spoke no English. During the insurrection, Estelí had been a stronghold at different times for both the FSLN and the National Guard. As the bus slowed down at the military headquarters, the beautiful Sandinista next to Noel Corea strapped on her pistol belt and applied blush-on to her cheeks.

It was very hot, and the children who came to the bus were sucking soft drinks out of plastic bags that had crushed ice in them. Barefoot children with skinny dogs surrounded a woman from California who was taller and blonder than most of the Americans on the bus. They asked to look through her sunglasses, which she was happy to let them do. A little girl offered her one of the soft drinks in a plastic bag, which she took. The woman had only a few raisins to offer in return, but when these were gone she thought of taking the little girl's picture. The little girl, who was perhaps six, did not seem to know what a camera was for, but she liked the woman and was happy to stand in front of her lean-to to be photographed. The woman from California snapped a Polaroid. As the outline, the ghost, the white shadow, and finally her own image materialized before the little girl, she wept. After the California woman took one more picture for herself, the little girl ran off to her friends holding her own miniature in her hand.

The neighborhood next to the army base was a collection of

shacks where people lived and sheds where they worked. A man came out of his home and said he had learned *un poco inglés* from a young American who had worked in Estelí. "You not *gringos*, you *amigos*," he said. "We don't want fight *yanquis*, just we want live and ron our leetle fag-trees."

We asked what kind of work he did. "Obre dere," he pointed across the dirt road. "I work in the desk fag-tree." He showed us inside the shed where he built chairs and desks, a factory by Estelí standards. During the Somoza era the wood for the factory had come from deep in northern Zelaya, where Somoza owned forests. Now it was from a smaller, but local, forest and was cheaper.

When he brought us inside the military camp, Noel Corea asked, in English, that we put away our cameras. He forgot to ask in Spanish, and the two Cubans continued photographing— sentries, a man doing push-ups, a machine-gun emplacement, two *milicianos* smoking cigarettes—until they were asked not to in their own language. In the company headquarters, a wood-slatted army room like army rooms everywhere except for the color picture of Sandino, a captain told us that Jalapa, the town northeast of Ocotal where we had originally been scheduled to go, had been attacked four days previously and three civilians had been killed. Jalapa was in what he called the parrot's beak section of the border with Honduras. If he was aware that the American invasion of Cambodia had also been in a section called the parrot's beak, the captain did not mention it. The contra plans, he said, called for taking either Ocotal or Jalapa. We would go instead to a border redoubt to the west, called El Espino, which had also been attacked but not for three months. He showed us a relief map of the area; contra camps were marked with blue circles. "We know they are there, but it is difficult for us to reach these camps in remote areas," he said. "They are protected by planes from Honduras imperialistically violating Nicaraguan airspace." A characteristic of military briefings, especially Sandinista military briefings, is that no fact is ever as happy alone as it is when accompanied by a message.

The captain introduced a senior revolutionary *comandante,*

Javier Carrión. We were surprised to find ourselves suddenly confronted with one of the heroes of the revolution. Carrión, whose rank was equivalent to brigadier general, looked young, fierce and tired. One of his eyes was red. If Richard Gere grew a small mustache and stayed up for three nights, he might resemble Comandante Carrión, who had been the guerrilla leader in charge of the Estelí region during the war against Somoza. Carrión tapped the map with his pointer. "The contras want to occupy a little territory north of here and name a government. Your government will then recognize it, and we will have a state of war between the United States and Nicaragua. Three times they have tried to take Jalapa. Now they are trying for Somoto, which we will have to evacuate. You will pass through Somoto today, but there is no activity there now."

A ripple of fright passed through the room, and of something else that, by comparison, made fright attractive. This was only modestly scary, after all. The contras would probably not be stupid enough to blow up a busload of *yanquis,* even *yanquis* they thought were being propagandized by the Sandinistas, when they needed *yanqui* help so much. But the other presence floating among us, among the Americans, was the prurient sense of consorting with the enemy. We were here looking at his maps and listening to his plans and putting dollars into his economy and about to allow ourselves to go into a marginal combat zone with only his protection against forces supported by our own government. We could say we were only trying to find out for ourselves, some of us as journalists, some as inquisitive travelers. But we could not deny that our very presence in what amounted to enemy headquarters was an offense against the policies of our leadership. When was obedience to the United States government a patriotic necessity, and when did patriotism reside in a hard look at the putative enemy? Comandante Carrión was not giving the answer.

He could only do what his own patriotism demanded. "We repulsed them here," the *comandante* continued, tapping the map with his pointer on a village called San Fernando, "but five hundred of them have turned up"—tapping to the east—"in this area around Murra. We believe there are now approximately two thousand contras here in the northern mountains.'' He squinted his red eye at the map, then turned back to us. ''The villages are far apart. A squad of fifteen well-supplied contras can cause a lot of trouble. They are organized into U.S. Army task forces and burn the coffee with flamethrowers before it can be picked. We arm the *campesinos* and they help defend their own land. The problem is, farmers can be overwhelmed by the contras, so we send the *milicianos* to the countryside. The *milicianos* help with the harvest while they become our first line of defense. The regular army backs them up when they need help and is involved in the big confrontations.''

The mention of coffee reminded one of the privates to bring everyone glasses of the homegrown product, which got stronger the farther one was from Managua. American Nabisco cookies were brought out with the coffee, but they were no match for it. A man from Albuquerque asked Carrión why the less-trained militia was used in the front lines instead of as backup. Didn't that turn them into cannon fodder?

''The regular army is always out looking for the contras,'' the *comandante* said. ''We are trying to catch them in large numbers before they break up into their task forces. In the last three weeks we have killed two hundred and fifty-three contras and lost seventy government troops. But that seventy in a country our size is like seven thousand for the United States. The regular army is also needed to protect our major towns, like Estelí, and the military bases themselves. The *milicianos* are used in the villages and on the farms.''

''What about Cubans?'' asked a lady from New Jersey. Everyone but Comandante Carrión looked at the two Cubans who were traveling with us. Neither raised an eyebrow until the question was translated into Spanish. Then one of them tilted his head at the lady from New Jersey and shook his finger at her. At that point the Sandinistas had not acknowledged having any Cuban advisers in the country.

''I don't know any Cubans,'' Comandante Carrión said, and smiled, breaking enough ice to allow his audience to laugh briefly. "But I will say to you that we must do what we can to let our revolution survive. If we are attacked, we must fight back, and we have to take help from wherever it is offered as long as our independence is not compromised."

"You told us Somoto and other places are being evacuated," a man from California said. "That creates a free-fire zone. We did that in Vietnam. Doesn't that mean you're afraid the people in those towns are sympathetic to the contras?"

"I would say people in those towns are terrified. Some of them have relatives in the contras and also in the FSLN army. What can they do when the contras are around? If they defy them, they may be tortured and killed. They may also be kidnapped or sometimes persuaded to go into the contra army. Whether they like it or not, the contras will get food from them. What we want to do is cut off the contras' sources of supply and places to hide. Most of the supplying is done from Honduras, by both air and land. We have to cut that, too. Evacuating certain areas is the only way to make sure the contras can't protect themselves behind other Nicaraguans."

"You're still talking about free-fire zones, then," the Californian persisted quietly. "That's what we did in Vietnam."

Comandante Carrión persisted even more quietly. "In Vietnam you were the invaders. The war was supported from Washington. This war is also supported from Washington. The contras are there because you want them to be. Without Washington, we have dissidents, we have an opposition, we have some people who cannot live with the revolution and go into exile. But we have no contras and no war. This war is made from abroad, not from Nicaragua."

Heading north, we crossed a river and wound into a series of high hills called the Mesetas de Estelí. The FSLN woman had armed herself with a rifle before leaving the military headquarters. Noel Corea said he did not need one for the area around El Espino. "The contras are near, but they are not there," the former Nicaraguan consul in New York said, as if his enemies might be in Queens, but surely not Brooklyn. "A pistol will do."

Tobacco farms were spread through the Mesetas de Estelí. The tobacco plants were covered with cheesecloth to shield them from the sun. We passed a large hemp plantation privately owned by a prosperous rancher. In a gorge, women were washing white clothes and drying them on gray rocks. At Condega, a town built at the foot of a small hill, a cemetery climbed up the hill from the houses and shops. The townspeople have left one of Somoza's DC-3 planes permanently stuck into the top of the hill where it crashed when they shot it down. Miraculously, in the local story on its way to becoming folk tale, the pilot of the plane was not killed. Condegans were so grateful to him for not crashing into their town itself that instead of capturing him they sent him home. They kept his plane perching above them, an angel of mercy in the middle of their cemetery.

Less than ten miles from the border, outside Somoto, the town being evacuated to deny sanctuary to the rebels, we passed a man coming south carrying what appeared to be his principal possessions: a shopping bag full of clothes, a guitar, and an AK-47. "This *campesino* is going in the direction of secure areas, so he is probably pro-FSLN," Noel Corea said, "but his brother-in-law, who knows? The people here are in danger, especially at night, and if his brother-in-law has been hurt by inflation or he has a cousin who was in the National Guard or he is told by his priest the Sandinistas are atheists . . . ."

Somoto was mostly abandoned. With wooden railings for tying up horses in front of the boarded-up stores, an empty town square, puffs of wind sending tumbleweed across the deserted streets, Somoto looked like a Nevada boom town vacated a century ago when the silver lode gave out. From here to the border we were in a no-man's land. By the side of the road were several more farmers carrying rifles. They had come to pick a few ears of corn or try to find stray livestock, Noel Corea said, and would be south of Somoto before twilight.

Three hundred yards from the customs office at El Espino the bus stopped. The border here was hilly, with deserted farms on the Nicaraguan side. The patrols were *milicianos*. This meant contra attacks were not expected. "They will come again at

Christmas," Noel Corea said. He led us off the highway to a small hill.

A sergeant and three privates came to lead us up the hill. Motor traffic was approaching the customs houses on both sides of the border. A dozen small trucks and old cars were waiting to be waved through to Nicaragua on the Honduran side, and about half as many were going north from Nicaragua. Both sides of the border, though well patrolled, seemed entirely peaceful, almost somnolent in the afternoon sun, except for one detail. The Nicaraguan side had been destroyed. Its customs office was a new shack about a hundred yards back from the actual border. The few structures at the border itself were leveled. Like a mule blown over by a cyclone, the old customs office was knocked onto its side, still perfectly intact except for no longer being on its feet. A direct hit on a house had collapsed the roof and scattered the furniture. Chairs were splintered and sent into the backyard; two broken beds had wound up in the front. Crockery lay in shards as if waiting for someone from a museum to come and reconstruct its society's family customs from the jigsaw images in its glaze. An iron stove stood upright, ready to be used again. A doll was in a ditch, its arms and one leg blown off. The house next door looked all right except its roof was missing.

One of the *miliciano* privates was a freckled, dark-haired girl looking very fresh and serious in her new fatigues and bandanna. She reminded me of the pictures of young Israelis working on kibbutzes in the Golan Heights. The enemy was not there but could be there anytime. "We did not expect them in El Espino," she said, "because we are on the main road between Nicaragua and Honduras." El Espino is on the Pan American Highway, which runs from Alaska to Tierra del Fuego at the foot of Chile and is the principal route throughout Central America. "No one here was armed except the six *milicianos* at the border post. Two were killed right away. Everyone in this family"—she pointed to the collapsed house with the upright stove—"was killed. The four border guards who were still alive ran back to a trench three hundred meters down the road. The contras were coming through on the way to Somoto, to take it by surprise as they had surprised the guards at El Espino. But the four *milicianos* in the trench stopped the contras for eight hours until at midnight help came from the regular army. In this way Somoto was saved."

"But after that, since we could not spare enough troops for a garrison there," Noel Corea said, "we knew we had to evacuate Somoto."

"They had bazookas and mortars and one tank"—the militia girl was back into her story—"and the tank was the hard one to stop. One of the *milicianos* captured a bazooka and put a hole in the tank with it, so the tank had to turn around and go back. We lost seven Nicaraguans, two offices, two houses, two businesses, and a café. Some chickens, I don't know how many, and three pigs. When the main force came, the contras ran at once. Of course, we could not chase them into Honduras, but Somoto was still ours and the border was safe again." The war against the counterrevolutionaries was producing its own legends as the war against Somoza had.

The Honduran side was undestroyed, with several cafés and houses, a truck depot and a gas station. The militia sergeant and his three privates discussed among themselves whether there were too many of us and whether our clothes were too brightly colored. They decided to split us into two groups. How much of this was a show, how much genuine wariness? "There will not be any firing," Noel Corea said. "These are precautions." He checked himself. "But if there is any firing, go down to the ground slowly, not fast. Don't run. Stay still. Don't be scared. This is safer than a lot of places in New York City. Wait a while, you get used to it, just like in New York." The sergeant and the militia girl led our group up the hill, the militia girl pointing below to the abandoned school she had gone to in the abandoned settlement of El Espino.

A zigzag trench was cut along the path up the hill. The sharp angles could absorb the concussion of a grenade fired into the trench, preventing it from killing more than one or two people; they would also prevent anyone with a machine gun from mowing down a whole row of soldiers, since there was no straight line to shoot along. The sergeant, who wore a camouflage uniform and was more in charge with each step we took up the hill, said that the contras were not the only troops who came across the border. Occasionally they were joined by Hondurans. "We captured a Honduran soldier on a night patrol last week," he said. "We didn't want a big incident, so we just returned him." He sounded like a fisherman who had thrown a trout back into the stream because it was not regulation size.

At the top of the hill, we could look down on the border crossing and directly over to a hill in Honduras that could have been a mirror image of the one we stood on. Perhaps their hill was slightly higher, with a few more soldiers patrolling it. Honduras and Nicaragua, two small countries to begin with, were reduced further now to the two sides of a theater, the audience in each peering down at the stage that was the border crossing, each also part of the show. A half-dozen Nicaraguan *milicianos* were posted around us on the hilltop as lookouts. The sergeant who had led us up the hill, very much in command now, redeployed them slightly. For our benefit? Or was he a manager moving his outfielders around when he sees a pull hitter coming to the plate? One of the *milicianos* held an American antitank weapon on his shoulder. "Captured from the contras," he said. *"Muchas gracias."*

The sergeant in charge of the top of the hill asked if he could borrow my binoculars. Well, sure, I guess so. He pointed them at Honduras. *Mira!* look at that *cabrón* with the bazooka! He passed the binoculars to the freckled *miliciana,* who found a goat she liked in Honduras. She used the binoculars' zoom lens to find a machine gun camouflaged in shrubbery. She said she had not known it was there, but the sergeant said he knew. He borrowed the binoculars again anyway. The other soldiers all took their turns. First glimpse of the opposing team. *Ay, yi, yi,* they must be sweating in those uniforms. So much *equipo!* Are those M-16s or Ahkas? That one holds his rifle like my little brother.

Consorting with the enemy had not been enough; this was helping them look at *their* enemy, which was *my* side in this war. Instead of vertigo, this hill could give you the terminal schizes.

Hey, let me have those things back, you've looked long enough. Why don't you get your own goddam binoculars? Well, you're poor, you're always poor. But my guys frown on this, you know. Hey, buddy, they say, that's aid and comfort *and* Japanese binoculars. Zing, we could yank your passport. Zing, how'd you like an IRS audit, or . . .

Zing, a single shot echoed from behind a hill smaller than the one we had been watching on the Honduran side. We all began the slow-motion dip to our knees when Noel Corea stopped us. "Target practice," he said. *"El pájaro grande,"* the sergeant said, pointing to a vulture that circled the small hill where the shot came from. "The contras are behind the hill and they are restless. They have no farm to go home to like I do, no jobs to go back to when they stop fighting. They have only the money the CIA gives them to betray their country. They get bored. They look up and see the miserable bird and no matter how ugly it is it has more freedom than they do. So someone takes a shot at it." The vulture still circled.

A quarter mile away on their ridge, the Hondurans looked across at us. One of them had a bazooka delicately balanced on his shoulder, perhaps the same type exactly, and from the same factory, as the one shouldered by the *miliciano* on the Nicaraguan side. One of the Cubans with us had a telephoto lens and took a picture of the Hondurans. The sergeant said the contras were using AK-47s, like the FSLN, only the contras had the Chinese version. The United States had captured them in Vietnam and at last had found a use for them. The Cuban with the camera said that some of the contras' AK-47s were now Russian because the Cubans had had them on Grenada. When the United States took over Grenada, the Cubans left their weapons behind, and, according to the Cuban, some of these were now being distributed to the contras. The Russian and Chinese AK-47s used the same size ammunition.

The militia girl looked at the hill the shot had come from and said to the sergeant, *"Peligroso"*—dangerous. The vulture swung over to our side of the border. When we started back down the hill we could see that part of the road below was still buckled and torn where the mortars had fallen during the attack on El Espino. "The Hondurans don't need those guards," the sergeant said. "We are not crazy. If we attacked their border post, even chasing the contras who attack us, the whole United States Army would be here in an hour. I will go back to my farm soon, God willing, but we will not lose El Espino to the contras."

The sergeant packed us on our bus, then lit a Marlboro one of us had given him. The bus was quiet as we left El Espino. The meaning of the border might not be clear, but its impact was. The border was unique. I was reminded of those individuals whose life and art reflect one another so faithfully they cannot always be separated. Like Janis Joplin and Edith Piaf, singing as well as living tragically, the scene at the border was performed and it was also real.

As though it were going downhill, which was true only part of the time, the bus bounced south much faster than it had come north. "The only way to describe the border to someone who wasn't there is so it comes out scary," said Nancy Cooke, whose parents had not wanted her to go even to Managua. She was the kind of person who remains cheerful through damage, whether to herself or others. Since she walked with a pronounced limp, Nancy Cooke had stayed with the group that did not climb the hill but went along the road. This meant her view of the border zone had not been as sweeping as the panorama from above but that she had been able to inspect the mortared homes more closely. "Yet it somehow isn't scary," she said. "I mean, you see a ruined house and you know someone lived there who is now dead. You're not scared, and you don't get mad right away, at least I didn't. You get curious—how do people get so they do this to each other? You hear a shot and even then you don't dive down or get scared out of your mind. Again, you're curious—how can someone want to do that to someone else, on any side, for any cause? Then you try to remember the forces of history, all the Somozas all over the world, right and left, the people who know only power and how to keep it, and it slowly dawns on you, yes, somebody with a loving mother and a crazy brother-in-law just might be driven wild enough to do that to somebody else who has an adoring little sister, an uncle who drinks too much and a crazy brother-in-law of his own. And by the time you get that far"—Nancy Cooke laughed at herself—"anybody who *did* want to shoot you could have spent half an hour lining you up in his sights. Maybe I'll get mad later at what we saw, and frightened for having been there at all, but my first response is just wonderment. How can this go on, how can we be part of it —part of it? I mean, how can we *cause* so much of it?"

The tension of the border gave way to jokes, singing and political discussion on the bus back to Managua. It was generally agreed that in the situation they face, no one could be surprised that the Nicaraguans had passed a fairly strict draft law. The law would drive some more of the middle class away, but it would standardize service for everyone else and put the country on the war footing that realism dictated. One of the Cubans shared a flask. An American had a canteen with *Flor de Caña* in it, and he shared that. Noel Corea was still serious. "If someone has religious beliefs that make him opposed to fighting in any circumstances, or if pacifism is a matter of principle with him, we won't send him to fight," he said. "But we will still draft him into military service and put him to work in a support capacity behind the lines."

The need for getting to the border and then out of the border region prevented us from stopping for lunch until five o'clock. It was a lunch of leathery steak and flagons of rum slightly diluted with Coca-Cola. Most of the Americans tried to drink only a little of the rum, but the waiters in the country restaurant felt they were not doing their job unless they kept filling every glass in sight. After the meal, the bus had not gone far when two of the riders, a man from Denver and a woman from Wisconsin, who had not previously known each other, remembered they had not used the bathroom at the restaurant. The bus stopped and both leaped off into the bushes, full of rum and relief that the border was behind them. It was dark, so they stayed near the bus. While the man was apparently fumbling with his fly, he said to the woman, "Hey there, how'd you like to come over and help me get this thing out?" "I'd love to," she said, "but I forgot to bring along a pair of tweezers." Most of the people on the bus chuckled a little, but the two Cubans almost fell off their seats. So they knew English. With all their elaborate pretense of understanding only Spanish, who were they spying on—us? Checking out Nicaraguan border posts? Were they really with *La Bohemia,* or were they with Cuban intelligence? For that matter, were they Cuban? Were they possibly Hispanic Americans sent to spy on other Americans in Nicaragua? They themselves, obviously, were not saying. Noel Corea shrugged—"That's Nicaragua Libre, my friends"—and the bus rolled on.

Everyone was glad to have been to the border, no one was sorry to get back to Managua. Stage-managed or authentic, the day left Nancy Cooke glowing. She was originally from Red Bank, New Jersey, and had gone to live in San Francisco, where she worked for an agency that promoted understanding between the United States and Central America. It was not the border alone that animated her now; she had the preparation of her job. The border served her, she said, as a kind of catalyst for the expression of all she had been thinking about for months. "Oh, what a time to be in Nicaragua," she said. "The world watches this experiment and can't believe the unlikeliness of the location, this wretched place that earthquakes and tyrants have barely suffered to exist.

"If they make it here, everyone else will want the same independence. It will be a beacon for Latin America. If they don't, if the revolution falls of its own dead weight or with a push from the *norteamericanos,* no one will dare try again until far into the next century. The light will be out. They know it in Washington, they know it in Managua. Just knowing it makes you giddy."

The bus dropped me off at the Intercontinental, which had become a Mayan Christmas tree. Long strings of colored lights climbed up its sloping sides. A white star was at the top, above Howard Hughes' old asylum. "Jalapa!" Noel Corea slapped out the word. "Ocotal and Jalapa are where we are being tested now, not El Espino. I hope it was fun, though. Good night."

XVII BROTHERS

REVOLUTION IN LATIN AMERICA has been described as a disagreement among the rich over how to treat the poor. Some of the rebel leaders in El Salvador, for instance, went to the same exclusive schools as the officials of the government they want to throw out. Fidel Castro was a lawyer from a landowning Cuban family before he was a revolutionary. Among the Sandinistas, with a few prominent exceptions such as the minister of agriculture, Jaime Wheelock, this phenomenon has been much less in evidence. Daniel Ortega and Tomás Borge, the most powerful revolutionaries in Nicaragua, both came from lower-middle-class families that had no connection with the old elite.

In the chronicles of Nicaragua, however, the names of a few families reappear like those of actors who play numerous parts during their long careers. None of these families has been more enduring than the illustrious Chamorros. Originally from a noble Spanish family in Seville, the Chamorros came to the New World in the eighteenth century. Settling in the old agricultural capital of Granada, they became members of the landed Nicaraguan aristocracy that established the Conservative Party. In the small telephone directory for Granada, running only twelve pages, are

206

to be found thirty-six listings under the name Chamorro, including two for townspeople—presumably the offspring of marriage between cousins—named Chamorro Chamorro. Throughout their long history the Chamorros have never been allies of the Somozas, whose own roots were in the Liberal Party of industrialists centered in León.

In 1849 the first Chamorro in power hanged the first recorded Somoza, who had tried to take the former's mistress as well as his presidency. The Somozas stayed down for several more generations, and the Chamorros stayed up. In 1916 a Chamorro who was the Nicaraguan foreign minister negotiated what became known as the Bryan-Chamorro Treaty with the American secretary of state William Jennings Bryan. The treaty gave the United States exclusive rights to construct any future canal across Nicaragua. Since the Panama Canal was already in operation, this part of the treaty was simply for the purpose of heading off any competition from the British or Europeans. The treaty in effect turned Nicaragua into a protectorate of the United States, helping to justify the arrival of Marines whenever internal stability—frequently defined as American commercial interests—was threatened. The later Chamorros were less friendly to the United States, particularly after the ascendancy of the Somozas, whom the Chamorros periodically tried to unseat by both political and military means.

One branch of the Chamorros went into publishing and bought what became the leading opposition paper in Nicaragua, *La Prensa*. After the murder of Pedro Joaquín Chamorro, *La Prensa*'s editor, coalesced the opposition to the last Somoza in 1978, the family was briefly courted by the Sandinistas. Violeta de Chamorro, the widow of Pedro Joaquín, was a member of the first FSLN junta after the revolution. She resigned in protest against the government's leftward direction, but she remained in Nicaragua. In the early 1980s, all three newspapers in Managua —two pro-Sandinista, one anti-Sandinista—were edited by Chamorros.

The split in the Nicaraguan upper class was epitomized in two sons of Pedro Joaquín and Violeta de Chamorro. Pedro Joaquín,

Jr., edited *La Prensa,* which opposed the Sandinistas as it had once opposed the Somozas, and Carlos Fernando edited *Barricada,* which was the FSLN's own official party newspaper. Though the Chamorro brothers were both combative young men, they were utterly different in every other way.

In his *La Prensa* office, where clutter had accumulated until it had become archaeological, Pedro Joaquín Chamorro fought his daily battle with Sandinista censorship. At thirty-two, he was every visitor's favorite oppositionist. He had a good command of English and was suavely handsome, with eyes that remained smiling when the rest of him scowled. Buoyant in his agitation and a little scattered in his anti-Sandinista jibes, which gave him an appealing air of vulnerability, Pedro Joaquín was a spirited critic whose complaints were numerous. He was not trained as a journalist but loved being an editor; before his father's murder he had been in the advertising department. He had enjoyed selling and persuading, and he did not try to disguise his relish in attacking the regime. "How can they instruct me to call Pastora a contra or Robelo a contra?" he asked rhetorically. "They fought for what we all fought for—freedom. I'll tell you who the contras are—the Sandinistas! They're fighting against the revolution we all fought to bring about. They're the real contras."

After several years of trying to puzzle out the Sandinistas and coexist with adversity, Pedro Joaquín found his frustration growing. "I don't know what I'm going to do if this keeps up," he said, rushing on in a torrent. "It's not only the paper and the censorship, it's the schools. My kids are in French school—most of the *comandantes* have their children there, too. It's supposed to be private, but the government decides even what time to give the kids recess. *Recess!* And history—history starts with Sandino and ends with Carlos Fonseca. A private school!" Then he backed up again and made a little half-turn. "Frankly, it hasn't been so bad lately; the censorship has been less the last couple of months. But again, they can come down on me anytime. I resist as I must."

He was jaunty. To "resist as I must" was a kind of nutrient for Pedro Joaquín Chamorro, having the secondary effect of a stimulant for his rhetorical flourishes. Plenty of people of his class in Managua agreed with him, at least in part, about the Sandinistas, but Pedro Joaquín behaved as if he represented the only opposition of consequence. In a way—*La Prensa* being the principal adversary voice—he was right. Although measurably less focused, he recalled a peculiar insouciance Churchill displayed in the long moment after the fall of France and before the United States entered World War II; he rather liked standing alone, and with all the desperation of his position he took a perverse enjoyment in the long odds. Pedro Joaquín was vain enough to show a distinct fondness for his own voice, if not quite programmatic enough to want a political constituency for himself. I felt he would not have minded having his own talk show.

At the Escuela Primaria Franco Nicaragüense, attended by Pedro Joaquín's children, the director of curriculum confirmed that the education ministry had suggested a time for recess so that the children could join a new city-wide sports program. The teachers had decided in a faculty meeting to let those children who wished to participate in the Managua sports program have their recess at the new time; the schedule stayed as it had been for the rest of the school. Only one *comandante*—Agricultural Minister Wheelock—had a child at the school, though several lower officials of the government did. As for the teaching of history, a class tracing the revolution had been instituted since 1979, but it was not mandatory and the rest of the ancient, medieval and modern history courses remained as they were.

Exaggeration, while it emphasized a showboating side of Pedro Joaquín, the anti-Sandinista as stand-up entertainer, did not invalidate his criticisms of the government. "The point is, the educational system is state-controlled," he said. "More than that, it is party-controlled, since there is no distinction between the party and the state. The army belongs to the party, too. The Sandinistas make sure all roads to power are narrow, and they stand at the checkpoints. Elections here will not test their power, only confirm their legitimacy in their own eyes. What validity can an election have when the press is censored and the Sandinista Defense Committees run voter registration? Of course we need a revolutionary party, but the Nicaraguan people were never told the FSLN would be the vanguard *forever*. Nicaragua is like a car going along a road the FSLN maintains. They sell the gas and oil, control the spark plugs, the cylinders and the steering wheel. You wouldn't have too much trouble fixing the race at Indianapolis if you could do that with all the cars there, right?''

Behind the metaphors he cheerfully dispensed, Pedro Joaquín was making charges that could, to a degree, be checked. Teachers I spoke to confirmed that the educational apparatus in Nicaragua has been reorganized to reflect the revolution, especially in history and economics courses. Political science has a decided anti-imperialist bias. Those teachers who have studied in the United States feel that our political science, on the other hand, has a decided imperialist bias along with a belittling of Latin America. The significance of the literacy campaign has been to make literacy—and literature—accessible to most of the population. Like anywhere else, the danger of literacy in Nicaragua is to increase the ability of propagandists to communicate, just as its glory is to increase the availability of ideas and the pleasure individuals derive from a broader acquaintance with culture. It is, Plato contended, the chance you take. Which way Nicaragua would go could be debated but not yet determined.

Similarly, block associations known as CDSs—Sandinista Defense Committees—keep the streets safe, reduce crime, issue good-conduct certificates to those who want passports, scholarships or government jobs. "Good conduct," of course, can be a matter of political obedience. CDSs do not run voter registration, as Pedro Joaquín charged, but they do help potential voters register. The CDSs perform helpfully in distributing coupons for scarce commodities and somewhat more pointedly as morale builders for the revolution. Their ideological cheerleading is desultory and varies depending on the neighborhood. But the CDSs are also organized for *vigilancia*. CDS leaders justify spying on their neighbors by alleging that the counterrevolution has tentacles everywhere. If that is true, so has the revolution. The fact that this spying is also desultory only makes it a greater source of anxiety. They may not be looking, they probably won't notice, surely they can't hear . . . or else they may. The argument goes that if someone has nothing to hide he has nothing to fear. That was also the argument of those who proposed loyalty oaths in the United States during the 1950s. It has never been proved that the way to build a free society is to institutionalize the devices of control.

The FSLN and the Nicaraguan government are identified with one another, as Pedro Joaquín Chamorro charged, far more than the party in power permeates the entire state in what we like to call the Western democracies. By this criterion of pluralism, however, Mexico does not qualify as a Western democracy. Since 1929, Mexico has been governed by what the writer Mario Vargas Llosa calls "the discreet dictatorship" of the Institutional Revolutionary Party. Though other parties in Mexico exist, they have had no chance to win an election or form a government. But the Institutional Revolutionary Party has been able to absorb and display a wide diversity in both domestic and foreign affairs. The left-right spectrum within the party is usually broader than that between liberal Democrats and conservative Republicans in the United States. The question in Nicaragua is what direction the Sandinistas will take when they are no longer in the continual state of emergency the counterrevolutionaries have forced on them. What will they do if peace breaks out? Will they consolidate like Castro or will they diversify like the Mexicans?

When he showed me the mechanics of censorship, Pedro Joaquín was ready with examples. Here was the report of a local police car that killed a pedestrian and injured two more while driving around at night without its lights on. Here was a picture of a Soviet jeep that had hit a traffic sign in Managua and gone into a ditch. Here were stories on the boxer Alexis Argüello, Poland, Afghanistan, the Pope, deployment of Soviet SS-20 missiles in Europe, former President López Portillo of Mexico, a plane hijacked to Cuba, Soviet submarines sighted off Scandinavia, a Nicaraguan supreme court decision to release from prison a former member of the National Guard, a Nicaraguan drug addict shot in the street by a policeman with an AK-47, and a local union dispute. All killed. "For this I fought Somoza," he said. "For this my father died."

Since *La Prensa* is an afternoon paper, Pedro Joaquín would send the government censor a photocopy of the front page at eleven-thirty each morning. The interior pages would have been sent over the night before; they were usually returned by noon. By the time the censor's office had looked over the front-page stories and indicated changes, it was between two and two-thirty in the afternoon. *La Prensa* kept a backlog of approved filler stories that could be inserted to make up for paragraphs or whole reports that were censored. Pedro Joaquín said he was not allowed to leave blank spaces because that would indicate there had been censorship. At three o'clock the editors phoned the censor back to say which fillers they were using. Only then could the presses run. Pedro Joaquín said the paper generally used about 25 percent filler material but that it had run as high as 50 percent. A few times so much had been cut he had simply refused to publish the paper at all. On other occasions, he had objected so strongly to the censorship of specific stories he had been allowed to run them. "Pressure from the United States has cut two ways," he said. "The military pressure gives them an excuse to censor me, and the political pressure makes them want to keep me in business."

Pedro Joaquín claimed the Sandinistas were losing their popularity. "In the eyes of most people this government is not fulfilling its promises. They're losing their hold on the people's affections. If you did a poll on the three most popular Nicaraguans, you would find they were Alexis Argüello, Archbishop Obando and Edén Pastora." I did in fact conduct such a poll informally on the streets of Managua, and the results made me wonder who Pedro Joaquín was in touch with when he spoke of "most people." Daniel Ortega and Tomás Borge were the two names most frequently mentioned, followed by Archbishop (now Cardinal) Obando y Bravo, Sandino and Pedro Joaquín's own assassinated father. (The poet Rubén Darío was also mentioned; I did not always stipulate that I preferred to hear about the popularity of living Nicaraguans.) The one opposition politician named was Alfonso Robelo, the former junta member who had joined the counterrevolutionaries since leaving Nicaragua. Neither Edén Pastora nor Alexis Argüello was mentioned at all; when I asked about them, I was told that the former was erratic and the latter had been misled by the contras since he retired as a boxer. Pedro Joaquín accurately predicted the mention of Archbishop Obando, who had become a strong critic of the revolution.

Despite his anger at the Sandinistas, Pedro Joaquín remained close to his brother. He could not account for the diametrical opposition between them politically. "My brother is a Marxist-Leninist, pure and simple. We don't agree. The state defines itself in terms he is comfortable with and I am not. When we get together, we discuss everything. I am annoyed at him right now for allowing a former *somocista* opportunist who is now a minor Sandinista functionary to say something nasty about me in *Barricada*. But we'll talk about it. We have good relations. Between us we have no forbidden subjects."

In his combativeness, Pedro Joaquín seemed to combine attributes of a Nicaraguan happy warrior—like Al Smith in the United States, and later Hubert Humphrey—with an admirable journalistic tendency to make healthy mischief for those in power. He was so cheerful in adversity I imagined his brother, securely ensconced in the compatible environment of a government he agreed with, would be ebullient about the Sandinistas and their prospects.

Carlos Fernando Chamorro, however, was the opposite of this expectation, and of his brother. He was confident enough about the Sandinistas, but no one, having met Carlos Fernando, would conjure him even in a dream as ebullient. Where Pedro Joaquín was exuberant and diffuse, Carlos Fernando was stern and focused. Pedro Joaquín was clean-shaven, with an open, inviting countenance; Carlos Fernando's imploded features insisted on privacy, and his drooping mustache gave him almost a dour aspect. Though he was twenty-seven, five years younger than his brother, he was as self-possessed as a corporation that resolutely refuses to sell stock to the public. A Managuan who has known them all their lives gave a tidy summary of the brothers. "If I had a cure for cancer, I would tell it to Pedro Joaquín and the world would be using it within a week; if I had a secret I would tell it to Carlos Fernando and it would be safe forever."

In his office at *Barricada,* the FSLN newspaper, Carlos Fernando Chamorro was fervent. When he spoke of his father, it was not with personal recollection but with an appreciation for the political effect of his death. "My father won the court case proving he had not libeled the plasmapheresis business," he said, "and the public conflict ended. Dr. Pedro Ramos, who was the visible owner of the plasmapheresis center, with Somoza in the background, left for Miami. We thought it was over. Then came the assassination on the tenth of January, 1978, and the immediate admission by the gunman that Ramos, a known confederate of Somoza, had financed the killing. On the eleventh of January, a mass demonstration marched all the way from the *La Prensa* offices to my mother's house. When they burned the plasmapheresis center, this was a natural explosion of the people's fury. They also set fire to a textile plant and to the Banco Centroamérica. It was complete rage."

Of his own anger he said nothing, but Carlos Fernando was where he was, and his position in the government provided testimony to the radicalization of one upper-class youth. When Patty Hearst, from the most prominent publishing family in the United States, briefly became a revolutionary during her captivity, she claimed to have found the truth her family had consistently suppressed. For Carlos Fernando Chamorro, heir to the most celebrated publishing name in Nicaragua, conversion consisted in extending the truth his father had died to reveal. It was truth he spoke of, not objectivity.

"For me, there is no journalism that is neutral," he said. "Everyone has concrete interests. The only difference is that we in *Barricada* say openly where we stand. We defend the principles linked with that truth. To work as a journalist within a political party is to demonstrate your principles in your daily practice. I am not a mouthpiece for the party. As much as any teacher in a classroom, I am an educator."

Carlos Fernando illustrated his points with examples. "*Barricada* is candidly for the revolution and for those who support it," he said. "*La Prensa,* with a pretense of fairness, *claims* to represent everyone's interests but is in reality very narrow. It is dishonest about its narrowness. It is a newspaper which once was independent but which has now come to represent very strongly the interests of one class. I know this"—he did not smile —"because it is the class I come from.

"As an educator I do not blindly support everyone in the government. *Barricada* is the FSLN newspaper, but we keep our distance from the government. In fact, there are people in this government who are often madder at me than at my brother. We have just done an exposé of the government's mismanagement of the toy industry. The assistant minister for internal commerce is furious and has attacked me in my own paper. I will respond to the attack in a few days, but the point is that we investigated and exposed government errors. We also ran a series highly critical of the educational system. You think the bureaucrats liked that? But the parents eventually thanked us, and we helped reform the system a little."

The difference, Carlos Fernando said, between his kind of criticism and his brother's was that he wanted to improve the revolution while Pedro Joaquín was trying to tear it down. *La Prensa* proposed no alternatives; *Barricada* was always looking for ways to help the revolution on its own terms. I asked why criticism had to contain a prescription; was there not plenty of value to society for a journalist merely to point out hypocrisy, dishonesty, broken promises on an official level? Beyond that, who is to say precisely what is constructive and what is only a sneer? Isn't the social purpose of the free flow of information and opinion to encourage an intellectual marketplace where individual citizens can make their own choices?

Carlos Fernando was not budging an inch. "The conservative press in this country capitalizes on errors only to make the reactionary process legitimate. We criticize to strengthen the revolution. After my father's death, over half the *La Prensa* staff left. Of the new staff at *La Prensa,* half of them work openly with the contras in both Honduras and Costa Rica. They are actively trying to tear down their own society from within. They have no interest in freedom of information, they care only about restoring their own class to power.''

The lines between friend and enemy, between right and wrong, seemed so clearly drawn to Carlos Fernando that I wondered whether he ever entertained doubts about anything. "The party has internal problems we debate freely among ourselves," he said, which I took to mean also that Carlos Fernando might occasionally debate within *him*self, though he would not put it that way, "but these problems should not be discussed in public. Premature discussion would lead to a complete misunderstanding by the public. It would lead to a loss of conf—"

But wait, don't I hear a traditional upper-class mistrust of the majority?

"Not at all. We *always* listen to the people. We are always in a dialogue with all sectors of our society. In a very important sense, the FSLN Party cannot learn anything *except* from the people. But where misunderstandings can arise, for example, is if we were to debate in public the allocation of Nicaragua's resources. We have terrible scarcities right now, scarcities of practically all consumer goods. If we start publishing stories about these scarcities, we will cause a complete panic and everyone will run to the store and hoard everything he can get his hands on. Then where will we be? We won't have shortages, we'll have nothing.''

That justifies the government censor who in effect becomes a newspaper editor?

"I don't like censorship. *Barricada* is censored, too. I have to submit every piece of copy to the censor's office the same as my brother. But we are talking about survival here. We are under attack by both weapons and dollars. Reagan will do anything he can to destabilize us. We don't want another *El Mercurio* in Nicaragua.'' He was referring to the newspaper in Chile, heavily supported by the CIA, whose stories allegedly helped bring on the military uprising that overthrew the government of Salvador Allende. "We don't want restoration of a police state and the oligarchy that ruled before. Look around. We don't have assassinations here anymore. In El Salvador and Guatemala the right wing rules by assassination. In those countries and in Honduras and even in Costa Rica, which is in terrible economic trouble, there is no wide access to the press among unions, women, farmers, small merchants. Here all segments do have access to the press, including the upper class which supports *La Prensa*. Look at the CDS block associations. North Americans come down and tell us they're totalitarian. Totalitarian? My God, after Somoza we had no means of distribution at all and no way of knowing who was where and what was needed. The CDSs helped in the literacy and health campaigns, and they help distribute the burden of our shortages more equally. Most of the time their vigilance is just an excuse to get together and have a few drinks. They help the social life of the *barrios* more than anything else.''

But the mere existence of the CDSs and the institution of censorship both give the government a way to check continually on people and supervise what is discussed publicly. Don't censorship and the CDSs both stop people from criticizing the government?

''That's not the question. The question is this: What happens in the United States if you have enemy armies coming down from Canada and up from Mexico, both supported by a superpower who also has its navy on your Pacific and Atlantic coasts? You have people inside your country who want to see those armies and that superpower succeed. Are you going to have censorship and neighborhood defense committees, or are you going to open your arms and welcome the enemies who want to destroy you? That's the question.''

Carlos Fernando Chamorro had the certainty of a true believer. Whether Sandinista controls were obstacles to freedom would remain beside the point as long as Nicaragua was under attack. He was a convert who had not only found his religion but also his own place within it. Having selected and fashioned a revolutionary mold for his character and ideals, he had poured himself into it. He and his brother continued to reflect the polarities in Nicaraguan life. In the months after I saw them, Pedro Joaquín

Chamorro left his country, joined the contras and became head of their broadcasting operations, while Carlos Fernando Chamorro, continuing to run his newspaper, was promoted to chief propagandist for the Sandinista government.

Barricada, after Carlos Fernando's promotion, remained the official FSLN Party newspaper. *La Prensa,* after Pedro Joaquín's voluntary exile, was closed by the government in 1986.

XVIII WORKERS

RECIPE FOR A COMMUNIST: Preheat a Third World dictatorship whose principal devotions are to its own maintenance and anti-Communism; coddle an oligarchy that controls 90 percent of the national wealth; skim off an educated middle class through exile or intimidation; chill dissent by suppression; crush peasants and workers with hunger and debts that make progress impossible; let foreign corporations drain the country of raw materials; stir in an army that reports only to the dictator and operates through terror and torture; garnish with corruption; combine all ingredients with sponsorship by the world's biggest economic power; simmer forty years.

It works well. What is produced is the exact opposite of what is intended by the original anti-Communists. The Communists themselves cannot do it nearly as successfully. From Batista to Diem to Lon Nol to Somoza to Marcos and beyond, Communist subversion has not been as effective as American support.

Revolutionaries themselves are aware of what has made them. "The United States has never learned the lesson," said Ernesto Cardenal, a poet, priest and the Sandinistas' minister of culture, "that in supporting cruel and corrupt dictatorships, it only radicalizes the population, causing the very thing it does not want: socialist governments." It may be premature to claim that the United States "never" learns. Richard Nixon himself has said, as quoted by the New York *Times* in 1984, "The Communists at least talk about the problem, and too often we just talk about the Communists." But he made the observation ten years after leaving the presidency.

Communism has not thrived in the industrial countries where Marx predicted it would root but has required the specifics of oppression by the few of the many. Once an oligarchy is firmly in place, the popular alternatives that enabled the world's capitalist democracies to flourish must be foreclosed. A major power such as the United States can do this by effectively locking the Third World dictator onto his throne, staking its own international prestige on the survival of the oppressor. If the oppressor should fall, the major power's credibility suffers. Again, see Batista, Somoza, et al. When this has been accomplished, it is only a matter of time before a rebellion occurs that links all the social segments not directly profiting from the dictatorship.

Those most opposed to the system of ownership that has characterized the dictator and his associates will be the Communists. They want their society to start over again; they want to redistribute virtually all property, recast all the social and economic relationships that have disenfranchised the majority of their countrymen. They will form the army, fly to Moscow and Havana for training, map the strategy for unlocking the dictator from his throne. Other political, religious and cultural interests will join the rebellion passionately and articulately, but the Communists will have the plan for how to reorganize the country after victory, and they will have the army.

After the victory, there is a moment when the revolution's united front might survive. Many groups helped overthrow the old regime and have a chance to participate in the new order. The Communists themselves, usually theoretical Marxists with no governing experience, may be wary of a tight embrace with Moscow. Too many of them have died in what has been essentially a war for independence. A coalition is formed that looks for international support. This is when the United States turns its coldest shoulder. Communists are part of the new government; they must be ostracized. The revolutionary regime falls into the lap of the Soviet Union, which has until then spent far less to win a new ally than the United States has spent to keep its old ally.

The process follows well-established patterns. In Latin America, hoping to forestall a succession of Cubas, the Kennedy Administration announced the Alliance for Progress. Under the Alliance, foreign aid was increased while economic and agrarian reforms were encouraged. Credit unions, modeled on those in the United States, were created in many small communities throughout Latin America, raising hopes for economic advancement among the peasants. As most of the countries were under military dictators whom the United States continued to support, the reforms did not get far. Hopes raised by the social part of the policy were dashed by the political part. *"Alianza sí, progreso no"* became a bitter joke among Latin Americans.

Aware that the policy had not worked, Richard Nixon canceled it and substituted one of "trade not aid." Aid cutoffs were harsh, but in a sense Nixon was encouraging a new maturity among Latin Americans as well as abandoning the hypocrisy of supporting both reform and dictators simultaneously. The effect of the trading-partner policy, as well as of the unfulfilled promises of the old Alliance, was to propel Latin Americans toward fending for themselves in other ways. The impulse toward political independence followed. Communists have been the beneficiaries of the process, not its originators.

During a factory tour I asked a Nicaraguan official about the Russians. "We like you *norteamericanos* much better," he said. He had met only one Russian, who had made a favorable impression on him, but the official was expressing the Nicaraguans' general amiability toward anyone from the country where so many of their relatives live. "We all have cousins in San Francisco or Houston or Miami, and we have all been brought up admiring many things about the United States, so many things. Especially your prosperity and what it buys you." Since we were in a factory, I asked the official, whose name was Allan Chavarria, about the quality of Soviet machinery. He laughed. "No comparison. Yours works, half the time theirs doesn't. American equipment is preferable in almost every detail. But we have no choice."

In the revolution as spectator sport, a factory tour is obligatory. See the workers in a workers' paradise. No Nicaraguan, certainly not Allan Chavarria, claims the workers have anything like a paradise, but it is the premise, and promise, of all socialist revolutions that a revolutionary life is a life transformed, most pointedly where the dignity of labor is concerned. Not entirely by intention—he is a committed Sandinista as well as a sort of union public-relations man—Allan Chavarria led me into a workers' gripe session in the last factory we saw. Once we were there, however, he seemed as curious as I was.

"If you want a chicken to grow you have to give it chicken feed," a muscular, unshaven machinist bellowed, quoting a Nicaraguan proverb, "and if you want me to do a good job around here you have to give me more money and a longer vacation." It was a grievance that could be heard, with countless variations, in any factory or union hall in the United States. It hardly bespoke a paradise. But it was a grievance that would seldom have been given voice, and never so loudly and directly in front of a foreigner, when Nicaragua had a government of which the United States approved.

I had met Allan Chavarria at the headquarters of the Central Sandinista de Trabajadores, known as the CST, the state-supported labor union. Except that part of its roof was open to the sky, the CST main union hall bore a resemblance to the plain Baptist churches in the rural south, with rows of benches leading up to an altarlike podium. Behind the podium were pictures of the Communist trinity—Marx, Lenin and Engels—as large as the images on a movie screen. Allan Chavarria introduced himself as the national secretary in charge of propaganda for the CST. In Spanish, *propaganda* means only public information and education and does not have the sinister connotation of the word in English.

For a public-relations man, Allan Chavarria was modest,

teacherly, patient. He reminded me more of a researcher than a propagandist. Allan Chavarria said he was thirty-three years old and had begun his career working in a cosmetics factory but now spent most of his time on worker education for CST. As he described this procedure, "education" does not reduce itself to Marxist indoctrination. It is more a consciousness-raising process that involves the way a worker conceives of his work, feels toward his colleagues, uses his leisure time, treats his family, relates to his society in general. Allan Chavarria's own life had taken him along the same route. Though he described himself as a Catholic, he lived with a woman he was not married to and they had had a child together. "My parents are not crazy about this," he said, "but they know I am committed to my family and they adore their grandchild."

A sign at the entrance to La Perfecta, a milk-processing plant, gave the same advice as saloons in the old west: "Deposit your weapons here." Next to it was a list of all the employees who had pulled night guard duty during December. Employees often showed up for their shifts with their AK-47s strapped to their backs and would begin guarding the plant as soon as they finished work for the day. The guards' purpose was to prevent sabotage or attacks by contras and "Yankee invaders," as a sign on a bulletin board warned.

The last armed attack on La Perfecta, ironically, was led by Daniel Ortega himself. The episode and its consequence have become one of the adventure stories the revolution feeds on. On a hot night in August 1966, Daniel Ortega led a commando raid on the milk plant. It was no theatrical gesture to dramatize the plight of Nicaraguan babies by stealing milk for a few of them. The twenty-one-year-old Sandinista urban guerrilla had a more practical objective: the money in La Perfecta's safe. Sandinistas called this kind of operation an "economic recovery." The commandos found the money and escaped with it, but one of their members was caught by a National Guard patrol. The leader of this particular patrol was a notorious sergeant named Gonzalo Lacayo. To fall into his hands, every young Sandinista knew, was to be subjected to treatment the brutality of which was matched by its creativity. In due course, Daniel Ortega's squad member was tortured to death. He apparently revealed neither the names nor hiding places of his companions, because there were no further arrests.

Daniel Ortega gave the money from the raid to the Sandinista central command so that it could be used for the daily operating expenses of revolution—to buy more weapons, support bigger attacks against Somoza, help the guerrillas in the mountains survive. He turned his own attention to planning the brief sequel—conclusion, as far as his squad's morale was concerned—to La Perfecta. He had Sergeant Lacayo followed and learned when he would be most likely to be alone on a Managua street without his bodyguard. In various versions of the story, this occurred when Sergeant Lacayo was collecting his weekly bribes or emerging from a whorehouse. In all versions, Daniel Ortega's commando squad very soon gunned down Sergeant Lacayo in public. The following year, Daniel Ortega was arrested during his subsequent "economic recovery" at a bank and began his seven years of torture and imprisonment.

Rattly, ancient Ford trucks pulled into La Perfecta carrying milk to the plant. They appeared held together with rubber bands and soldered coins. Allan Chavarria explained that with American spare parts unavailable, creative solutions were needed when the trucks broke down, which, at their advanced ages, they frequently did. Ammonia began to seep from one of the plant's refrigeration tubes while we were there, but the leak was fixed quickly. The man who made the repair, exchanging the old rubber tube for a newer plastic one he had taken from another machine that had broken down, said he was grateful we were only visitors and not the safety inspectors.

According to a plant official, what had happened at La Perfecta since 1979 was typical of perhaps 25 percent of Nicaraguan businesses. La Perfecta remained under private ownership after the revolution. The owners got new loans from the National Development Bank. After eighteen months, when there were virtually no improvements at the processing plant, employees began to suspect that the owners were decapitalizing, sending their borrowed money out of the country. The workers, whom the revolution accorded a status roughly analogous to that of stockholders, won the right to examine La Perfecta's books and check them against what they saw going on. They found discrepancies, the kind of discrepancies that correspond to white-collar crime in the United States—fraud, defalcation, embezzlement. They hired a lawyer who went to the department of justice, and after an investigation that resulted in the owners' flight to Miami, La Perfecta was nationalized.

"It was not that capitalism did not work well in Nicaragua," Allan Chavarria said. "Capitalism probably worked too well here. It did everything Marx said it was supposed to do. It raised some of us up, it cast all the rest of us down, creating a textbook case of class antagonism. In the United States you have strong owners, too, as we had here. But you also have strong unions with their own interest, a strong government with its own interest, many kinds of popular pressure. All this restrains the capitalists. We had no restraints here. The result was pure capitalism, which for us was the same as pure plunder."

In the plywood-and-corrugated-tin union office at La Perfecta were color photographs of three boys from the plant who had been killed by the contras. There was also a map of the Soviet Union showing what crops and products come from each region. A bookshelf was filled with well-thumbed novels—*Don Quixote* to *For Whom the Bell Tolls* to cowboy adventures—the plant workers had been able to read since the literacy campaign. Before the campaign, whether they could read or not, there had been no bookshelf for the workers, according to the officials.

Because of a shortage of cartons, the milk was poured into transparent plastic bags at La Perfecta. Because of a shortage of milk, reconstituted powdered milk was often mixed with the whole milk before being decanted into the plastic bags. Because of a shortage of workers, some of the machines were not running, and because of the spare parts shortage, other machines were not functioning properly. Despite all this, the atmosphere at La Perfecta was cheerful. I could have understood defiance or determination or discouragement more easily. The plant was well lighted, and except for the replacement of cartons by plastic bags, which are common throughout Latin America, most of La Perfecta's equipment looked modern and clean. The workers did their jobs with what appeared to be an alternating current of diligence and relaxation. "Hey, man," one of them said as we passed his machine, which was churning out popsicles, "this is the revolution, right? I've been here nine years, but we're producing more now because we are producing happily because we are producing freely. That's no bullshit. We're organized, we're defending ourselves, and we're in a hard situation but we're going to survive." He grinned so broadly neither Allan Chavarria nor I could tell whether he was trying to put one of us on and if so, which one. "Hey, because that's what the revolution does, man," he said, throwing us each a popsicle. "So how do you like it?" he asked, without specifying whether he meant the revolution or the popsicle.

Unlike La Perfecta, the textile factory Allan Chavarria took me to was nationalized the instant the Sandinistas assumed power. Textilera de Nicaragua, or Texnicsa, had been owned directly by Somoza and in the latter stages of the insurrection had housed National Guard units. The FSLN had attacked and destroyed part of the plant. According to the assistant manager, when the FSLN captured Texnicsa, Somoza had it bombed. In the fighting, so much of the factory was wrecked it could accommodate only two dozen workers in 1979. When I was there Texnicsa had 1,670 employees, with plans to expand to twice that number. "Go anywhere you want here, talk to anyone you like," the assistant manager said as Allan Chavarria and I entered the large plant. "After all, this is Nica Libre." He meant liberated Nicaragua, and he also meant the national cocktail. The assistant manager knew, of course, that Allan Chavarria was a union official, but Chavarria himself went off to talk to other employees at Texnicsa, rejoining me from time to time. The manager let me wander where I wanted, answering questions when I asked them but not pressing.

In order to emphasize the amount of reconstruction that had taken place under the Sandinistas, the assistant manager had clearly exaggerated the destruction caused during the war. A few of the buildings were new and renovated, but literally an acre of equipment—huge sewing machines mostly—was antique. Though he could not account for the contradiction between the destruction he described and the old machinery, intact except for worn-out parts, the assistant manager proudly pointed to mechanical looms from both England and the United States that had been manufactured before World War I. They had survived the war against Somoza but not the spare-parts shortage. I stopped counting when I got up to two hundred sewing machines that were shut down. Most of them were Singers from New Jersey, but others were from West Germany, England, Switzerland, Ohio, Pennsylvania and Massachusetts. Bulgaria has been providing the newer machinery, and Japan has been taking up some of the slack in spare parts. Mexico has replaced the American dyes that were cut off. What Nicaragua itself contributes, in addition to labor, is the cotton, the finest quality of which comes from León.

If hundreds of machines were idle, thousands were busy. Most were giant, industrial-sized Singers. Texnicsa was operating on three shifts, twenty-four hours a day. It was the biggest textile plant in Nicaragua, and the management planned to make it the biggest in Central America within two years. The manufacturing environment was similar to that in postrecession Detroit. Everything was clanging, whirring, pumping, chiming, humming, ringing, clattering, throbbing, hissing, booming, sounding and resounding. All the Singers everyone has heard. Chain-stitching here, binding there, mending and hemming and tacking and netting and twining and weaving. Regardless of politics and the revolution and counterrevolution—if they can ever be disregarded even for an industrial instant—Nicaragua was visibly in production at Texnicsa.

Making spare parts had become a small industry in itself at the textile plant, as it is throughout Nicaragua. In one large shed, men and women were fashioning replacements for broken flywheels, blades, rivets and screws. Because metal is among the many scarce materials in Nicaragua, hard rubber and plastic were in use as substitutes. A damaged steel gear might be replaced with a plastic one that would not last as long as metal but would get the machine back in operation quickly. When the big American companies pulled out of Nicaragua after the revolution, some of them took back all they had, from railroad tracks to the smallest wrenches. As a result, stories circulate that sound like bad Polish jokes about how many hours it took how many men to remove a simple nut from its bolt.

Reminders of the war were plentiful at Texnicsa. Photographs were displayed of three workers who had recently been killed fighting the contras; two were in management, on the plant's governing board, and one was a machinist. The remaining sixty Texnicsans on military duty continued to receive their factory pay while they were at the front. Posters saying the defense of the country could be hazardous were common around the factory, coupled with injunctions to produce more shirts, pants, uniforms, tents, cots and knapsacks.

A bedroom-furniture exhibit in the plant meeting hall was a reminder of a happier aspect of life. Prizes for production, punctuality, discipline and ingenuity were common at Texnicsa, but this bedroom set was going to be given away to the winner of a raffle. In a society where industriousness and determination had suddenly been elevated above all other virtues, the maintenance of a prize for blind good luck—corresponding in religion to the unmerited favor of God—was a sign that the Sandinistas did not ignore the morale value of the Irish Sweepstakes.

It was next to the bedroom set that the grievance session took place in which the burly machinist demanded higher pay and a longer vacation. His complaint gave others nerve. A woman said she and her colleagues had not been granted use of the patio outside the plant dining hall when it was their turn. A cloth dyer said his Swiss dyeing machine was mixing up colors. Two men who worked on adjacent Singers were angry at the man who worked next to them because he had been late twice that week, holding down the number of shirts their section was able to produce. Others pleaded for incentive pay and bonuses in addition to a basic salary raise, which they also wanted. A young dyer who was newly married pointed toward the bedroom set and said, "If we don't get a raise, maybe I'll win the double bed." An older man told him he didn't need a double bed for what he should be doing.

In the warehouse for processing raw materials, soft ropes of cotton from León, ropes as big in diameter as the trunk of a redwood tree, were being divided into smaller strands by a thin old man working a German machine manufactured in the 1930s. Somoza I could have bought it from a Hamburg industrialist, or received it as a gift, the Third World on its knees before the Third Reich. Had this man worked this same machine over the decades, growing old along with it? No, he had been at Texnicsa only two years. He carried the small strand of cotton to another machine that divided it into still smaller strands, which a third machine could then spin into thread. Before coming to Texnicsa the old man had worked in a slaughterhouse all his life, starting when he was twelve years old. It had been owned by a friend of the Somozas who had closed it down and left the country after the revolution. Any way you looked at it, he said, work was struggle. He liked the cloth because it was so much cleaner than the slaughtered animals, but he was glad he did not have to work with the dyes. Even the ones that were not red looked like the blood of something to him.

A man with thick straight black hair and a lined, leathery face paused at his Belgian loom. His hair and his forearms looked vigorous; his eyes and mouth sagged. He was forty-three, he said, but he knew he looked ten years older. He had been at Texnicsa twelve years. He had lost a son and daughter to Somoza. The daughter was pregnant when a National Guardsman named Urcuyo charged her with sabotage. She did not even know a single Sandinista. Urcuyo had had his eye on her for years—he came from the same *barrio*—but she had rejected him for another man. The other man Urcuyo didn't touch. After his daughter was picked up for questioning, the loom operator never saw her again. His son went after her, and he, too, disappeared. *Por cierto* it was a better life since the triumph of the revolution —he had more money, he was calmer at the plant and at home, he got much more encouragement to do good work. The plant gave him food when he needed it, though Somoza himself often gave free lunches at Texnicsa and always provided huge meals if they had to work on holidays. Prices were going up too fast in the last few months. His wife complained more than he did. Thank God he still had four children at home. The revolution gave him a better chance to become a foreman, though he liked his loom well enough. One of his sons was a great pitcher, another Dennis Martínez if he could keep his concentration. He had his hopes for his children and also for himself. He had his memories, too. Urcuyo got away after the triumph.

At the head of the row of looms in the long gray room where cotton was spun into cloth, the Texnicsa employees had made their own Christmas tree. First they had stuck up a thick wire for the trunk and fastened thinner wires onto it for the branches. Then they had wound raw cotton onto all the wires. From the cotton branches they had hung balls of all the colors of yarn they manufactured at the plant, along with red and green ribbons tied in bows. Silver and gold thread had been braided to look something like tinsel before being woven through the branches. At the top was a star made of white cloth, and cotton dolls leaned against the bottom of the tree. "Did you see a more beautiful tree anywhere in Managua?" Allan Chavarria asked rhetorically. A few feet away someone had spray-painted the wall, not neatly but boisterously like subway graffiti, "*Feliz Navidad.*" He had then added, improbably in English, "Happy New Year." A setup for visitors? Spontaneous holiday cheer? One never knew in Nica Libre.

Over a drink at the Intercontinental, Allan Chavarria gave his summation: "Our real freedom in this revolution is to try to remove misery, fear, ignorance, and want. They were our closest companions before and we are not rid of them yet. Perhaps you saw today that now at least we can exert ourselves to win the struggle against them. Another day you may see that we will defend this revolution as long and as well as we need to. People here are still much like their parents. That is Nicaragua. We remain what we always were except for *esperanza.*"

XIX   AMERICAN EMBASSY—III

ONE MORNING NEAR THE END OF MY STAY, I was on my way to the American embassy when I was handed a message that said Daniel Ortega would see me that evening. I was glad I was going to the embassy, because the officially perceived national interest of the United States would surely prepare me better for Ortega than a day spent looking at the confusions, or being briefed on the wonders, of the revolution. My unofficial preparation for Ortega had begun the night before when I had sat briefly in the Intercontinental with an American journalist from a midwestern paper. The Sandinistas failed singularly to charm him, sometimes failed to show up for appointments he had thought were chiseled in marble. When they did show up they impressed him as arrogant hypocrites. His paper had supported them originally, but he was on his way home to reverse its policy. His last night in Managua he had decided he hated the whole country and was pouring as much of its *Flor de Caña* into himself as he could find. "Where do they get off, lecturing us on how to run our country when they can't even feed their own people?" he asked. "You couldn't *give* me this country, and if you did I'd throw it right back at you."

231

I was conceding Nicaragua was not mine to give when the waiter brought the reporter his check. He refused to pay it. When he also refused to let me pay it, several worried waiters surrounded us and tried to persuade him to go. He did not feel like it, he wanted another drink. He told the waiters where they could stick their stupid little country. Communist bastards. When one of the waiters tried to help him up, the reporter shook him off so threateningly the waiter retreated to a corner. Seeing how intimidated the group was, the reporter suddenly changed his mind. He allowed that leaving was the only good idea he had heard in Nicaragua, so I escorted him to the door before he could change his mind again. "We're going to turn this fucking country back into a colony," the reporter said as he wobbled toward a taxi. "That's what it was, that's what it deserves to be. Teach them a lesson. The next time I come back here will be with the United States fucking Marines, and let me tell you it can't happen too soon."

Having errands in the vicinity of the embassy, I had gone there early, though my appointment was not until lunch. It was demonstration day again, and the small band of Americans protesting U.S. policy contrasted not only with the midwestern reporter of the night before, but also, as they intended, with the seventy-five Americans working for their country inside the embassy. Americans living in or visiting Nicaragua were as subject to polarization over the revolution as Nicaraguans. On both sides of the embassy fence was the unasked question: Who was more American in December 1983—the idealists come down to help the Nicaraguans, and by extension the Sandinistas; or the diplomats inside, arguably as full of ideals, come to serve their government with the belief that in this direction lay patriotism?

In high, quavering, mostly female voices, the demonstration began with several verses of the hymn for all movements, "We Shall Overcome." A few of the protesters looked as if they could have done their first singing on behalf of the suffragettes. We are not afraid, went the second verse. Others in the group would have sung for labor solidarity in the '30s. We'll walk hand in hand, we'll walk hand in haaa—a—aaaannd. More of them had sung for civil rights in the '60s. Truth will make us free. In the '60s and the '70s they sang against war. We shall live in peace. In the '80s they were singing for Nicaragua. Deep in their hearts they did believe, lifting their voices against the early-morning traffic that drowned most of their words. The cars in Managua were not big on mufflers.

A little blond boy wandered away from his pregnant mother to the embassy fence to look at the security guard, a handsome bearded man in civvies. The coffee-klatch aspect of the demonstration seeped in as friends discussed where to get mayonnaise and who was going home for Christmas. A CBS news crew had been sent to cover the protest, with its correspondent Bruce Morton in charge. They were not finding anything to shoot. The little blond boy, separated by only the fence from the embassy grounds, asked the security guard his name and job. "Fred Mecke," the security guard said affably. "I'm here to take care of all the security at the embassy." The little boy asked where he was from. "All over, I guess," Fred Mecke said. "The first place I was from was New York, but all I have left there now is a safe deposit box, uh, just a box in a bank with some old stuff in it." "Oh," said the boy, who looked a couple of months shy of four. He began to play with the vertical bars in the iron fence around the embassy. "Careful now," Fred Mecke said.

A chant woke everybody up. "USA/CIA/OUT OF NICARAGUA/ RIGHT AWAY." The chant seemed to clear people's throats, and they became talkative.

"I heard Jim found extra work as a translator."

"Most of our family are in the St. Paul–Minneapolis area; my aunt's never been out of St. Paul."

"It's my one day off—can you meet me for lunch after I get my hair done? I'm free till two when the kids get home."

"Are you still with the National Council?"

"I'll have to wait until I see my physical therapist in Los Altos."

Bruce Morton of CBS News counted carefully up to thirty-eight participants and then did a mock report on the small demonstration, pretending he was on camera. "A surging throng of angry protesters stormed the embattled embassy's gates this morning in tense Managua . . ." He let his voice trail off, and he and his crew left shortly.

Small trickles of protesters continued to arrive in Volkswagens and minibuses. A couple of dozen Americans who had come down to take part in a peace vigil on the Honduran border showed up looking tired. Most had landed in Managua the night before and were on their way later in the day to the north, where their group, known as Witness for Peace, was concentrating its efforts.

A minister read a statement from another minister linking racism, poverty and war. Doug Murray, the pesticide specialist whom I had seen several times around Managua and at the previous embassy demonstration, remarked that the statement originally came from yet a third minister, Martin Luther King. "But hey, there's only so much truth around," Doug Murray said pleasantly, "so we have to keep repeating it." Murray was wearing a San Francisco Giants cap and had an old copy of *The Sporting News* rolled up and stuck under his arm. He could have been on his way to work in Marin County instead of Managua, or sneaking off to Candlestick Park for a few hot dogs and a beer to soothe him through a Giant loss.

Working as a safety inspector with responsibility for pesticides at the Nicaraguan ministry of labor, Doug Murray knew that some of the weed and insect killers being used were dangerous to workers. "Historically there's been no regard for worker safety," he said "and you can't turn that around overnight. In most cases, because of the economic noose from the United States, what a farmer sprays is the only insecticide he can get, and he has to use it or else not only his family but his whole community suffers. So I try to get them to be more careful, but I don't shut them down the way I would at home."

Doug Murray justified his double standard by the difference between what he perceived as selfish agribusiness at home and the meager subsistence farms he was finding in Nicaragua. I asked how much longer he planned to stay.

"The point is, I matter here. In Nicaragua I feel unseparated, after a long time, from the part of myself I value most. I think the reason all of us are down here is there's nothing going on for us now at home, and no prospects, no way to make ourselves felt in our own society. We've become strangers there.''

Doug Murray's feelings were representative of those expressed by Americans who came to Nicaragua to help the revolution. Disillusionment with the United States was general among them, coupled with a despair that their disillusionment was so out of fashion as to render them voiceless at home. In their expatriate sentiments, there had been a well-understood if unwritten compact between the United States government and the principal organs of mass communications to bury the aspirations of the planet's dispossessed in a sea of indifference and complacency. By contrast, they saw Nicaragua as a land of opportunity, a reborn society where individual effort could have visible effect. While they found the political and social atmosphere at home lacking in compassion, that was the very emotion they described as being abundant in Nicaragua. I asked Doug Murray if there were not abuses and inadequacies in the United States that needed the kind of commitment he was willing to make in Nicaragua.

"No one at home cares right now," he said. "Whatever part of the national character is dominant in the United States now—rolling back everything progressive, telling other countries what kind of government we'll allow them to have—doesn't seem to include me. You get your degree and you bang away at some meaningless job for a few years, or a teaching position where you feel alienated from your own subject, and you finally get so frustrated you just have to get out. You come down here and immediately your attention quickens, your energy begins to come back to you, you regain a little credibility with yourself. Meanwhile, when you see what people read in American papers every day about this so-called Leninist police state, you wonder why the invasion didn't come a year ago. You know they're not awake yet to any of the realities of life in Central America. You think to yourself, My God, what can I do so the folks back home won't sleep through this one?''

Where do you feel freer, in the United States or in Nicaragua? "In the United States I can say any fool thing that comes into my head. In Nicaragua I am helping build a society. The social and political structures of the United States—and, I suspect, of the Soviet Union as well—are not set up with the interests of the majority in mind. Those structures serve power, they maintain power in its place and mandate prosperity for those who hold it. For everyone else, it's 'See ya later, buddy' "

"NO TO THE CONTRAS/NO TO THE MARINES/DOWN WITH REAGAN'S WAR MACHINE." An old standby helped the early-morning juices flow. The assemblage had now reached sixty.

The Americans from Witness for Peace neither chanted nor demonstrated in any vivid way. True to the name of their organization, they stood quietly and watched. Among them was Russell Christiansen, a lawyer from Bangor, Maine. He was fifty-two years old, a father of four, with reddish-brown hair and a red beard beginning to show gray. "Some of us have got to die," he said when I asked him why he was going to the border. "The cause of peace has so little visibility in the United States now, and I believe it's the only cause worth dying for. By going to the border, we dramatize this in a general way. If some of us die, we bring the cause home to our countrymen in a very personal way." He spoke calmly, unrancorously. If individual sacrifice was needed to bring peace, Russell Christiansen was willing to be the individual who made the sacrifice. "We stand in solidarity," he said, "not with the Sandinistas but with the people of Nicaragua."

The little blond boy was trying to reach through the bars and touch Fred Mecke, the security guard. Fred Mecke took a step backward and told the boy to be careful. They grinned at each other. The little boy looked back at Russell Christiansen, whom he had never seen before at the weekly embassy demonstrations. Russell Christiansen was also smiling.

"I'll see you at the border, then," Russell Christiansen said to me. No, I said. But I added a question: Where are you going to be? "At Jalapa." I don't think so, I said, having already caved in to my least appealing instincts.

Someone pointed to Fred Mecke and said he was a suspicious type. His companion said she knew what he meant; the security guard could easily be CIA. The man said he knew a former Peace Corps volunteer who came through Managua and swore he had seen Fred Mecke in Bogotá, only he had no beard then and very little hair on top of his head. No hair in Bogotá, said the woman, but dark hair in Managua *and* a beard sounded like an agent to her. CIA oozing from his pores. The man said it might not have been Bogotá, and it could have been one of the embassy's other security guards. This leaves us with the clear inference, then, that Fred Mecke either was once in Bogotá or he was not, and while there, if there, he was clean-shaven and bald, or not. If a well-trimmed beard and a hair transplant made him CIA, then the CIA's insinuation into the key fabric of American life was complete, since the Agency was now obviously in control of the New York advertising business.

At last the little blond boy did what he had been trying to do during the entire demonstration. He managed to get his head through the vertical bars protecting the embassy. His mother, who was holding up a placard about imperialism, noticed this and yelled for her Raybert to stop that before he got hurt. When he tried to pull his head back out, Raybert found he had gotten stuck. His mother beat Fred Mecke to the bars and tried to pull Raybert's head out. She could not, and Raybert cried so hard no one could hear the reading of an open letter to the Organization of American States urging it to adopt a resolution telling the United States to disengage its military forces from Central America. Fred Mecke approached the fence and looked down at Raybert, not interfering at first. When he saw Raybert's mother was not going to extricate her little boy, he reached down with the forearms of a body-builder—possibly a CIA body-builder, of course—and pulled the iron bars of the fence apart so Raybert could get his head out. The freed Raybert looked up in awe at Fred Mecke the way the little boy in the Coca-Cola commercial looks at Mean Joe Green. He got the smile from Fred Mecke just before he collapsed sobbing into his mother's arms, causing her to hand her placard to a friend so she could put Raybert over her shoulder.

The security guard was in a reflective mood as the demonstration broke up. "There's just about every way to look at this situation that you could dream up," Fred Mecke said. "I've been in Nairobi, Addis, Khartoum, South America, El Salvador when it was so bad you couldn't have your family there. Nowhere have I seen the variety of ways to look at a situation that we have here. For example, in my job as security guard, I'm supposed to protect people, but around here it's so safe a lot of what I do is just hand-holding. Now is that because the population is so tightly controlled, or is it because everyone's so gung-ho for the revolution?"

How prepared is the embassy for an invasion?

"All U.S. embassies have shredders. In an emergency it just takes a flick of the switch and a few minutes to destroy the most sensitive documents. You always have to have contingency plans for whatever might happen, and you also have to know not to believe everything you hear. This country is one tangled place— for their people, for our people. Sometimes I liken Nicaragua to a Fellini movie."

The American embassy was calm, as usual, and the people inside did not act besieged. I liked the members of the staff I met, the staff liked and respected Ambassador Quainton, and the ambassador went around—as he had emphasized to me—without needing a bodyguard. Besides the official hostility between Washington and Managua, there was only one problem around the embassy. Everyone insisted on being referred to as a "foreigner" or a "Western diplomat" or just a "Westerner."

I recall lunch in the embassy commissary with two such Westerners, a man and a woman, who had numerous contacts among Nicaraguans during their terms of service in-country, as diplomats like to say. They were friendly and enjoyed their work, which involved knowing most of what went on at several levels of Managuan society. The first thing they told me was that the midwestern reporter had not been content with swearing vengeance on Nicaragua the night before at the hotel. At dawn he had called the embassy to demand that President Reagan send *Air Force One* to evacuate him from the evil clutches of the Sandinistas, who had announced on television (he said) that they would never permit him to leave the country alive. He was not an ugly American, then, or not *just* ugly—he had gone crazy, too. Nicaragua could do that in December 1983.

The man and the woman who were my hosts had completely different kinds of jobs at the embassy, and they frequently disagreed about Nicaragua, but neither had any doubt that the Sandinistas were more to blame for their difficulties than the United States was.

"They're aiming at total control over the life of the individual," the man said.

"They're eliminating the freedom to live as you like," the woman said. "To go back a little, I was liberal-to-radical, I taught college and opposed the Vietnam War. I was very sympathetic to so-called wars of national liberation. I don't doubt for a moment the Sandinistas' commitment to a better life for the poor when they first came to power."

"But the system they set up is an all-encompassing one," the man said. "It takes over your life and exists primarily to keep the Sandinistas in power. The first two years they concentrated on supplying new services to the masses. After that they consolidated their power into this system that subjugates more than it liberates."

Did the hardening of the party line coincide with U.S. support for the contras?

"It's whose ox is being gored," he said. "Are the Sandinistas reacting to our reaction or are they simply being their Marxist-Leninist selves when they crack down on dissidents? After a point I'm not sure it matters."

"The system seldom takes the form of physical abuse," she said. "It uses a steady, insidious abridgment of individual liberties. I guess you can tell I've taken a giant step to the right since I've been here."

"Health care was spread around to more people at first," he

said, "but the quality declined. Those who had nothing before now have something, but it's not as good as what was being offered before to those who could afford it."

"It's the same in education," she said. "Enrollments have doubled and tripled, but the quality of education received at the universities has declined sharply. The leveling of quality has been dramatic, according to our friends here. The intellectuals stayed, you see, because the level of violence was very low once the Sandinistas had won. Now they're not so sure what to do."

I asked them who their friends were.

"A professor who recently gave a series of lectures on John Cheever at the National University," she said. "Other friends like that."

"If you mean," he said, "that our friends are an educated elite, that's probably true."

"I guess we do look at things from the point of view of the upper middle class, not the lower class, but a decline in quality is a decline in quality," she said.

A Nicaraguan who specializes in John Cheever must be as rare as an American who specialized in Alexander Pope at the time of our revolution.

"We are pleading guilty," she said, "at least I am, to the charge of knowing educated Nicaraguans. So?"

The man interrupted with a remark that the opposition to the Sandinistas was growing and not limited to the elite. I asked how the man and the woman, as foreigners in Nicaragua, felt about the United States funding the contras.

"The contras," he said, "are a bunch of louts. In all candor, that's what they are, louts."

"But funding them," she said, "is pale in comparison to the Sandinistas' support for the rebels in El Salvador."

"We have to do distasteful things," he said. "That's part of hardball, the same game the Sandinistas are playing as soon as they invite the first Soviet adviser onto their turf, which also happens to be the North American mainland."

"Which isn't to say," she said, "that we don't have earlier sins to pay for."

"We have sent ambassadors to Nicaragua," he said, "who thought the Somozas walked on water."

"If you look back," she said, "from the Marines to the Somozas, we do have quite a bad record to live down."

If one were a Nicaraguan, I had to ask, at what point would one say the United States had stopped adding to that record?

It was some relief to all of us when lunch was over.

Leaving the embassy, I hitched a ride with a Nicaraguan who was employed there. He said he was a servant at the embassy and thought "de world" of the Americans he worked for. He was from the East Coast and had worked on cruise ships to Tampa and New Orleans. "For de life of me," he said, "I can't figure out why Mr. Ray-gun don't love de Nicaraguans. Why Mr. Ray-gun love de Grenadians so much, Skipper?" He explained that the people of Grenada had been the beneficiaries of American intervention while Nicaragua was being left to the Nicaraguans, which had always been a bad idea. The revolutionaries themselves were the worst of his countrymen, because they had no experience governing and no profession except the military. "We need Americans down here to straighten things out," he said. "Only bad experience I ever had with Americans I was working cruise liners and got me some nooky off American girls and the chief say, 'Charles, you get you ass offa my ship.' I was just doing what they wanted me to do. Other than that, I always find Americans a happy bunch of folks to work for. Nicaraguans are making a mess. To tell the truth, Skipper, I like to see Mr. Ray-gun find the biggest bomb he got and drop it on the lot of them."

XX DANIEL ORTEGA

MY FIRST QUESTION TO DANIEL ORTEGA was a mistake I almost did not recover from. "What's new?" I asked.

At the time—December 1983—he was coordinator of the ruling junta and was already treated as the head of state whenever he traveled abroad. Later, at the Russian Tea Room in New York, I saw a tableful of other Nicaraguan officials, including the foreign minister and the ambassador to the United Nations, scurry from the room in order to reenter *behind* Ortega. The protocol marked the distance between Daniel Ortega in the 1980s and his bank-robbing days of the 1960s, his seven prison years, his five years as a guerrilla fighter in the 1970s. One diner remarked that even in the United States the Sandinistas have to eat Russian food. Soon after the evening at the Russian Tea Room, he was elected president of Nicaragua and assumed the position by law that he had been occupying in fact for five years.

At home, both before and after his election, he was much more comradely. People still called him Daniel, and children loved to touch him whenever he walked among them, as I had watched him do at Purísima. When I saw him alone in Managua, it was late in the evening and I had been waiting half an hour, which is nothing by Nicaraguan standards and very little by any standards considering my appointment was with the *de facto* leader of a country under armed attack. Furthermore, of course, the attacks were supported by my own country.

As he entered the office in Government House where I had been told to await him, Daniel Ortega smiled, the only time I saw any expression on his features except for straight-ahead, direct earnestness. We sat next to each other but at right angles so that it was easier for us to look at each other than if we had been side by side on a couch. His interpreter, a Canadian woman, sat on the other side of me, which meant I was somewhat tennis-matched between the two of them. Neither of us was comfortable enough in the other's language to speak it in what was, after all, an on-the-record interview. I remembered that the first Somoza had originally been chosen by the Americans largely because he was so fluent in English. From that day forward, until he told the American ambassador "I'm a goner" after his shooting in 1956, Somoza I only gave orders and went slumming in Spanish. When he partied in New York, did his biggest business, deliberated with the sundry ambassadors from Washington, or *took* orders, the language was English. His sons spoke still better English, knew still more colloquialisms, though most of these were a decade out of date. By the time of Daniel Ortega, it had become doubtful that another Nicaraguan head of state would ever speak English for the record as long as the revolution lasted.

He was dressed in casual fatigues. The universal green of fatigues is not pea or lime or kelly or forest—nothing so vital—but resembles the husk of an avocado after at least one week of rot. No complexion can stand up well in fatigues. No matter how clear or nut-brown or pearl-white, all skin becomes sallow in fatigues, a footnote in the catalogue of reasons for civilization to do away with war. In Daniel Ortega's case, the fatigues did what they could to drain his tan and add to his appearance of being in a continual brood. The *comandantes* of Nicaragua keep their private lives as private as gossip will allow, but the Junta Coordinator was known to have been married once, to a woman who later became director of the Sandinista Defense Committees, and with whom he had one child. For most of the time since his release from prison in 1974, he had lived with Rosario Murillo, a poet who became president of the Sandinista Association of Cultural Workers, with whom he had four more children, all born since the victory in 1979. Now, at the age of thirty-eight, he liked to jog three miles several times a week and to work up to twenty hours a day.

So I said Hello, groping for the icebreaker as we settled into our chairs, and What's new?

Fifteen minutes later I was still taking notes, still had not opened my mouth again with another question. The first question was going to be the last, then. I had thought such a question would get us off on a fairly informal footing, give him a chance figuratively to kick off his shoes after a hard day and say anything he liked. Jesus, your government is driving me crazy. Why didn't anyone ever tell me it was easier to run a revolution than a country? How are you finding Managua—if you do find it let me know where it is. (But he never makes wisecracks, not even bad ones.) It's been such a long day why don't we have a cigar, maybe a drink; or if Reagan could see the spirit in our *barrios* and on our farms, he'd know how popular this revolution is and he might think again before arming our enemies. All these remarks, except the one about Managua, are part of the arsenal used by Fidel Castro to disarm visitors while at the same time letting them know it is all right to talk about virtually anything.

I had surely done nothing to warrant confidentiality. Whoever Daniel Ortega might not have liked in the nine-member Directorate, what his problems were with the ministries of labor or agriculture, how he planned to counter the next American military initiative—I would get nowhere near any of this, and we both knew it. But I had hoped for a middle ground of informality between rhetoric and intimacy. What I got was closer to the former, but rhetorical hardly describes Daniel Ortega's presentation. His words poured from him quickly and densely, with passion. He felt his revolution and lived it every minute of his life. He was not the most charismatic of the Sandinistas—that would always be Tomás Borge—only the most sincere. Forget about humor, don't look for subtlety, never mind the ability to see the other fellow's (or country's) point of view, settle for sincerity, count on Daniel Ortega to say what he means. As he went on, I began mentally discarding other questions I had prepared—about the revolution, about Nicaragua's relations with other Central American countries, about his diplomatic strategy with the United States, about foreign trade, about Soviet influence in Nicaragua and so forth. The answers, I realized, to each of these questions would be infinite variants on the same theme: It's up to Washington. Washington will decide how much we are pushed toward the Eastern bloc, whether our private sector can survive and thrive, how we are perceived and treated by our neighbors, whether the revolution can remain peaceful. Washington will decide all this because the power cards in this hemisphere, both militarily and economically, are held in Washington's hand.

What *could* I ask, then? A country on the traditional fringe of the American empire suddenly declares its independence. So what? It can't jump the seas and locate itself elsewhere, it can't become prosperous overnight. It can't go for a swim and wind up in Southern California even if it wants to. It *can* have ideas that are not those of the empire. It can—at its peril—align itself with the empire's enemies, daring the empire to strike back, which it probably will in one way or another. If the empire's enemy is fascism, as it was in the 1940s, dictators on the fringe of the empire will flirt with it, as several Latin leaders did during World War II. If the enemy is Communism, the flirtation is equally sweet to the revolutionaries of the 1980s. It is not *their* countries that Communism allegedly enslaves. Allende is recalled with affection; Castro is treated with respect in the Latin countries simply because he said no to the United States and lasted for a generation. If Latin Americans have been colonized and imperialized it was by Portugal, Spain and the United States, not by Communism. If their educational systems have been narrow, it was the narrowness of an uncompromising Catholic Church, not of Marx. A revolution in a small, poor Latin country could not be expected to get very far, but for the moment of its existence it would be permitted to have an idea of its own, perhaps a philosophy. What was Daniel Ortega's?

In *The Book of Laughter and Forgetting,* Milan Kundera told of the enthusiasm he and his friends had when Communism first came to Czechoslovakia. Their dream was "the creation of an idyll of justice for all," Kundera wrote. "People have always aspired to an idyll, a garden where nightingales sing, a realm of harmony where the world does not rise up as a stranger against man nor man against other men, where the world and all its people are molded from a single stock and the fire lighting up the heavens is the fire burning in the hearts of men, where every man is a note in a magnificent Bach fugue and anyone who refuses his note is a mere black dot, useless and meaningless, easily caught and squashed between the fingers like an insect." Soon the enthusiasts were celebrating the triumph of their brave new idea for transforming their society, celebrating in a fever because in addition to installing the new order, they had also triumphed over the evil that had prevailed before. "They danced all the more frantically because their dance was the manifestation of their innocence, the purity that shone forth so brilliantly against the black villainy . . . suddenly they were all singing the three or four simple notes again, speeding up the steps of their dance, fleeing rest and sleep, outstripping time, and filling their innocence with strength. Everyone was smiling . . . and before long not one of them was touching the ground, they were taking two steps in place and one step forward without touching the ground, yes, they were rising up. . . . " What happens in Kundera's idyll, as in the history of Czechoslovakia, is that one by one all those dancers who do not subscribe to the state's Communist orthodoxy are forced out of the circle. Once outside, they become black dots to be squashed.

Not every revolution becomes despotic. Czechoslovakia was long enough ago, far enough away to have no close relationship with Nicaragua. Even Cuba was no clear model. Despotism flourished both with and without revolution. But it seemed, in the light of Marxist history, pertinent to ask for Daniel Ortega's ideas on freedom. Could Prague's fallen dancers become Managua's ostracized dissidents?

Meanwhile, the Junta Coordinator was still pouring on the heat to my first question. It turned out that asking Daniel Ortega what's new was like asking a patient in a nursing home how are you. It's your mistake, and you're going to get the full catalogue before he even pauses for breath.

"Nothing is new," he said, "in the sense that our offers of amnesty to the contras and to the Miskito elements who have been fighting against the revolution are all in the context of goals we have set long before. Our internal actions have been planned for a long time and are only now being implemented. Our external diplomacy is all based upon the search for peace that has always been our intention. To the government of the United States, anything we do that they like is in response to the pressure they apply on us. Their pressure makes us work harder, yes, makes us treasure our independence with even greater tenacity, but our policies have been decided on by us and are not the fruit of their policy of force."

Ranging backward to the FSLN struggle in the 1960s and 1970s, forward into the peace proposals of the Contadora countries—Mexico, Panama, Colombia and Venezuela—Daniel Ortega took the offensive. Nothing was new about FSLN goals, which had been promulgated by Sandino himself and by Carlos Fonseca since the beginning of the struggle. On the other hand, the opportunity to realize those goals was new in Latin America. The literacy campaign, an electoral law allowing true pluralism for the first time in Nicaragua's history, *campesinos* working their own land—that was what was new. They would welcome multilateral dialogues with their neighbors or bilateral ones, they would talk anytime with the United States, and they would support Contadora peace efforts. They rejected only the idea of talking to Nicaraguan traitors, since they felt this group did not deserve negotiating status with the country they were betraying.

Through all his discourse, Daniel Ortega's eyes were trained on mine, and I never saw him blink except when I was finally able to ask a new question. What lifted his words beyond rhetoric was his concentration. His whole being, even his dark, drooped mustache, emphasized the gravity with which he spoke. The scar above his right eye, reminder that he had been beaten almost to death by Somoza's men, was the exclamation point to his resolve. If Daniel Ortega had been dumb as an ox, he would still have been formidable, because his concentration was as fixed as the arrangement of the Big Dipper. Since he was in fact far from dumb and had studied and thought about his country for at least twenty years, ever since he began protesting against Somoza III as a teenager, Daniel Ortega presented a learned as well as nimble adversary in any debate. Every muscle fiber and all his protoplasm seemed collected into a lifetime meditation on the essence and existence of Nicaragua. He had no tact. His strongest admirers were agreed that Daniel Ortega had lost the Kissinger commission on Central America completely by presuming to lecture them on the historical misdeeds of the United States in Nicaragua. This stern young man had only his focus on Nicaragua, but in most of his forums it had been what he needed.

What was needed to govern, however, was clearly distinct from what was needed to win a war. The pursuit of visible military goals, the ability to give and take orders, was not naturally bonded with the ability to delay, compromise, parcel out patronage, manipulate public opinion, decide between factions or win elections. For anyone living with the reality of oppression, revolution becomes as necessary as air. The true peril begins with victory, when rebels have to convert their ability to destroy into an ability to build. Power is to a revolutionary what the apple was to Adam, or nuclear fission was to physicists. Nothing can ever be the same again. "In some sort of crude sense, which no vulgarity, no humor, no overstatement can extinguish," J. Robert Oppenheimer told scientists at MIT two years after Hiroshima, "the physicists have known sin; and that is a knowledge they cannot lose." Oppenheimer might have been talking about revolutionaries who come to power. The plight of the Sandinistas was what to do with the forbidden fruit now that they had tasted it. How would the experience of governing replace the innocence of revolt? It was not easy to say Daniel Ortega was wrong to ascribe the emergency in his country to actions taken by the United States, but it was not yet easy to say, either, how good a peacetime leader he might ever prove to be. When he at last finished with what was definitely not new in Nicaragua, I asked Daniel Ortega why he had recently said the FSLN would never give up power, either by votes or by bullets. Did that mean he would not honor the legitimacy of an election if he lost?

"Oh yes, I am happy you asked me that." Suddenly he was a southern senator on *Meet the Press* who has just been asked why he always votes against civil rights if he's so progressive on other social issues. He talks states rights. In Nicaragua, denigrating bourgeois electoral politics is how you pacify the Marxists on your left, but you can't say that, so you say: "No leader of any political party anywhere who has confidence in his party's ability to win an election is going to talk about losing. I was merely affirming my own faith that the FSLN will win the elections."

Well, yes, never mind that the way the statement was made indicated that the Sandinistas, like the Institutional Revolutionary Party in Mexico or the Congress Party in India, intended to continue governing their country for the foreseeable and controllable future. The revolution was not negotiable. To suggest to a Sandinista in the 1980s that perhaps one of the traditional parties such as the Liberals or Conservatives might again run the country was the same as it would have been to tell an American colonist of the 1780s that since he had won the Revolution he would no longer have to recognize the king of England but he would still be governed by Whigs and Tories in London. *Somocismo* without Somoza is the way Sandinistas describe the programs of most of the parties to their right. All right then, Mr. Coordinator-that-is-and-President-to-be, what is your feeling about socialism? Is it inevitable in Nicaragua?

"We are provincial and small. Our capitalists aspire as much as our socialists. Before the revolution we had a very few rich people exploiting a large number of peasants. In the middle were the artisans and small shopkeepers. The few who exploited are gone. We welcome all others because we need them. Large industry never had much role here, but we want to attract outside investment and we are formulating a law that will safeguard the funds of foreign companies and countries. There will continue to be private business here; capitalism will continue. The main problem is that some businessmen resisted a fair distribution of our national resources and saw a threat to their interests when we insisted on collecting taxes. Somoza often let them off with bribes, no real taxes. The revolution has no problem with the private sector. We consider businessmen necessary and funda-mental to our hopes, but it must be a private sector with public responsibilities, a private sector answering to the expressed needs of the people.''

The state will make all the rules for business?

"No. The government cannot tell the private producers what to produce. But what we do have a real need for is full-capacity production in sugar, cotton and coffee. We will do what we can to stimulate growth and production in areas where we must have the commodity to export. One problem is that we now need to produce three times as much coffee, for example, to buy one tractor as we did five years ago. Farm prices have risen much more slowly than industrial prices, and we are basically a farming country. We continue to need our businessmen, anyone who can bring in foreign exchange from the world market. The business-men whom we do not have good relations with—and we have very good relations with many—are those who disagree with the revolution politically. They have mixed their producer role with their role as politicians. They condemn us politically, but they are still doing very well economically. Without the aggression from the United States, our private sector and our public sector would both be doing much better.''

It must be very different to be a revolutionary fighting for power and actually exercising it. What have you learned since coming to power in 1979?

"So much. We have changed many things from the way we thought they would be. Planning a government is much different from actually having to govern. Planning, in fact, is one of the things that changed. We learned we are much less a planned society than we thought we might be.

"Everything in our attitudes is different from when we were fighting Somoza. We were involved for so long either in clandestine operations or actually in prison or hiding. You never feel free. Now all of us have the new feeling of liberty, a whole different style of living. I feel great pressure in my work now; before it was pressure from the enemy. You always know you can be killed at any moment. At the same time you are yearning to fulfill other tasks. Now the tasks are still there to be done. There are still so many children without shoes, children who have to quit school to work on farms; throughout our society no level is without its great challenges. And over all, we face the daily aggression from the United States. We have to defend what we've won. When the war pressure is finally relieved, we will go much faster in reconstruction. Then Nicaragua will truly be an example of development in Central America."

Everything wrong in Nicaragua, then, might be forever blamed on the United States. Among its American supporters, Nicaragua often seemed to be given a free ride past criticism, since whatever was missing from the revolution could be laid at the door of a policy that surrounded the Sandinistas with hostility. I asked if Ortega would acknowledge mistakes made by the Sandinistas themselves.

"We've made our errors. Shortly after the triumph of the revolution, we outlined an economic order that has had to be changed often. We predicted inaccurately. We have had to ask for more massive credits than we wanted to. We thought we could normalize Nicaragua much sooner, in the short term, but of course we didn't know there would be the war from the North Americans. We also made internal errors of management. There were mistakes on the Atlantic Coast, not only with Miskitos but with everyone there. Our censorship—aspects of that have been mistakes. The relationship with the church has been too confrontational at times. We are making the effort now for more dialogue between us. We never had any religious problem with the church, none at all. It has only been a political problem. The church has opposed us on political issues, and we have opposed it on political issues, never on religious issues."

What was a political issue for Daniel Ortega and the committed Sandinistas could be a moral or even theological one for other Nicaraguans. As seen by both the government and its opponents, simple survival was at the heart of most arguments. Resistance to the draft, for instance, was regarded as close to treason by a government fighting for its life and the continued existence of its revolution against foreign domination. But to certain of the priests counseling young Nicaraguans, draft resistance was obedience to the Fifth Commandment against killing, a moral imperative in a pacifist philosophy, and above all the surest way to stay alive during a war. Both sides wanted to survive, each believed it was obeying the same religion, and each found a different path to survival.

In a country inspired by revolution and assailed by doubts as to the revolution's direction, Christ was where you found him. "The message of Christ is peace and reconciliation with your enemies," a conservative priest told me. "Where is *sandinismo*'s other cheek?" A leader of one of the Christian base communities, also a priest, asserted an opposing value. "Christ's option for the poor and the revolution's goals are the same," he said, as if debating the conservative priest even though they had never met and were a generation as well as a hundred miles apart. "The only way to sustain this revolution is to defend it." As it was in its own earliest days, Christianity has become controversial again in revolutionary Nicaragua. In the avowedly Marxist countries, atheism is promoted above any religious belief and churches are tolerated, if at all, with suspicion. In Nicaragua, each side claims God's favor. Like other Sandinistas, Daniel Ortega was promising that if the church would stay out of what he considered politics, the politicians would be happy to stay out of religion and have the church continue to thrive in Nicaragua. The dispute was not only between church and state but among Christians themselves as to where Caesar's realm ended and God's began.

Turning to foreign policy, I asked how Ortega thought a small country and a big country should get along in an area of the world traditionally under the hegemony of the big country.

"Now this is the question we ask ourselves. Isn't Nicaragua entitled to respect and to rights that other nations have? All we want in our relationship with the United States is mutual respect. We believe we are entitled to that after all these years. Of course, we would like also to have cooperation, we would like to have a new economic relationship, but those are extra: first, just respect. This means respect for our territorial integrity, respect for our right to self-determination, respect for our right to form our own friendships. The United States has strong economic relationships with, for example, the USSR and with China. Why should you object if we too form economic relationships with those countries?

"Since we have at last gained our independence, it is natural for us to have a relationship with those who befriend us. But there is the naturalness of geography, too. Geography tells us the United States is our biggest and most powerful neighbor. You think we don't want friendship with such a neighbor?

"But what does the United States want? We recognize the legitimate security concerns of Washington, and we have offered many times to satisfy those concerns. We will never become a base for an enemy of the United States. We want to survive as an independent nation in this hemisphere. Washington seems to want us to die before negotiating peace. The policy of the United States has become incomprehensible."

Carlos Fuentes, the novelist who observes both Central America and the United States indulgently from his midway position in Mexico, has said that American acceptance of the Mexican revolution was not granted until Mexico was strong enough to prevent the United States from crushing it. I asked Daniel Ortega if he thought this was a period in which Nicaragua had to prove itself to the United States before we would acknowledge its independence.

"No, the current policy is just incomprehensible, as I said. Most Latin Americans are simply resentful of the imperialist attitudes of the United States toward Nicaragua. If the United

States had worried once, only one time, about democracy during all its invasions of Central America and of Nicaragua in particular, if the United States had used the postulates of Jefferson on democracy and applied them here, there would never have been the need for a violent revolution in Nicaragua, nor in El Salvador, nor Guatemala nor anywhere else. But instead, every time you come you install a dictator who hates the people and who sets up a government that is the very opposite of your own democracy and all you say you represent.

"After your own War of Independence, the model of a federal democracy based on ideals of freedom as embraced in the struggles of Washington and Jefferson became the model also for the independence struggles in Latin America. But the dream died. The Monroe Doctrine was announced, then treaties and loans were imposed on us. We were given virtually the status of protectorates, all in the name of American national security, all long before the existence of a Marxist state anywhere in the world. We were invaded again and again; no leader could spring up among us who refused to take orders from the United States or he would not remain our leader. Communism was not your enemy. Our independence was your enemy."

He would claim, of course, and had on numerous occasions, that Nicaragua's independence did not mean dependence on the Soviet bloc, that Nicaragua was merely a desperate nation finding help where it could. Then I might say there were worse things on the globe than U.S. hegemony and if he was going to become a tool of Soviet policy he'd start finding out what they were. Then he'd say Nicaragua will *never* be anyone's tool, and we'd have gone nowhere. So I skipped independence and went instead back to freedom. Freedom in Nicaragua, if that was what the revolution had brought, felt radically different from freedom in the United States. What was Daniel Ortega's concept of freedom?

"I always think of freedom in the plural. Freedom is for the people here, not for the individual. Freedom has an integral character linking the individual to the group. It is not simply what the individual feels, it is the action of the individual within society which organizes the rights of each to the benefit of all. Society limits, of course, those aspects of individual freedom that go against the common effort in all phases of life—spiritual, moral and material."

Did I understand that correctly? (The fact is, I couldn't believe my ears. He was, I thought, not defining freedom but unfreedom, at least where an individual is concerned. The individual was the whole point; freedom existed for me principally as a right granted to the individual to protect him from the group.) You believe in freedom that exists only for the group, not for the individual?

"There is room for the rights of the individual, too, but in the revolution we consider the rights of the people first. In a situation of economic and social injustice such as we had in Nicaragua, it meant a complete lack of liberty for those affected by the many injustices. Those perpetuating the social and economic injustice felt themselves to be free. Everyone else was trapped by the injustices of poverty, exclusion, disease, unemployment. The revolution comes and redefines freedom to correspond to the new interests of society, which are justice, equality and opportunity for all who have been denied these rights in the past."

We had arrived now at Daniel Ortega's idea for the revolution he was administering. It was easy enough, I said, to understand the need for restructuring a society that benefited only a few. But when you institutionalize what you call freedom for the people at large, aren't you excluding the possibility of freedom for the individual? Freedom as I think of it does not exist in a group but only in the possibilities open—or not open—to an individual. What you call freedom for the people I believe most Jeffersonians would call the tyranny of the state.

"Your freedom, sir, is a monster." He had actually said it. Our one national icon was, for him, grotesque. He became even more intense than usual, perhaps because he meant what he said even more than usual. He did not pause for emphasis but raced on for emphasis, faster than ever. "A monster, that is what your freedom is to us. The result of the kind of economic freedom that existed under Somoza was exploitation. What the United States called stability was, to us, repression. What the United States called freedom was, to us, oppression. You have a truly monstrous mechanism in the United States, and when it was exported here it satisfied a few individuals at the expense of all other individuals. The mechanism was so monstrous and powerful and loud that when the masses cried out against it the machinery drowned their cries.

"This mechanism still exists. It will be used against us in any invasion, and it is being used at home to try to convince the American public of the need to invade Nicaragua. So far the public has not been convinced, but the Administration proceeds anyway with its plans to overthrow us. Don't these actions go against the rights of the people of the United States as well as against Nicaraguans? And when American boys start getting killed here, will your government simply lie to the American people about protecting American lives and interests, thus controlling public opinion through emotional blackmail? And will you then call this freedom and democracy?"

Ortega was mixing economics with politics, laissez-faire capitalism of the Somoza era with a U.S. government public-relations campaign of the 1980s aimed at convincing Americans that justice was on the side of the counterrevolution. In Nicaragua, where open intellectual forums and workers' collective bargaining rights have both been traditionally suppressed, freedom to speak and freedom to exploit ignorance for one's own profit are perceived as very close. I told Ortega that the issues of intervention and national interest were noisily debated in the United States. When they feel the government exceeds its mandate, many Americans become agitated and vocal. I asked why that same freedom of expression did not exist in the new Nicaragua.

"We have very noisy debates here, too, and you have heard them. The opponents of the FSLN on both the left and the right are highly vocal. And their complaints are printed in the papers, especially *La Prensa*. Because of the national emergency, and only because of it, we feel we must have an official censor. Our country and our revolution are under attack. We do not wish to help the enemy penetrate our lines; we want to give him no information that can be helpful to him. We don't want him to know about our crops any more than about our troop movements. Those things which demoralize us could help defeat us. Some—and only some—of the material which openly supports the contras is censored. Some things are censored that are silly. How much freedom of the press did the fascist propagandists enjoy in the United States during World War II? Wasn't it thought unpatriotic just to print material that might encourage the enemy? I don't like censorship, and I hope it will end soon. Freedom to speak and write is crucial to the revolution."

The question of freedom is wild in Nicaragua, like a child's wind-up toy whose adjustments are off-balance. You turn the key in its back and release it, but you never know where it will go. In Nicaragua it flies all over the room, all over the country. If the question is out of control, what can the answer be? If you are an American in Nicaragua, the question of freedom—for whom, to do what—becomes a boomerang. What we call free enterprise, which made America prosperous, tossed up a few millionaires and left everyone else impoverished in Nicaragua. Free elections —and there were always several choices on Nicaraguan ballots —led to dictators. (One of these, Nicaraguans never forget, had even been an American dictator—William Walker.) The elections had not really been free because of vote buying, cheating and ballot stuffing, but the winners had always been able to wave numbers at their critics. The other freedoms Americans prize had never had a place in Nicaraguan life anyway. Foremost among these is freedom of expression.

Freedom of expression is traditionally the freedom on which all the others stand. It is not an abstract but a practical matter. This freedom is either present or absent. (It is not quite an absolute—yelling fire when there is none and publishing military secrets during wartime are examples of expression most states forbid—but it is close.) If freedom of expression is absent, any attempts at freedom in economic, political, cultural or religious life will be severely restricted. Nicaragua had no strong history of respect for freedom of expression, nor had Marxists. When strict Marxists have come to power, they have often operated on an assumption that they alone possessed the truth about society, as if their theories were mathematical proofs or the chemical formula for sulfuric acid. It was unnecessary to debate the proportional relationships of sulfur, oxygen and hydrogen when these have been scientifically established. It was undesirable to permit untruths to circulate when the truth has already been revealed. What prospects had the Sandinistas, with their Marxist orientation and their Nicaraguan heritage, of instituting the freedom of expression Daniel Ortega said they favored? How was the United States helping?

Suppose a different kind of war from the World War II example used by Daniel Ortega. Suppose a war in which a country several dozen times larger than the United States but in the same hemisphere, a kind of metastasized Brazil, deploys its troops along our southern border while playing war games in northern Mexico. Its government supports hostile armies drawn from the most renegade and discontent elements in American life. These armies are encamped on both the Canadian and Mexican borders, from which they make frequent, deadly forays into Michigan, New York State, California and Texas.

Brazil warns us repeatedly that if our troops follow the rebels back into Canada or Mexico, it will regard us as having attacked an ally and will invade us. Our settlements along both borders are in danger. The citizens of, say, San Diego, El Paso, Detroit and Buffalo can never be sure at night that when they wake up in the morning, assuming they do, there will not be rebels in their backyards. Would we, under these circumstances, be mistaken to conclude that we were in a *de facto*—though undeclared—state of war with Brazil? Would we be able to leave in place all the civil liberties we are so proud of? Would the newspapers be free to print ads for the carnival in Rio, and columns extolling the virtues of Brazil and the American insurgents it pays, and would the television networks be free to include nightly reports on the heroism of these insurgents as they burn farms outside Buffalo, kidnap children in San Diego? Would our ministers, searching their souls for a moral way to confront the danger, be free to preach draft evasion from their pulpits? Would our government be likely to want to negotiate with the rebels, whose military leaders are not only in the pay of Brazil but were formerly supporters of the most brutal regime that has ever run our own country?

All this is what the United States asks Nicaragua to accept. At the same time, we insist that Nicaragua's censorship is totalitarian.

Freedom of expression, then, can be related to the independence of a nation. This independence itself can be a function of size—of *relative* size, size in relation to one's neighbors. The biggest guy on the block has more freedom than one of the littlest. It may not be the law according to the rights of man or the Declaration of Independence, but it is the law of the jungle, and the hemisphere. Curiously, the very freedoms Americans insist upon at home were those the United States had historically helped deny Nicaraguans. The United States, having pioneered in modern times in evolving a system of government intended to protect the weak from the strong, the poor from the rich and even the uneducated from the educated, was free to behave in international affairs as though only the strong, the rich and those educated to "buy American" were qualified to rule. Anyone who thought differently had to have as many missiles as the Soviet Union—or be under its direct system of protection—to be a credible adversary. Thinking the American way entails its own definition of freedom and slavery. The survival of many, the historian Walter LaFeber has observed, can be sacrificed to preserve freedom for a few. "Latin Americans bitterly observed," LaFeber wrote in *Inevitable Revolutions,* "that when the state moved its people for the sake of national policy (as in Cuba or Nicaragua), the United States condemned it as smacking of Communist tyranny. If, however, an oligarch forced hundreds of peasants off their land for the sake of his own profit, the United States accepted it as simply the way of the real world."

One cannot know the status of freedom in Nicaragua. It shifts from day to day, place to place, crisis to crisis. Joan Didion wrote of El Salvador, "Terror is the given of the place." In Nicaragua the given is uncertainty. What course will the revolution take in six months? What will the United States do? How will the contras react? Each question was doing a majestic float through a whole constellation of uncertainty, tailed by freedom's comet, no less uncertain.

Freedom in the revolution was at times as loose as anarchy; at other times a government line was as tight as an edict from the medieval church. When he considered freedom, Daniel Ortega seemed less totalitarian and Communist than Catholic and Spanish. He was not setting up a state whose function was to extract obedience from its subjects, as in the Leninist monarchies. He was new enough in his job, and idealistic enough, to be using the state as an instrument to achieve social goals set by the foremost revolutionaries, like bishops deciding between orthodoxy and heresy. When the orthodox ideals had been decided, the expression of an individual's free will had a correspondence to that in the days of exalted canonical power.

In the ecclesiastical debate over free will, those who supported its existence (as against the position that all acts were divinely predetermined) maintained that God had granted human beings free will to be able to choose to serve him in a variety of ways. They were free, as well, to choose not to serve him and to do evil, but only once. As soon as they exercised the will to do evil, they could be punished, or banished, as God had cast out Satan from Heaven. In that sense, one is free to act against the social goals of the state only until one has done so. But the revolutionaries of Nicaragua could be counted on to change their minds far more often than medieval bishops had. The Sandinistas had a saying: "We try something this week; if it works, next week it becomes policy; if it doesn't, next week we try something else." The margin for freedom, for experiment, was therefore far greater than it had ever been when all ideological roads led either to Rome or to the see of the cardinal in Madrid. The Sandinistas wanted the church to emphasize Christ's option for the poor. They wanted to decentralize the religious hierarchy as well. But all the talk about change, all their actions on behalf of what they called the *clases populares,* could not obscure the Sandinistas' fundamental debt to the traditional church when it came to thinking about freedom.

"We are Christians, finally, on the concept of freedom," Daniel Ortega said in the way of someone who had discovered, through talking about a subject, exactly what he means. "Christians before we are anything else. From the French Revolution we have learned much about the rights of man, much also from Jefferson, as we have learned from the United States to dream of our national independence. And then Sandino. It means so much to us to call ourselves Sandinistas. He was not only a man who resisted the United States, he was not only anti-imperialist. He also tried to improve the conditions for workers in the fields and the cities. He stood for true liberty. Sandino was assassinated before he could fulfill his dream, but his dream lives. We have educated ourselves in Marxist thought to give a certain guidance to the social and economic policies of the revolution. We do not isolate Marx from universal thought; our Marx is not applied mechanically or automatically to the problems of Nicaragua. We move forward with universal ideals of progress and justice.

"But our idea of freedom itself comes to us directly in a deeply Christian sense, deeply Catholic. The fact is that in the United States you began with the individual and worked out toward the people as a whole. This was also the Protestant way to salvation. Everything the government did not absolutely need you saved for the individual. That left you uncontrolled by the government, which was desirable as an ideal, but it also gave a few people the opportunity to become more powerful, hugely more powerful, than anyone else.

"In our case we start from the people as a whole, as a group, the way Christ considered humanity as a flock. His crucifixion was for the salvation of the whole flock, not just the strong ones. In our revolution we, too, begin with the idea, the need, to serve the multitude, and the multitude in Nicaragua has historically been extremely poor, ignorant and subject to early death. We serve the people as a whole and we work toward the individual himself from the multitude. We want the rights of the individual to flow from the needs of the people. You proceed outward from the individual to the group, we work inward from the group toward the individual. We think in this way our many individuals can learn to act with humanity in solidarity with what is good for

XXI   THE BORDER—II

"VIVA SOMOZA" WAS TOO SHINY TO BE OLD. It was not the kind of joke Sandinistas made. The farmers who lived in these mountains outside Estelí would not be likely to have a can of iridescent spray paint nor to put it to use in this manner on a rock alongside the main road to the border if they did have one. That left the contras. I asked Roberta Lichtman, a knowledgeable American journalist living in Nicaragua who had agreed to guide me in the north, whether the block lettering was likely to be recent. It could be two months ago or last night, she said. But the sign did not leave grave doubts as to the contras' political sympathies.

We had started from Managua before dawn. As the sun came up, we passed a hill where the revolution was underwriting both caffeine and nicotine, coffee and tobacco plants cohabiting in the parched, mottled soil. A family was traveling south. The wife carried a basket on her head and a large sack on her back. Two small children walked behind her, each carrying a double sack and bent low to the ground. Behind them the husband rode on a horse; he carried nothing but the tall sombrero on his head, and the horse had no saddlebags. "That doesn't mean they're not

263

committed to the Sandinistas,'' Roberta Lichtman said as she steered our rented Toyota around a curve away from the family. "They may be prorevolution but completely steeped in the old ways of *machismo*. Or they may be contra sympathizers waiting for the day when feudalism returns to Nicaragua and the dominance of the old patriarchal church is restored.'' Either way, the Sandinistas had their hands full.

We stopped in Estelí for breakfast, less than thirty miles from Honduras but only halfway to the part of the border we were headed for. In the main square outside the cathedral, a sergeant stood almost at attention, following us with his eyes. Though he did not appear to be on duty and had a paperback tucked under his arm, he glared at us. Here was the only Nicaraguan I met who was visibly and markedly hostile to Americans. I thought at first he might be physically sick in our presence. Yet he wanted to talk. He would not give us his name but said proudly that he was a member of the Special Forces that hunted the contras in the mountains. Nodding toward the cathedral, he said Sandinistas had hidden in it. Somoza had responded by shelling it with U.S. mortars, bombing it from American planes.

"If the Guardia had ever seen you talking to a man they were suspicious of, like me,'' the sergeant said, "they would have disappeared you. Sssssst.'' He drew his index finger across his throat. "Like that. Before, I worked in a tile factory. Then came the fighting against Somoza and his supporters in the United States.'' He hissed the words "Estados Unidos.'' "After the triumph, I can never go back to the tiles. The army sent me to train in Cuba. The trainers were Russians, who were very affectionate to us. They showed us how to detect the slightest noise in the mountains, how to determine without moving where that noise came from and what probably caused it. They were like your Rangers, or Indian scouts—fantastic, these Russians. If we were sick, we saw Russian doctors. I never knew such medicine existed.

"Look inside the church. Still destroyed. Then go into the neighborhood around the church—leveled by American planes for Somoza. We still don't have the money, or the men, or the materials to fix this neighborhood. Look around, and remember who is responsible.'' The sergeant prepared to leave and changed to an at-ease position, which required him to remove the paperback from under his arm. He softened only a little, less with conviction, I thought, than in observance of leave-taking formalities. "Perhaps your government is one thing, your people another. *No sé.* I don't know." He got into his jeep and drove off fast.

The book the sergeant carried was *La Hija del Capitán, por* Alejandro Pushkin. The novel followed the true story of an illiterate Cossack who led an eighteenth-century peasant revolt, briefly impersonated the dead czar, Peter III, and tried to abolish serfdom. Pugachev, the Cossack, won notable victories with his peasant corps before being defeated by the combined armies of Peter III's usurper and widow, Catherine the Great. Betrayed by another Cossack when he tried to escape, Pugachev was taken to Moscow and beheaded. The Special Forces sergeant's fondness for a story about a Russian peasant uprising could be assumed.

Inside the Cathedral of Estelí, an obliging sexton showed us a pew where six Guardia had died. Their commander had previously given them orders to bombard the church, which they had done, almost killing the priest. After taking hostages into the church, the Guardia had held out for several hours against a rebel counterattack. Finally, one of the Sandinistas had rushed into the church and thrown a gasoline bomb. The six Guardia had apparently been incinerated on the literal spot. The sexton pointed cheerfully to the floor in the pew, where ghost outlines of several bodies could be seen. "Look how the tile is charred still. Here was a torso, over there an arm, and another arm, a leg. This head and this head and this one. All burned stiff, crisp. I carried them out myself, in bundles, like sacks of charcoal. See the outstretched arm and spread hand here. Why don't you have a camera?" If only peace could be declared, the sexton obviously felt he was in possession of a Satanic version of the Shroud of Turin. Oh, it was no Momotombo or Tipitapa—the principal Nicaraguan volcano and a resort on Lake Managua—but the sexton could easily have judged that the Guardia fossils in his custody ranked somewhere between a stalactite cave and the Monimbo Indian market as a potential magnet for the peacetime tourist dollar.

Sandino's guitarist wandered into the church, an eighty-year-old arthritic musician named Pedro Francisco. Not only his age but his military bearing and height—over six feet—were reminiscent of Stanley Atha, the last Marine in Nicaragua. Pedro Francisco had spent many hours entertaining his commander, several years running from Stanley Atha and his cohorts. Most of Pedro Francisco's teeth were gone. His mouth had not caved in, his jaw still declared itself, and his eyes had their light. He wore a battered sombrero, his worsted suit was tattered, but all three buttons were buttoned and he wore a neatly knotted if frayed tie. Pedro Francisco had never gotten over being trapped once, in Jalapa, by the Marines. "My two brothers were killed; I expected to die. By God's grace Sandino got us out of there to the Río Murra and back to El Chipote. He had me play Mexican songs all night. Later I grew coffee until Somoza took my farm for his friends. I moved to Estelí and worked in a lumberyard. I was too old to fight during the insurrection, but twice I warned the FSLN here when the Guardia were massing to attack." His bony fingers, his slender, attenuated body, his drawn face and high cheekbones, even his walking stick and thin tie all gave Pedro Francisco the elongated look of a figure slid down from an El Greco canvas. He hummed to himself as the sexton gently led him toward the altar for his devotions.

A sign two blocks from the cathedral stated that a hardware store had stood there and listed the names of thirty-four heroes and martyrs of the revolution who were killed by the Guardia, along with a doctor who evidently had his office above the hardware store. A large tree with yellow flowers, called *amarquita* in the neighborhood and resembling an acacia, grew next to the plaque. The tree had somehow survived the bombing, a young woman in an army uniform told Roberta Lichtman and me, and the new building would be constructed around it.

The young woman, introducing herself as Leida, took us another two blocks into an undestroyed *barrio*. The homes were old, built around a tiny plaza, all still standing. Along with her uniform and a pistol at her side, Leida wore blue eyeshadow, with a touch of mascara. When she smiled she showed a gold tooth. She was smiling when she pointed out the casing of a five-hundred-pound bomb that had fallen in the plaza and failed to explode. "We leave it here, a monument to *yanqui* know-how," she said. A young man rested against the base of the bomb, disobeying a cap he wore that said, in English, "Get Cracking." He had shrapnel in his arms and legs from a bomb that did go off. "This *barrio* was saved," Leida said, "because the FSLN was able to drive the plane away before it could circle back and drop another such *monumento*."

I recalled the film footage I had looked at showing the fighting in Estelí during the last months of Somoza. A lady standing in the rubble of her home covers her face and cries, shuffling away from the camera after the National Guard has finished bombing Estelí. "He's no good," a man says to the camera in English. "I'm talkin' about Somoza. We don't like him." The National Guard has temporarily recaptured the bombed neighborhood, in September 1978, and its commander orders his troops to clean up the bombed homes. A soldier mounts a John Deere bulldozer; two others start up tractors. The civilians are cursing at Somoza in English, and the soldiers either do not understand or are indifferent.

The footage shows the Estelí movie theater standing alone on one block, the only building intact. Two nuns walk in the center of the street, and a child pulls a hand cart that holds adult clothing on top of a large cooking pot and a baby on top of the clothing. A fat man wearing no shirt picks his way over bricks and pieces of roofing that have fallen onto what used to be his floor. His house is like a breakaway set in Hollywood, because no walls prevent the camera's view from the street into his kitchen. He lifts a bowl that appears unbroken and shatters it against the bricks. Another man passes the camera on a donkey, momentarily obscuring the fat man in his home. The house's front doorway frame is upright, though it is surrounded by no walls. "He calls himself our *padrón*," the fat man says, reaching his doorway and speaking English to the camera, which has been walked closer to him, "but the country don't recognize him. The army keeps him there, like his brother and his father. See what his planes and tanks do, look at my stove. He has five percent of the people with him. He buys them, and they steal and kill for him, they control the rest of us for him. The man is an abomination. He's a motherfucker. Forty-five years is long enough, no?"

"The National Guard will be obedient to me," Somoza says calmly in Managua at a news conference, "and we are pledged to keep Marxism out of Nicaragua." His eyes are weary and his jowls are slack. The dictator gives the impression of a player approaching endgame, continuing to move his pieces around the board as he watches them bleed, knowing the game is up but waiting until someone in Washington calls checkmate. "They say it's the rifle gonna make Somoza go. I say it's the rifle gonna make me go." He smiles dismally at his slip. "I mean stay."

As we walked through a partially rebuilt *barrio*, Leida explained that when she was not on duty in the army she managed a radio station in Estelí. Her husband worked in agrarian reform near Ocotal, and they saw each other only once a month. It wasn't ideal, but it was all they could manage during *la emergencia*. The emergency was invoked in Nicaragua in the same way, and with the same frequency, as "for the duration" was used to explain virtually every abnormality from product shortages to drinking problems to neurotic love affairs during World War II in the United States. Leida's toddler was entered in a child-care program in the manner of well-educated working mothers everywhere. This part of her life, at least, was parallel to that of her counterparts in the developed world.

Leida straightened her uniform when we approached the Sandinista headquarters. The day before, her unit had supervised the release of thirty-two contra prisoners. They were being sent home for Christmas in line with the limited amnesty for all insurgents except the leaders. "Most of them were only collaborators," Leida said. "They took messages back and forth, or they gave food and shelter to the contra soldiers. The ones I talked to could not even read the messages they were given. The literacy campaign and other programs of the revolution had never gotten to them. I think we began to reach them while they were held prisoner. They are nothing like the contra leaders, the former Guardia, whom we will never permit back. The government does not lead the Nicaraguan people on this. The government follows us. In the French treatment of Vichy leaders after the Second World War, was power-sharing ever considered for one moment? That's what we're talking about here." She hurried into the army post to get out of uniform and over to her job at the radio station.

An hour northeast of Estelí, Roberta bumped us to a stop at a military roadblock. The sergeant in charge apologized for stopping us, explaining that there were dangers. Why did we want to go beyond this spot? We were *periodistas* and here were our credentials from the press office in Managua. Where are you trying to go? His friendliness amounted almost to a plea. Well, Sergeant, we're heading up to the border to see what's going on around Ocotal and perhaps Jalapa. At the mention of Jalapa he wagged his finger and shook his head. The contras threatened the road running to Jalapa from Ocotal. Jalapa was secure, but don't try to get there after dusk. The road stayed almost exactly parallel to the Honduran border, always a few kilometers south. Be careful. He waved us on.

We headed east from the Pan American Highway on the small road that went to Ocotal. Stanley Atha had chased Sandino in this area, the province of Nueva Segovia. On one side of the road a field of sugar cane climbed a hill, and on the other, several acres of tobacco incubated under its netting. A man in a black sombrero rode a donkey and pulled a reluctant mule behind him by a rope. Tomás Borge came on the radio in an FSLN commercial, saying that education was the best way to defend the revolution. He was followed by Daniel Ortega inviting all those who had left the country to come back; radio stations in the north carried well into Honduras. "You are Nicaraguans," Daniel Ortega said, "and Nicaragua needs you." The next song was a ballad that began, "Don't lie to me if you love me, *por favor*." At the edge of a cornfield a billboard carried the declaration: "All Segovia Unites Against the Yankee Invasion."

Jouncing toward Ocotal, we crossed the Río Coco. The contras had blown up the bridge twice in attempts to take the town that had been held by the Marines against Sandino in the 1920s. If the contras were able to take Ocotal, as they had tried hard to do in at least three offensives, they would establish a "capital" and call for international recognition. A town of Ocotal's size—with a population estimated at between 35,000 and 45,000—would give credibility and visibility to the insurgents' struggle.

Ocotal was baked and bustling. It is a pretty town in the sense that the adobe houses are painted different colors and the local dress has room for variety. But the military were everywhere, in cafés and patrolling streets. A glance at the Honduran mountains to the north was a reminder of how near the contras were. A sign of Sandinista popularity was the large number of civilians armed in Ocotal. A hostile or wavering population would be under the gun, not carrying it. But Ocotal also gave the sense of lull, of an interval between the acts of its drama. It was Saturday, a market day, and Ocotal was enjoying the fact that it was not where the current action was.

Sandino's silhouette was stenciled on lampposts, homes, restaurants and stores all over Ocotal. Yet Sandino himself had been virtually blown out of the town in 1927. He attacked the Marines and their National Guard trainees, who had barricaded themselves in Ocotal's city hall. For once, Sandino outnumbered his enemies; he had two hundred troops against thirty-nine Marines and forty-eight National Guardsmen. Sandino also had the help of numerous local citizens who disliked having the Marines around. All morning on July 16, 1927, Sandino besieged the Marine-Guardia force in the city hall. The Marines had superior firepower but they were surrounded and could not hold out indefinitely, which Sandino was prepared to do. It would be an immense victory for him if he could kill or capture several dozen Marines in one stroke, and a humiliating defeat for the United States. To those in Ocotal, the siege looked successful.

That was the morning. In the early afternoon, five De Havilland biplanes soared out of the mountains and dropped down on Ocotal. In what is believed to be the first dive-bomb attack in history, Sandino's forces were pounded with bombs and strafed with machine-gun fire. They ran, but in a few minutes they were massacred. Several accounts put Sandino's losses at one hundred dead. The Marines had one dead and one wounded; the National Guard had no dead and three wounded. Sandino changed tactics. Defeated by airpower, he did not strike in such force again. After Ocotal he split up his command into small, fast patrols that made hit-and-run attacks wherever they could find and isolate Marines and Guardia concentrations.

The contras of the 1980s have several advantages over the Marines of the 1920s. They have better air support than the five De Havillands, though the De Havillands got the job done. They have excellent radio communications, the lack of which was a key complaint of Stanley Atha's. Their firepower is, of course, superior. They also have a recent example that shines before them. "The contras have one major advantage," an FSLN soldier told the journalist Pete Hamill. "History. They know how we did it."

They do, and they do not. Around Ocotal, for instance, they have destroyed grain silos, trucks, a lumber mill, a coffee-processing shed, an electrical generating plant, an oil pipeline, several bridges and farming co-ops. Most families, as I heard everywhere in the border region, had stories of kidnap, rape, torture. Marxists themselves are hardly innocents in revolution; Peruvian insurgents have engaged in widespread terror, while the Salvadoran guerrillas have committed many kidnappings and occasional acts of terrorism. But this is not the way the Sandinistas won Nicaragua. As the party in power, the Sandinistas have been charged with individual acts of suppression, to some of which they have admitted, ascribing these violations to a United States policy that isolates them and puts them on the defensive. Suppression and terror are not, however, the means they used to gain power. Working patiently, the Sandinistas used urban discontent combined with rural poverty and oppression to gain the sympathies, by 1979, of virtually every anti-Somoza element in the country. The contras build their base from fear, not sympathy. "Why are you doing this to us?" an Ocotal farmer asked

Pete Hamill. "I never learned to read. Now my children are learning to read, and the Yankees send the contras to burn down the school. *Por qué? Por qué?*"

The day I was in Ocotal, the contras attacked and destroyed a farming cooperative not far away. The co-op, known as El Coco for its closeness to the Río Coco—one of Nicaragua's longest and most important rivers—had recently sent twenty men into the Sandinista militia and had a drastically reduced defense force. Some of the members of El Coco had relatives in the contras, who knew the co-op was underdefended. One of El Coco's leaders, Wenceslao Peralta, was the older brother of a contra named Crescensio, who had vowed to the Peralta cousins he would either destroy Communism or die. At dawn, the contra force surrounded El Coco and began firing. El Coco's defenders later told Jeff Nesmith of the Cox News Service that they jumped quickly into their foxholes and returned fire at their attackers. "We are going to kill you, hole by hole," the contras yelled to the families trying to protect the co-op. "We are going to eat you alive."

Aciscla Mattei Polanco, a sixty-nine-year-old grandmother, remained in her cabin protecting her three grandchildren, one of whom was a fifteen-day-old baby, while her husband and two sons fought outside. At the beginning of the attack, the baby cried. Señora Polanco tried to keep the baby quiet, because the contras fired in the direction of the crying. Petronila, Señora Polanco's twelve-year-old granddaughter, was hit in the head by a bullet and died quickly. Shortly after, a shell exploded inside Señora Polanco's home and a fragment hit her eight-year-old granddaughter, Francisca, in the upper body. Another fragment broke Señora Polanco's right arm. Francisca told her grandmother she had a pain deep inside. Señora Polanco told her not to cry so the contras would not know there was anyone inside the cabin. Francisca obeyed her grandmother and lay quietly at her side. After a while, Señora Polanco realized that Francisca had died.

The baby still cried, so Señora Polanco picked it up and carried it outside in her good arm. The contras, Señora Polanco told Jeff

Nesmith, laughed at her and called her names, but they did allow her to leave with the baby. In fact, they said they would kill her if she did not leave. When they had wiped out or driven off El Coco's defenders, the contras raped two women and a sixteen-year-old girl, then shaved their heads and cut their throats. The men captured by the contras were executed. Between sunup and noon, Señora Polanco lost her husband, two sons and two grandchildren.

The Peralta family survived. "We will return to El Coco, we are the children of Sandino," Wenceslao Peralta said. He did not seem so sure whose child his brother, Crescensio, was. "I would not kill my brother on purpose, but I don't know who is on the other side in a battle. If I am fighting and he is with them, whatever happens, happens." Crescensio's sentiments, as expressed to relatives he visited later during a contra foray near El Coco, were similar. Like the Chamorros at the other end of the social scale, the Peralta family contained Nicaragua's divisions within itself.

Graffiti in Ocotal unintentionally linked Sandino with a philosopher he probably never heard of. The point, emblazoned in spray paint, is that made by survivors of the Holocaust. "The Past Will Never Return," the signs proclaimed in several places, presumably to emphasize that it has been learned—as George Santayana advised—and therefore will not have to be repeated.

We were warned at a gas station to fill up and hurry up. Most gas stations would be closed on Sunday, the attendant said, adding that the road to Jalapa was unsafe as soon as the sun fell below the peak of the highest mountain. Jalapa was only about twenty-five miles away, but most of the road was unpaved, bumpy and filled with hairpin turns. It was three o'clock Saturday afternoon.

We started right away. I had worried that going to the border a second time might turn out to be like seeing a suspense movie with the suspense removed. The first time through, you were caught and held by the turns of plot, but the second time you were mostly aware of being manipulated. The music, script, acting and decor all became self-conscious. Here was where they hooked your interest in the fragile little revolution you didn't want to see hurt. Here was the villain barging across the border. What would happen when the little revolution got too close to the border for her own comfort and safety? Bang, bang, some people are dead; bang, bang, bang, it really gets hairy. Boom, the sky is ripped by planes, just as in the 1920s. Everyone hides. But hey, here they come, defenders of the faith, the rescuers. They're grim, they're determined, they're tough, they're humorless, they give lectures, they believe their own rhetoric, they're—the Sandinistas.

We were not, however, manipulated into picking up Rodolfo Octavio Morales Gallardo on the road out of Ocotal. He was a twenty-eight-year-old off-duty cop, hitchhiking home to spend Saturday night with his school buddies and go to church in the morning with his parents. He had been waiting two hours for someone to go toward Jalapa. He said it was almost too late to start.

Rodolfo Octavio thought it might be the last time he would get home before the invasion. He was more than prepared for post-revolutionary Nicaragua. It was not that he anticipated the time with pleasure, only that he knew exactly what he would be doing, the way a young American might plan a junior year abroad. "We will return to the mountains," he said, "where you will look for us. Here and there the patriots will die. But you won't stay here forever, and we will." He was not cheery, but he was far from solemn; he had simply had the future foretold by someone in whom he had utter confidence.

With the fighting at its present level in the mountains, Rodolfo Octavio would not marry. "For me the times are too uncertain," he said, tilting his head from side to side, leaving the impression that perhaps the times reflected a struggle of his own. "Another problem," he said, "is that my police work is sensitive. I have a girlfriend, and that's okay. But if I wanted to marry, someone would have to investigate my wife—her background, other members of her family, her own loyalty, everything. I don't want to do that to a woman."

Does that mean that around here everybody has at least one relative with the contras?

"Maybe. Or they just know someone. There are things that are *privado* that should remain *privado*."

Rodolfo Octavio liked roller coasters. He continually urged Roberta Lichtman to drive faster around the hairpins, helping her hit every boulder or pothole in the road. When I asked if this was necessary, he said our Toyota and our kidneys were not what was important; the important thing was to be in Jalapa before sundown. Ocotal was in a kind of bowl; climbing was the only way out of it. We might have been in the mountains of New Mexico in midsummer, except the road was dirt.

Half of Rodolfo Octavio's family were in Los Angeles. They had sent a plane ticket once, but his mother had used it instead of Rodolfo Octavio. She came back with two dresses and a radio.

Two nights before, Rodolfo Octavio said, the contras had taken part of the road through the mountains, but they had been chased off at dawn. He described this as if the FSLN were flushing rabbits out of a vegetable garden, perhaps by waving their arms and shouting. We passed over a bridge across a wide stream that ran through the village of San Fernando, which had an FSLN garrison because it was under frequent attack. Germans had settled here once, and some of the children in the plaza were blond.

The dirt road from Ocotal to Jalapa would provide the ultimate number of ambush opportunities for a director of Western movies. A hundred cliffs overlooking the winding road, five hundred overhanging rocks, fifty sharp corners where the extras could lurk, dozens of canyons for the Indians to ride out of, at least twenty-five gulches where the Dalton gang could wait. No place was available for the sheriff or cavalry to get a clear fix on things. If Newman and Redford had come to Nicaragua, *Butch Cassidy and the Sundance Kid* would be in its two millionth reel by now, its principals still untrapped.

By the time we climbed into Jalapa the sun had gone back of the mountains but the flat heat still sat all over. The town is in the foothills of the mountain range it was named for, Cordillera de Depilto y Jalapa. The one-story houses were mostly wood, some adobe, some brick. Everything was dusty with the dryness of bones. In a flash it changed. As if a scene had been rejected and a new backdrop rushed in, clouds floated overhead and dropped tanks onto Jalapa. The dust abruptly became spongy before winding up mud.

Before we let him off, Rodolfo Octavio told us lodgings were minimal—*"El hospedaje no es muy bueno, es deficiente."* This turned out to be a compliment Roberta Lichtman and I did not feel our eventual accommodations warranted. Jalapa had two decent inns with plank floors and simple cots, but the Witnesses for Peace—good for them, tough luck for the *yanqui periodistas* —had beaten us to town and taken all the rooms.

There were almost no cars in Jalapa. Boys switched their oxen toward the corral. Men and women carried small packages of food, walking with an intention belonging to country people whose steps are homeward. Jalapa was settling into itself at the end of a week. Windows and doors stayed open. In the warm rain a *bodega* kept its radio on full blast, sending "Walkin' in a Winter Wonderland," in English, as a twilight gift to its *barrio*.

Compared with Jalapa, Ocotal came in retrospect to seem overdone, too busy and anxious. Compared with Ocotal, Jalapa seemed a peaceful country village snuggled into a mountain. It was mercifully free of the Sandinista iconography, the stenciling and slogans, that were all over Ocotal. Jalapa would have been nothing more than a farm town if it had not been for the army garrison. Although it must have had a sharp impact on the local economy, the army post seemed to affect the atmosphere of Jalapa very little. Except for the radios and the very occasional television aerials, we might have wandered back several centuries into a rural hamlet that Cervantes or Oliver Goldsmith would sentimentalize in one line, satirize in the next.

But Jalapa only *looked* like a peaceful country village. "They took her away," a Jalapan told an interviewer from the Central American Historical Institute, remembering an attack by the contras. "She'd just given birth the month before. They gang-raped her. My son tried to resist them, so they killed him, pulled out his intestines and filled them with stones. Then they busted up his head and his legs and left his body, along with others, on the other side of the ravine. They cut my aunt's and uncle's throats and then cut out their intestines, too. They filled them with paper and dirt, and then they went and cut out their eyes. They also took one woman's seven-year-old daughter, raped her and then killed her."

At dusk on this Saturday Jalapa existed uneasily, the mountain's serenity juxtaposed with the war's inevitability.

Offering us Coca-Cola out his window, a young man said he would like us to stay with his family but since everyone was home from school there was no space even on the floor. At twenty, Omar Efraín González was a Jalapan who had been south to Estelí to study crop production and soil management. He was home on vacation, both for the Christmas holiday and to help harvest coffee. Because he seemed so self-reliant for twenty and because of a half-moon scar on his forehead, I asked Omar Efraín if he had been in the war.

"No, no, not yet, though I am ready as most of us are," he said. "It depends what the enemy's plans are." He was well aware, of course, that he was visiting with representatives of his enemy, yet he was friendlier, I felt, and considerably more familiar, than he would have been talking to a Russian. When I asked him about this, he turned out to have thought about the contradiction. "Well, we know the *norteamericanos*," he said. "We know you better than you know us. We can live with you. Can you live with us? The Russians, well, they are helping us. Perhaps we will get to know them better, but we don't know them very well right now."

Omar Efraín said many of his friends were harvesting on private coffee farms but he himself was helping at a cooperative. They had to be especially careful around Christmastime because the contras had a record of Christmas raids. "Last year the Barredas, a couple from Jalapa, were kidnapped and taken to Honduras, where they were tortured to death. The FSLN caught the officer in charge of the contra group when he sneaked back into Nicaragua. He called himself El Muerto—these are the names the National Guard always liked to give themselves. El Muerto is in prison now, because the revolution abolished the death penalty.'' (The story of the Barreda family was investigated and confirmed by human-rights organizations, including the Americas Watch Committee, which gave details of it in a later report on Nicaragua.) ''During a raid after Christmas they attacked sixty *campesinos* in a field, where they blew up a little girl with a grenade. My cousin told my father the contras kept shooting the dead and the wounded until their faces were masks of blood.''

Who likes the contras in Jalapa?

''You can't always know. I think it's people who don't like the changes. Some have money, but some are poor. They resent the FSLN. They resent everything. You hear always complaining from them.

''When the war is over I hope to be an agronomist and manage a farm co-op. If I am able I would like to travel, meet my cousins in New York. My aunt moved there before I was born. My brother has been to Mexico to study. He studied political science and he came back to join the army. He says the Mexicans aren't going to obey you any more than the Cubans. Everybody in Latin America wants freedom, you know.''

Would you say you're learning your opinions from school, from your family or from experience?

''I have very little education, mostly in agronomy. I have lived in my country twenty years, which maybe isn't such a long time to you but it's long enough for me to remember Somoza. My uncle had a small farm, only a few acres. When the big owner wanted it he pushed my uncle off. My uncle had no debt to him, nothing; the man with the bigger farm just came in and took what he wanted. The Guardia could take you off your bicycle or out of your car and just beat you for nothing, and rob you also. For nothing they would do this. We had tons of Guardia here in Jalapa. They'd hit you and disappear you as quickly as you can say it.

How did you get that scar on your forehead?

''High school students went on strike here in 1978, to express solidarity against Somoza. I was one of five helping to lead the demonstration. We had no weapons, we just marched a little. A lieutenant in the Guardia came to our house while my father was gone and dragged me away from my mother, who tried to protect me. He grabbed me and swung his pistol at my head, but I pulled away, so the pistol hit me on the forehead and left this scar. The lieutenant told my mother if I showed up dead, she could know he was responsible. We didn't have any more demonstrations after that, but I carried food to the *muchachos* in the mountains. This is the period President Reagan says we had freedom in Nicaragua.

Omar Efraín showed us a home where we could spend the night. The house had a few rooms for rent around what had once been a central courtyard but had become a refuse dump. Several chickens were pecking discontentedly at a pile of garbage that was choking some ferns. A single burst of gunfire, perhaps four shots from an automatic rifle, caused me to look at my watch. It was six o'clock and, being mid-December, almost completely dark. A skinny, smiling little girl who looked five and was probably seven showed Roberta Lichtman and me to two rooms. She collected what amounted to fifty cents from each of us for the rooms; the grossness of this overcharge was to become apparent. Roberta took the smaller room, which had no lock, insisting that since I had a pair of binoculars I would be better off in the larger one, which had a hook-and-eye lock on the inside.

It turned out to be sort of a trade-off. True, Roberta had no lock, but when the young girl showed me my room, she gave a little yelp: *"Araña!"* The word I did not know, the sight I knew well, though I had previously encountered it only in dreams. On one of the two cots lay a spider of a genus, class and wingspread that existed, I had always hoped, solely in fantasies and magicians' specialty shops. The spider was tan; it could almost have been lost against the cot's dirty brown blanket until it began to move. Its size was that of the outstretched hand of one of the taller centers in the National Basketball Association. With a touch of bravado, the little girl offered to take care of it. Could fifty cents mean that much to anybody? Oh no, I said, towering above her, let me. I raised a shaky two-week-old capitalist newspaper. *Araña,* oh sure, arachnid, spider, frequently poisonous, tricky bastards. Also the name of a fellow at the foreign ministry. I had to save the little girl, who was still somehow managing to show no fright. What a performer.

She smiled gamely at my newspaper, said don't bother and shooed the spider away with a hand that was much smaller than he. He? How did I know? Maybe it was the Empress of Tan Widows, a family I thought I remembered from the nightmare of Saturday-morning cartoons that also has Roboto and Skeletor in it. The spider didn't really go away. He only crawled—ambled? —to the bottom side of the bed. *"Oye,"* the little girl said to the spider affectionately, leaning down to look under the cot, "come on out, it's not your turn on the bed anymore." The spider stayed where it was, and the little girl chuckled as she left the room, still burying her feelings beneath her facade of good cheer. Once she got outside I heard her laugh loudly, at last giving way, no doubt, to her hysterical but understandable terror of the spider. I left the room, too. The spider could have my binoculars.

There was another burst of gunfire as Roberta and I went out to try to find something to eat. It seemed to come from the mountain but could have been an echo from somewhere in the town. No one paid any attention to it. The little girl's mother, our landlady, said we were brave to stay here. It was impossible to tell whether *aquí* meant here in her house or here in Jalapa, and whether she was referring to the gunfire or the accommodations, or whether she had heard the spider story from her treasonous daughter and was mocking me. I like to think I heard her reprimand her daughter for insolence as we left.

It was a pleasure to be outside. The gunfire seemed more remote than the spider, and it stopped anyway. A full moon rose over Jalapa, illuminating clusters of boys in clean shirts laughing as they hurried to their Saturday nights. Of course, it was also a contra Saturday night, and a contra full moon. Clouds were left over from the rain, and they masked the moon occasionally, converting the town's huts and houses into unfriendly shapes.

If you are a guerrilla in the mountains, I wondered, do you love or hate the moon? Conversely, if you're defending the town, do you want the obscurity of clouds or the clarity of the full moon? If you're a contra, you're a recognizable target if the moon is out, but at least it lights your way into town for a raid. Maybe you want the cover clouds provide. What would the PLO want, specialists in attacking border settlements? What would the Israelis want, the reigning counterspecialists? We asked a boy running along the dirt street, Which should we be pulling for tonight, the full moon or the clouds? Always a bright moon, he said, then we can see them coming.

But they're not coming tonight anyway, said a soldier in the Sandra Café, downstairs from the inn where most of the Witnesses for Peace were staying. They came twice already this week, the last time only two nights ago. It's a major effort, and they go back with nothing to show for it. They cut the road from here back to Ocotal an hour ago; that's enough for them tonight. Several of the Witnesses were in the café—Jean from Washington, D.C., Peter from Washington State, Dennis from New York and Joe from Philadelphia. Above the music, they shouted how glad they were to be at the border finally. The jukebox was playing too loud to hear the contras even if they were just rounding the corner.

Living in Managua, an American who had been there since 1981 had said to me, there is the danger of aggression, but in Jalapa they have to be ready every minute. The Sandra Café in Jalapa, then, was the other end of the line from the Intercontinental in Managua. But everyone was relaxing, having a noisy musical time.

An FSLN soldier, off-duty but in uniform, yelled at us above the jukebox. You're in the right place, he said. Jalapa is where the battle for Nicaragua is fought most fiercely now. Not the combat, or not only the combat, but the battle for the *campesinos*. At Purísima, the contras dropped *jabón* from planes, soap for all the people of Jalapa, in little Ziploc bags. Each bag also contained a picture of the Virgin Mary. We laughed at the little packages while we were using the soap, but some of the *campesinos* . . . *Yo no sé,* I don't know. Our own record is not spotless here, either in protecting them or in agrarian reform. Some of them are still waiting for land the revolution promised them right after the triumph.

It was a singles bar, the Sandra, as well as the only night spot in Jalapa. Young women danced with each other until the young men beat back their shyness, about half of them in uniform. The tortillas were steamy and good, the fried plantains crisp and juicy, but the rice was only fair, a bit pasty. The beans were too old, not just refried, Roberta said, but re-re-re-refried. The Sandra's dog knew perfectly well we did not like our meat and begged soulfully for it. A Witness for Peace said the leathery stuff was so counterrevolutionary we had better hope it was not the counterrevolutionaries themselves. We were on the point of giving it to the weeping dog when Roberta observed that the Sandra's proprietors might have other uses for their meat and would not applaud our disposing of it in this way just because we did not want it ourselves. We contented ourselves with the three-star plantains and tortillas. One Witness for Peace screwed up the courage to give his meat to the dog.

The Sandra's disco personality was in full throb by eight o'clock. Blue and orange flashing lights supplemented two purple lights that cast the unearthly pallor of a Billy Idol video over the dancers. The purple lights, however, did not flash or revolve and were there simply to repel mosquitos. Rodolfo Octavio, the Ocotal policeman we had given a ride to, showed up, dressed for Studio 54. The principal difference between the Sandra and its North American counterparts—except for the presence of mosquito lights and the absence of perceptible controlled substances —was simply that the Sandra got going so much earlier. By nine o'clock, the contras could have decimated the young *petite bourgeoisie* of Jalapa with a single mortar.

Down the street a Protestant evangelical meeting was taking place in the assembly hall of a school. Widely spaced gunshots were background noise to the service, but they did not require the minister to raise his voice. He combined born-again fundamentalism with liberation theology. Now and then he nodded at Marx. People who confessed to sin and believed in God's grace

The Border—II : 283

could receive absolution and await bodily resurrection. Redemption would come through Christ's suffering. The yearnings of the oppressed to be free would come through acceptance of the yoke to Christ, and the yoke was work, the work of building a just society. The fruits of work must belong to those who gather them.

Many of the worshipers had rifles, though very few were in uniform. A boy in a T-shirt, looking like the thirteen-year-old who had stopped me on the street my first day in Managua, had an AK-47 that was almost even with his head when he sat down. He leaned the Ahka against his folding chair while he learned about salvation. The Ahka kept slipping, so he kept propping it up. The boy was casual about the Ahka, as were the people around him; it could have been a broom he was going to sweep up with when the service ended.

After the minister finished his sermon, he asked all the children to come forward for a special blessing. The boy with the rifle watched other children his age going toward the minister. He made no move; he was a soldier now. It was clear, anyway, he could not go forward with his Ahka. It wouldn't stay propped up by itself, and he knew he was not supposed to lay it on the floor. So the Ahka's presence had finished his childhood. "Come now, children," the minister said, "we don't want to take all night. Each of us has his duty afterward." That did it; something did it. The boy decided he *was* still a kid, and he handed his rifle to an adult near him as he sidled out of his row. Full of purpose, he made his way forward to receive the children's blessing. He had found out there were times when it took more courage to be a boy than a man.

In no hurry to get back to our overpriced rooms, Roberta and I stopped by a CDS meeting that was drawing to a close. A Jalapa CDS concentrates on crisis preparation. How to give first aid to the wounded, how to put out a small fire (the fire brigade has to come for the big ones), the endless tasks of food supply, garbage disposal, maintaining minimal standards of hygiene while under attack. A short man, whom I recognized as having a room where

Roberta and I were staying, laughed at the mention of hygienic standards. Those could decline even before an attack, he might well be thinking. He winked at Roberta.

A woman asked if the FSLN thought there would be another eight-day siege of Jalapa like the one the previous year. It could come anytime, she was told, but the outer defenses were much better organized now. They hoped to stop the contras before they could penetrate to the town. The contras had been in the vicinity on Tuesday, again on Thursday, so they were sniffing around, no one could pretend they weren't. But the chain of defense—the army, the citizen militia, the CDS groups themselves—remained strong. The contras had better arms, a corporal said. The Jalapans had better organization and morale. That was because the revolution was for workers and peasants, who knew that the solidarity of the entire revolutionary project served . . .

I started to think, How bad could that spider be, anyway? The little girl had laughed at him, and maybe by now he had left the room to get some fresh air. I'd heard this song about the revolution being for the *campesinos* until I knew it by heart. How could they *always* want the same song? Did Jefferson go around boring Europeans with incessant sermons on individual rights? Was I a jaded Europhile yawning at the libertarian rubes? Nicaragua excited me, too—the suspense, the hopes, the caught moment of unlimited possibility exploding against the reticulate weight of walls collapsing in on the whole country. But I found revolutionary rhetoric as unsoothing as the rhetoric on the home front about contra freedom fighters. Perhaps the repetitions were necessary to Nicaraguans. Tension in Nicaragua was at such a pitch that they came to use rhetoric as muscle relaxant, Valium for frayed sensibilities and destroyed prospects.

Wait a minute, their rhetoric was over and the CDS people were asking *me* a question. Do we have poverty in the United States?

Do we! But be careful, practically any way I say this can lead to misunderstanding. Okay, yes indeed we do have poverty and it is not hard to find. In all the cities and many rural areas. But our poverty is often hidden, if a middle-class person is not actually looking for it. It is hidden not so much by the press or politicians as by the whole elaborate process of production and marketing and advertising and consumption. We make so much and we buy so much and we use so much that the poor, who are numerous, tend to be left out of the process and easily forgotten. Unless a social scientist or politician or journalist is focusing on poverty, either out of conviction or to make his reputation, we do not frequently have the poor in our consciousness. When the poor do get organized, we think about them and start programs to help them. Then we stop thinking about them again. Pretty soon the programs become more important than the poverty they were started to fight. The programs get criticized, cut back, and the cycle of poverty in America continues, with the poor still there.

It was *their* turn to have their attention wander. A farmer made a major statement that he still hated Cubans because some of them came to Jalapa to pick the tobacco crop in 1967. Since this was after Castro's revolution, well before the Sandinistas' success, I assumed the Cubans were exiles if Somoza brought them in. They apparently took jobs away from Nicaraguan workers. A woman asked me where I had gotten my watch. The corporal told the farmer that Cubans were now friends of Nicaragua. A boy said he had cousins in Los Angeles. This reminded me of the Nicaraguan I know whose mother was abandoned by his father shortly after the family moved to Los Angeles. She raised my friend and his sisters by herself. My friend was on heroin within a month of his discovery, at fourteen, that his mother's second job was not as a waitress but as a prostitute. *Hijo de la gran puta* —literally, "son of a big whore"—is not a phrase Spanish-speaking people level at each other casually. *Sandinismo* took my friend off drugs, where he has stayed, committed to the revolution and working for his government. The CDS meeting broke up, each of us in our separate cages.

Back at our lodgings, Roberta and I thought about sleep, she in the room that did not lock, I in the room that belonged to the spider. With so few civilian cars in Jalapa, the rumble of trucks in the night was very noticeable. It would fade, a roll of waves on a distant shore, then come closer until it was like thunder. The dogs and coyotes and birds of Jalapa would quiet down until a truck startled them into howl and screech. The night had cleared, and the clouds were too thin to cover the moon. There was no firing until a quarter to midnight, but it sounded as though it came from right outside the house. Four, perhaps five, shots. After a brief silence there was a bang right in the house itself. I heard the innkeeper laugh, so I went to see what had happened. The shots he didn't know about; maybe someone was drunk on a Saturday night, maybe it was a calling card from the contras. It wasn't much, listen, even the dogs aren't hollering. But the bang inside the house—that was what he had laughed at—was a chicken which had been scared by the gunfire and knocked over a pan in the kitchen. We heard a few shouts outside. I asked whether it would be a *miliciano* shooting off his rifle. The innkeeper said no, probably just a farmer. He added that there had, of course, been fighting around the town this week. He asked why I'd come. I couldn't remember.

Dogs were the radar of Jalapa. At twelve-thirty in the morning they went wild in the northern hills above the town. Occasional languid bursts of firing kept up through the night; a few times they were accompanied by louder detonations that might have carried more intent. A form of communications I could not decipher was being employed. Ahka chatter, mortar burp. It was like telephoning people you don't like in the middle of the night and hanging up as soon as they answer.

The dogs grew bored, letting many volleys of firing go without reply. They were a selective radar system for which casual pops were not worth registering. I whacked the cot the spider had *not* been on earlier, and, when nothing crawled, lay down. Gunfire was perhaps the wallpaper of everyone's life in Jalapa, and everyone apparently grew accustomed to it.

I wondered where the spider was and fell asleep.

Around one-thirty there was some staccato yammer in Spanish from Roberta's room, followed by a slammed door, followed by a knock on my door. It turned out our divison of hazards—she in the lockless room, I in the room with the NBA spider—had

been good for neither of us. The man who had winked at her at the CDS meeting was a traveling salesman in the room on the other side of hers. He was not only a traveling salesman but a traveling shoe salesman, and he had slipped into her room at one-thirty with some sample Wallabees. It was possible I had been hearing this story all my life, first as the kind of dirty joke nine-year-olds tell each other, later as a tale from Boccaccio, and finally as one of those quips that starts with, "What did the farmer's daughter say to the traveling salesman who brought shoes to her room in the middle of the night?" Oh well, it's only the old Wallabee routine, Roberta, it usually happens in the Sheraton lounge around ten P.M. So it starts later in Central America —why don't you just go back to sleep? Thanks for your heroism, said plucky Roberta, but he was drunk and anyway the Wallabees were not my size, by which time she was already stretched out, almost asleep, on the second, or spider, cot in my room. I felt a solemn duty to warn her about the spider. Bedfellows make strange wars, she mumbled, and was out.

With the traveling salesman's demoniac objective foiled and Roberta now offering the NBA spider a closer target—unless, don't even think it, he had switched cots during the ruckus—I hoped to get back to sleep. But there was at least one creature in Jalapa that did not buy the wallpaper theory of gunfire. The rooster in the next block subscribed to the antiquated notion that attacks begin at dawn. Throughout the night, every time so much as a single round was fired, Chanticleer assumed sunrise was just around the corner and it was time for him to go to work. Hey fella, I wanted to yell at him, didn't you hear about infrared scopes and other night sensing devices? How about giving a little credit to Yankee ingenuity? We can attack anytime we feel like it now, around the clock. So pipe down. But with every zing, blam, pop or whup, the cock crowed, gloating over his thorough knowledge of outmoded warcraft.

What the innkeeper referred to as calling cards were exchanged now and then all night. At five-thirty, dressed and more or less washed from my canteen, I stepped out onto the street to see how our car was. It was reassuring to find the Toyota unbothered and well rested. Americans and our cars, even if the cars are Japanese, can be counted on to comfort one another. A block away the fields started, and mists began to rise over the coffee beans the way steam would come off a hot cup of the finished product. In the purple light I looked down and picked up half a dozen fresh Ahka shells. So what? Only the rooster took them seriously. Something is happening but you don't know what it is, do you, Mr. Jones? asked Bob Dylan. Negative capability, replied John Keats, occurs when a man is capable of being in uncertainties, mysteries, doubts, without any irritable reaching after fact and reason. Some contra scout had marauded to within twenty feet of the house we were staying in, or else had not; some drunk had been taking potshots at a cat, or had not; someone had defended the honor of his wife or mistress, or protected himself against someone else who had, or any combination or none of the above.

Twenty-two Witnesses for Peace gathered in front of a church at six o'clock to wait for the bus that would take them to the fields. The image projected in the United States had been of the Witnesses for Peace getting themselves to some visible border and standing there. They would in effect dare each side to shoot at the other. When firing began, the Witnesses would witness it, bullets flying back and forth, occasionally dropping one of them in his morally superior tracks. In reality, the Witnesses were at the border to help with the harvest and hold peace vigils during off-hours. The vigils would occur in towns, in fields and occasionally at a border-crossing point itself. But the Witnesses were considered to be at the border the entire time they remained in the vicinity of Jalapa. The word "border" was as much a region of the mind by now as it was a line on the map. The Witnesses were at the border in the dictionary sense of being at the outer part or edge; the rim, brink, margin or verge: of themselves as well as Nicaragua. This was a secret to no one who was there.

Julie Knop, originally from Milwaukee, now living in a Christian ecumenical community in Georgia: "If you work for justice, you want to live it out, so I'm here. Back home I live with many conservatives. They know I'm here to conserve life. My parents voted for Reagan and they're scared I came here, but the last thing they told me was they're proud of me. I'm not scared, the gain is worth the risk."

Doug Milholland, a soft-spoken, blue-eyed carpenter from Port Townsend, Washington: "I'm a Quaker and a worker. What else would I be for but peace?"

Chris Moss, a computer analyst originally from England, now living in Philadelphia: "It's only an accident of history that Britain is not involved here. I feel moved by some sense of humanity and solidarity to join the best Americans I know."

Paul Gurwitz, a carpenter originally from Washington, D.C., later moving to Asheville, North Carolina: "We sit and talk about doing something. Coming to the border we're putting our bodies on the line and finding out if we really mean what we say."

Dennis Leder, a Jesuit priest from New York, and Joe Cassidy, a Philadelphia social worker, had been in the Sandra Café the evening before. Both said that coming to the border enabled them to serve simultaneously their social, ethical and religious principles.

"We're neutral as to support of the Sandinista government," said Betsy Moran, a staff member of Witnesses for Peace and coordinator for the delegation in Jalapa. She had spent six years in Central America, the first two in the Peace Corps in Honduras. "But we do support the Nicaraguan people in their struggle to survive against the contra attacks supported by the United States. We are for nonviolence, and right now the United States is being very violent against Nicaragua, which is not being violent against the United States. That's what it comes down to."

The Witness for Peace perhaps closest to his own border was Russell Christiansen, the gentle, red-bearded lawyer who had been at the American embassy demonstration in Managua. He had visited Nicaragua many times in the Somoza era, when he was frequently in Central America because his wife was Costa Rican. He was a former deputy director of CARE in both Honduras and Chile, and he had made several more visits to Nicaragua since the revolution. A graduate of Middlebury College and New York University Law School, he did substantial *pro bono* work representing indigents, and he had once run for the Maine legislature, losing by thirty-seven votes. In Jalapa, Russell Christiansen was an example of the effect the border had on nerve ends normally covered by the padding of civilization.

Russell Christiansen had come to Nicaragua this time, at the age of fifty-two, with his life almost literally in ashes. Just before he had left Maine, his office and home, which were in the same building in Bangor, had burned down. His personal and legal records, his notes on law cases, his clothes, his books, photographs of his children, heirlooms he had almost forgotten until he lost them, his curtains, his paintings, his address book—everything was gone. He had been offered, not long before that, the directorship of a group aimed at rebuilding friendship between Americans and Iranians, but at the last minute the funds for his position were withdrawn. Before that—several years before but strung together that morning in Jalapa in the same brief account —he had been painfully divorced from his wife, who now lived in Costa Rica with their two youngest children. The breakup had been complete, with Russell Christiansen becoming a stranger to the Costa Rican side of his family, stranger to a considerable portion of his own life. His two oldest children were in colleges in Texas and Florida, and he had had almost no contact with one of them since his divorce. When Russell Christiansen spoke of his children that morning near the border, his feelings simply overwhelmed him. "I can't think of the four of them without an aching heart," he said. "My son in Florida told me over the phone recently—after six years—that he accepted me again as his father. Next time, maybe we can tell each other we love each other." A plain enough statement, unadorned, and Russell Christiansen smiled when he made it, but his smile fought its way through sudden tears.

Having lost almost everything he once took for granted had clarified for Russell Christiansen the value of what remained to him. Though not unaware that his surname gave him a kind of allegorical stature among the Witnesses, he considered himself no Job and no mystic, the recipient of no specific divine favor or wrath. But he was ready to part with the most precious thing he had left. "As I told you in Managua, some of us have got to die," he said. "Americans started caring about Vietnam only when other Americans started getting killed. If that's what it will take here, that's what it will take. Misfortunes have not made me want to die; they've given me a greater appreciation of life. Thirty people in Bangor offered me places to stay when my home burned. That's more important than the loss, isn't it? But I wanted to come here because I believe in this revolution. I see this government serving the vast majority of the people, just as I saw the previous government exploiting the vast majority. So I'm willing to live in a danger zone and share the Nicaraguan experience. When I go, however I go, I hope others will take my place."

Russell Christiansen boarded the bus along with the rest of those keeping the peace vigil. When he got back to Maine he was going to start a legal clinic to help poor people. Until then, he was going to continue helping even poorer people.

Roberta Lichtman and I followed the bus that carried the Witnesses to the harvesting north of Jalapa. The dirt road led to Honduras, but the fields were all planted. Though we went only a few miles, I kept thinking we must be in Honduras. There being no bridge, Roberta nosed the Toyota through a stream widened and deepened by Saturday's rain. The bus plowed through perfectly. We stalled as soon as we got to the far side. Luckily, the bus stopped at the next field and unloaded. We forgot the car and hurried to catch up on foot.

Several farmers stood guard on the perimeter of the six acres of rice and corn the twenty-two Witnesses for Peace were going to harvest that Sunday morning along with an approximately equal number of Nicaraguans. The farm was private, but other farmers in the area had come to help in a cooperative harvest. Rafael Soza, one of the farmers standing guard with an Ahka, said this farm was much more exposed to the contras than his own. He grew beans and corn on the edge of Jalapa, and he had not been bothered much. Sometimes in fields like these—but more likely at farms farther off the road—the contras would come and have shoot-outs with the farmers. Though this week had been abnormally quiet, on four different days they had had to stop work on the nearby farms to defend themselves. Usually it was just a sniper. Sometimes they came in force and shot mortars into the middle of a rice paddy or cornfield, ruining part of a crop, scattering or killing workers.

Rafael Soza recognized a number of the contras in the area. "I know them all my life," he said. "Some are old *somocistas,* but not many. Some got mad when the Sandinistas wanted to make their farms cooperative. Some were coaxed into Honduras after the revolution. They didn't like it there, but when they came back the government had confiscated their land for redistribution because they stayed away too long and became collaborators. So then they collaborated more. Sometimes contras can talk the poorest people into going with them, since the poor think what the hell, it can't get worse. They find out." Rafael Soza was forty-nine, and he had eleven children, whose ages ranged from five months to twenty-six years. "And not one will ever become a fucking contra," he said.

"Pipe down," said another farmer on his way to start picking corn. The second farmer, unarmed, was not intimidated by Rafael Soza's Ahka. "No government is any good, but I didn't have to stand in food lines before. They let you alone then. Not me so much, but some people resent the shortages. This government doesn't bother me, neither did the other, so I feel about the same. Before, there was more freedom for business. You hear the business people complain. For me it's the same." He did not identify himself as Sandinista opposition, but he did not sound as if he would refuse a hungry contra an ear of corn.

In the distance we heard occasional firing, usually not in a burst, just a round or two. All small-arms fire, almost a domestic squabble. A woman stood guard over the rice cutters, her back to them, her Ahka pointed at the hills. A fifty-one-year-old farmer said he had been unable to harvest his own coffee last year a mile closer to town. He let his beans rot unpicked after the contras shot at him in the field. This year was safer, and he had been able to plant more of his land because for the first time in his life he had gotten a bank loan.

Pedro Pablo Rodríguez, owner of the farm whose crops were being picked today, was enthusiastic about the cooperative harvesting. "Before, two of us took a week to do what thirty of us now do in half a day," he said. "Look how quick it goes." The Nicaraguans picked corn and cut rice faster than the Americans, who were sweating more, talking less. A number of Nicaraguans had beckoned Americans into their rows in order to show them how to work more efficiently. "This is only on Sunday," Pedro Pablo Rodríguez said. "The other days of the week we each work our own land. Every Sunday during the harvest, we choose someone's farm and help him. Almost all of us have bank loans now. We produce more, we help each other, we do it faster. Don't even mention the old days. If I didn't have to face into the fire every day I'd have everything I need."

Listening to Pedro Pablo Rodríguez, a Witness stopped harvesting long enough to make a connection between the last American war and what she thought likely to become the next one.

"No, no, no, no it was not in vain, you tell yourself over and over again," said the American woman, who was not quite old enough to be grandmotherly. She put down the machete she had been using to cut rice and patted her brow as she presented a parcel of her life, like a gift, to anyone caring to listen. "Doug died for a purpose, that's what he did. He went over there to defend the country and its principles and especially its freedom, he went to do all that needed to be done. But it's 1968, it's Khe Sanh, and he gets killed. You lose a boy in a war, you don't want to believe it's a bad war, but you have a lot of time to think when your son is gone. A dreadful lot of time. You start to look at the war policies differently. After a while you see that no good, not one good thing, came out of that war, not for the Vietnamese, not for the Americans, and you learn about the lies you swallowed, and your son was made to swallow. You reflect. You love your country. You have a kid buried, and Doug never, oh, I mean *I* had a kid buried, *I* lost . . . " And here the woman paused, at her own border as much as the border between any two geopolitical entities, while she blew her nose and wiped her eyes.

The Gold Star mother was Mary Chatlos, a New Englander

who had moved to Los Angeles to live in a Catholic Worker community. Like the other Witnesses, she had come to Jalapa because she supported peace; once there, she found herself confronting her own past, which was not peaceful. She looked at the farmland that surrounded Jalapa, then up into the mountains that divided Nicaragua from Honduras. "I wonder if Doug didn't walk through rice fields like this on the other side of the earth," she said. "When I decided to come down, the Catholic Workers I live with wanted me to do it and yet didn't want me to, afraid for me and encouraging me at the same time. They like having a live-in grandmother. My own kids, they were scared to death. I had to take a trip all the way back to New England to reassure them. My son-in-law works for a computer company that helps make the Cruise Missile. We don't talk about that too much; we know where we both stand. So I came, and I came as a patriot. I'm here partly because I want Nicaragua to be left alone, but I'm here mostly because I love my own country. Here we are again, ready to go to war over a place when most of us don't even know where it is or what side we're on. If we invade, it will be years before we get out. I can't even imagine how many more Dougs there'll be."

If people sounded similar at the border, which was only an extension, after all, of the way they sounded all over Nicaragua, a country in crisis, it was because dancing on the barrel of a smoking cannon would be likely to produce similar sensations in all the dancers. Survival, determination, the love of existence and the faith it can be better; these collided with such immediate concerns as heat, thirst, the harvesting. A flickered wonder whether the car will start would quickly be replaced by the need to keep out of a machete-wielder's way. Where we stood, Honduras became the mountain just north of us; Nicaragua was squeezed into this valley the mountain squatted over. The world in a grain of sand. It was defensible terrain, but it would always be vulnerable to the heights.

Firing continued every few minutes, the border's Muzak, with an occasional mortar at greater intervals. While I was watching several Americans swing their unfamiliar machetes next to the defter Nicaraguans, I heard shots that came from an adjacent field in the direction of Jalapa. That could mean that Jalapa, the way back to the rest of the world, was out of reach.

Like all of Nicaragua, the border was contradictory. It was an unsentimental place, because survival there had nothing to do with moral virtue, only with quickness or luck. But the border also invited a sentimentality that produced the illusion of clear sight. Waiting to hear whether the road to Jalapa would be reported passable, I imagined the United States and Nicaragua reducing themselves to a house and its vicinity. Windows all over the house presented views Americans have of the world. In the front a great bay window gave onto all the continents and major countries. The rear of the house had many small windows, all facing Nicaragua. Nicaragua was out back, as we have always said; the yard was full of Nicaragua. But each window showed a different country. From the many windows could be seen equally many Nicaraguas.

Out one window Nicaragua looked like Cuba, a satellite of the Soviet Union. A second window showed Nicaragua in the shape of Mexico, vulnerable to collapse or a left turn, last domino before the Rio Grande. From the third window the Third World was in sight, Nicaragua holding the key to development in the underdeveloped countries. The fourth window featured the Free-World-versus-Communist-tyranny morality play, the East-West struggle in microcosm. The fifth window rebuked the fourth: The struggle was not East-West but North-South, the haves of the Northern Hemisphere defending their possessions against the have-nots of the Southern. Out the sixth window were—Jesus, here they come—all the refugees. Guatemalans, Salvadorans, Cubans; the Nicaraguans would make it an avalanche. Hispanics would be electing senators and governors, whole states would be Latinized, even the clocks wouldn't run on time. We have to do something.

From other windows Nicaragua could be seen as Vietnam, Chile, Afghanistan, as an example of class war, Christianity under siege, economic anarchy, revolutionary export. None of the windows showed Nicaragua as itself; with more light inside the house than outside, the windows essentially became mirrors. Like the mirrors perched at Sandino Airport, the spy mirrors for security, they reflected the observer rather than the country he was observing. Mirrors of intention and fear and self-esteem, none of them after a while showed as much about Nicaragua as about the United States. I recalled earlier American images, the national self as savior of Europe and Asia in 1945, then as fumbling giant knocked out by the Oriental underdog in 1975. I wondered what image of ourselves we would ultimately find in the Nicaraguan reflection of the 1980s. Which version of our destiny would we fulfill, which version affront? Perhaps it was only that in the end, every great nation gets the Nicaragua it deserves.

"This isn't much, nothing much at all, what we're hearing today," Russell Christiansen said. He flourished his machete at some weeds. "I've been on a coffee co-op even closer to the border where mines were going off at night around the farmhouse and during the day mortars were falling on both sides of the fields we worked in. All the *campesinos* were armed there, not just a few like these folks here. It gets a lot worse, you know, a lot more dangerous."

Thanks, I thought, and I really do mean thanks to all of you, but it also gets later, it gets too late to leave, and travelers, no matter how much they witness, are never quite Witnesses. Roberta Lichtman did not require strenuous persuasion.

There was not a flicker of life in our car. The water from the stream we crossed had drowned not only the spark plugs but the entire carburetor. A couple of the Americans took a break from rice cutting to try to help us. Chris Moss, the English Witness for Peace, applied his computer analysis to the situation and came up greasy. The same Japanese television crew that had filmed Tomás Borge's speech, diligently doing their own border scan, came by and tried jump cables. Nothing; our attempt at convening the United Nations did not start the car. A Sandinista army truck gave us a push, but all that came from the Toyota was a tired cough. We were talking about hitchhiking, a doleful project in a war zone, when a Jalapan farmer came by on a tractor and said he was also a mechanic. He removed our carburetor and drove off with it.

Home, at such a time, comes to be represented by the last place one felt relatively safe and comfortable. For me that was inside the car itself when it was running. If we got in the car, home would move off to Jalapa, a settlement with busy people and things to eat, not looking as though it would be wiped off the map easily. But once in Jalapa, home would recede to Ocotal, a larger town considerably more secure than Jalapa. At Ocotal home would withdraw to the Intercontinental in Managua, representing happiness to anyone stuck without a car in a field north of Jalapa. Only if we reached the Intercontinental safely would it be possible to be homesick again for real home.

The farmer was quick. After he brought back the carburetor and reinstalled it, he also drove the Toyota across the stream that had caused the trouble in the first place, taking it through the shallowest part of the bed. On the road back to Jalapa we picked up a soldier who had the rest of Sunday afternoon off and was going to have a good time in what was the big town for him. He had already begun the good time and was quite drunk. After we let him off he sat on the first street in Jalapa on a tree stump and laughed.

When we reached the other side of Jalapa, Rodolfo Octavio Morales Gallardo was waiting on the road to Ocotal, hitchhiking back now that his leave was over. He told us he had been waiting about an hour and was going to give it fifteen more minutes before quitting, which would mean loss of a day's pay in Ocotal. "I am surprised to see you," he said. "I thought you would have left earlier or decided to stay over. I opine you to get off this mountain before rain, fog, darkness and the contras make it inhospitable." When we mentioned we had given a ride to a drunken soldier, he was mad at us. "You don't give a ride to a soldier along this kind of road, no kind of soldier, especially not a drunk one, because he can't even try to protect you. If the contras stop your car along here and you have a soldier with you, it goes very hard with you. Like dead."

Okay, Rodolfo Octavio, you're a good cop.

On the road back, Rodolfo Octavio became, for him, quite emotional. He passed the time by punctuating the arroyos and sharp bends with the names of lost friends. "Here my school friend Sergio was taken and skinned alive, just on the other side of that stream Julio and Marta were kidnapped, there by the big rock the Benavides family, on their way to market, were ambushed, tortured, and vanished from the earth. One daughter escaped and told. Around this bluff they cut the throat of my girlfriend's first boyfriend, Tadeo. *A la frontera no pasarán,"* he said, using the FSLN's most repeated slogan, with some irony. At the frontier they shall not pass.

When we came to San Fernando there was still enough light so that Rodolfo Octavio objected only mildly when we said we wanted to see the town. The blond children in the plaza were descendants of World War II Germans whom Somoza I had allowed to settle on some of the land he owned in the area. An American living in Managua said there were "no known heavy hitters" among these Germans; they were minor-league Nazis who had decided a Latin American dictatorship would be more congenial after their defeat. Eventually they had moved on, and the blond kids were probably grandchildren.

The local Sandinista commander told us his garrison had been attacked in the night. San Fernando was known to have contra sympathizers among its citizens, which worried the Sandinistas enough to keep the garrison in a village that seemed too small to warrant one. The contras had come in some force, the commander said, bearing two mortars, eight grenade launchers and six M-60 machine guns along with their Chinese Ahkas. It had been more of a pursuit than a battle really, the contras running back up the mountains and leaving their weapons behind. The Sandinistas had captured these, along with several American knapsacks and a hammock one of them was swinging a child in. Others were reading and relaxing, enjoying the Sunday afternoon after the morale-boosting chase on Saturday night. Two of the men were cleaning the captured machine guns. "The contras lose all this, they don't care," the commander said. "They know your government will give them more."

Just outside Ocotal, a truck full of wounded Sandinistas passed us, barreling into town. The truck kicked up so much dust it became a grimy mirage of itself. Cattle came into the dust cloud and blocked us for a couple of minutes; they were dry ghosts by the time they crossed the road. We saw the truck again on a side street of Ocotal, with the last of its cargo being taken off the back by stretcher. In front of the small hospital two elderly men lay gently passed out in the dust with their own vomit for pillows. We made a small detour in the next block because men and women were dancing at a wedding while children played tag. An agile cowboy did tricks with his lariat. Rodolfo Octavio said goodbye.

It was dark long before we reached Managua. Coming down out of the mountains into the heavy tropical air, we could see faraway lights of a low-slung city, mostly one- or two-storied, like six or seven suburbs of Los Angeles all strung together. Anyone approaching Managua for the first time would have been deceived into thinking a real city lay in wait, with recognizable blocks of shops and small businesses and homes all platted without regard for the trembling earth.

The Intercontinental was happy with rumor. Ambassador Quainton's grown children had arrived for Christmas. So there would be no invasion right now—you wouldn't let your ambassador bring his family down just ahead of the Marines, would you? A prominent reporter was reliably reported to have already gotten a crush on an ambassadorial daughter. Was it true the Nicaraguans had received three new Soviet jets with offensive capability? Could be the last straw. A ranking Sandinista, everyone was talking about it, was in the cocaine trade. Cruising the lobby, tacking from group to group, an official from the American embassy could neither confirm nor deny his own story that an entire Sandinista battalion—think of it, 1,000 men at least, that translates to 100,000 in the States—had defected to the contras. There was not enough to go on yet. Mark your calendars anyway: December 18, 1983. It would mean the revolution was over.

XXII AFTERMATH

STOCKY, STATELY, FULL OF BENEFICENCE and wholly in his element, Miguel Cardinal Obando y Bravo moved around the old seminary on the outskirts (but then the whole city is outskirts) of Managua, blessing the students for the priesthood and chatting sociably with their rector and teachers. The visit was not for inspection or ceremony but only part of the many pastoral functions His Eminence was pleased to perform daily. It was early evening following a furnace of an afternoon, not yet cool, though the promise of relief was in the air and in the dying light. At the cardinal's approach one seminarian stopped playing his guitar, but the cardinal told him to continue; another asked if the Sandinistas' draft law was going to be applied to theological students, and the cardinal said not as long as he was there. Acolytes in shorts and priests in T-shirts gathered around their superior, cassocked and hatted but genial and unintimidating, under a spreading ceiba tree whose huge branches were filled with puffs of cotton and showy bell-shaped flowers. How the flower bells could survive unwithered in this season of virtually unrelieved dryness was one of the sundry mysteries that reminded me I was back in Nicaragua.

300

By April of 1986 the effective opposition to the Sandinistas inside Nicaragua had concentrated itself, like a purified compound that has been precipitated out of a chemical solution, in the person of this man of God under the ceiba tree. While he was an archbishop, Cardinal Obando had refused the present of a Mercedes-Benz from Somoza III and had mediated the safe passage on several occasions of Sandinistas who wanted to leave the country. He had been friendly to the revolution at first but had never been close to the Sandinistas and had turned against the leadership by the early 1980s. The Sandinistas accused him of siding with the old Nicaraguan ruling class and a conservative, hierarchic Pope against the legitimate strivings of the peasantry. Obando protested the Sandinistas' censorship, treatment of the Miskitos, military draft law, Marxist leanings, use of priests in their government, and their favoring of liberation theologists over the traditional church.

In 1985, on his way back to Nicaragua after being elevated in Rome by John Paul II, Obando offered his first Mass as cardinal to an audience of contras in Miami. Later, the Sandinistas suppressed a new Catholic publication that advocated draft resistance and canceled the broadcasting license of Radio Católica for failing to carry a speech by Daniel Ortega. Obando insisted he was only a servant of God. The Sandinistas claimed he was a servant of the imperialism that had brought misery to Nicaragua and of the counterrevolutionaries who would destroy the hopes of most of their countrymen. As Obando stood with the seminarians under the canopy of the ceiba tree, he nodded me in the direction of my car. The cardinal wanted to be alone with his flock, and he had already said he would see me later.

Managua was divided between citizens who thought Nicaragua was their country to do what they pleased with and those who saw themselves as perched on the doorstep of the United States and thought they had better mind their manners. Since both propositions could be argued with equal vigor, the situation displayed itself not so much in an unfolding continuous view as in the short burst. When I broke a Saturday lunch date on a Friday night and tried to reschedule it for Monday, the man I was calling said, "Monday falls into the category of the distant future, but try me midmorning." The crisis between the United States and Nicaragua had gone on so long that people had adjusted as they do in military occupations, fatal illnesses and impossible love affairs, pouring themselves existentially into each moment as if it might be the last. The short burst has its own limitations, of course, revealing what it does not have time to conceal, concealing what it does not have time to reveal.

Was the irony intentional or not when TACA, the Salvadoran airline, played Frank Sinatra singing "I Did It My Way" over its sound system as the plane landed at Sandino Airport? Possibly the plane's Muzak had been hijacked by a dissident Salvadoran who admired the Sandinistas; possibly it was a loyal TACA employee making fun of anyone foolish enough to get off in Managua instead of staying on until Panama. Coincidence, the most likely possibility in most parts of the world, is seldom a live option in Central America.

The two givens of Nicaragua, immediately visible and more solidly institutionalized than they had been in 1983, were poverty and war. By 1986, Managua was swollen to a population of over a million, approximately one third of the country. Refugees from villages and farms streamed into the city, pushed by crop failure and unsafe conditions caused by combat, lured by the hope of jobs. The city was becoming clogged with new *barrios* and squatter settlements. In the acres of lean-tos, plumbing was out of the question and electricity was often a matter of a few light bulbs strung on wires that hummed over a community of several hundred families. Huts were thrown up with whatever came to hand, corrugated tin, plywood, crushed beer cans, vegetable crates.

The contradictions, as always, were abundant. The government was trying to make the countryside safe and attractive and, to some degree, had succeeded. In the war, the Sandinistas had beaten back the counterrevolutionaries along the northern border with Honduras. The area around Jalapa was so much more secure than when I had been there in 1983 that refugees from other provinces were moving there to work and farm. Rural hospitals, attempts at improved public transport and education, and continued redistribution of farm acreage gave added incentive to settlers. The government was offering every bonus it could think of and afford to those who would go back to the land.

But the contras were not out of the fight for Nicaragua. Though the southern front along the Costa Rican border was virtually closed, the insurgents were promising to reopen it. Though they were unable to mount the large attacks of 1983 and 1984 in the north, they could infiltrate small bands of troops deep into the countryside, making farms in the interior less secure than those along the border. If they could contain the bickering among themselves and make efficient use of support from the United States, the contras seemed able to keep the war going indefinitely.

This was the success of the counterrevolutionaries and the United States: To be in Nicaragua in 1986 was to be in a state of what felt like permanent war. Hemorrhaging at the center, Nicaragua struggled to find a tourniquet in its own social policy and assistance from the Eastern bloc. Western Europe also provided help, but the military aid and the oil came from Moscow and its clients. Nicaragua had become a patient receiving intensive care. Living and dying, the citizenry was being bled more efficiently than it had been by Somoza III at his old plasmapheresis center, the "blood bank" Nicaraguans had called *casa de vampiros*.

The military were the new class of haves. If there were canvas, rubber and transportation, if there were fruits and vegetables and beef anywhere, the military had to have them. The rest of the population lived with shortages, power failures, breadlines. "This is nothing new—we have always been poor in Nicaragua," a textile worker told me. "The Sandinistas are inefficient at everything, even repression; what's the surprise things are sliding downhill?" a businessman asked. But beyond traditional Nicaraguan poverty or Sandinista mismanagement was the reality and permanence of the war.

As in other countries fighting long wars, some people were making money. There actually seemed to be more consumer goods available than in 1983, but most of them were in the black market. At the Mercado Oriental in Managua, naked children wandered from stall to stall, begging, but there was a brisk business in everything from beef to color television sets for those who had money. The prized toothpaste was what the Nicaraguans called Coal-gah-teh; a tube of it cost the equivalent of $4 at the official rate. Those who could not afford Colgate had to be content with Bulgarian toothpaste, the taste and contents of which were the subject of wry speculation. Bulgarian products, as I was going to find out in a more personal way before I was through in Nicaragua, were the butt of any joke about industrial quality.

Inflation was in the stratosphere. Even the official government exchange rate had gone up geometrically, but on the black market the dollar was worth seventeen times what it had been in 1983. Virtually any real product, from cigarettes to spark plugs, was a more effective unit of barter than the cordoba.

Yet the economy was not entirely a washout either. The coffee harvest of 1986 was bountiful and a great success on the international market. This had raised morale all over the country. The Sandinistas were given credit for another aspect of the harvest: They had protected coffee workers so well that the contras had not been able to kill a single harvester.

Cracked and parched near the end of the dry season, Managua still managed to be seductive in its old ways. People endured with a coupling of bravery and purposeful commotion. The whole city, from the lean-to *barrios* to the government buildings to the Intercontinental, needed a coat of paint, but that would only have disguised its longings and desperation. Seeing the city again, I was again surprised at the friendliness of Nicaraguans standing endlessly on breadlines. They still distinguished between American policy and Americans. "You're generous people but you don't understand Latinos," said an old man standing in line for bread in the Plaza España, which would be a centrally located downtown square if Managua had either a center or a downtown. "You send the contras to attack us and tell us this is pressure to make us have more democracy and less army. I don't like the army everywhere either, I wish we had much more *democracía.*

But when did a country *reduce* the size of its army and increase its democracy while it was being invaded?'' "It's bad here, waiting many hours in this heat for everything," the man next to him said, "but in Honduras they have no breadlines because they have no bread at all.'' The bread was being sold at the government's low controlled price. Some of those on the line admitted they were not buying bread for themselves but to resell at a higher price at a black market, where the bread would be marked up and sold again for a greater profit.

Two days a week the water was turned off in Managua. The night before a shutoff, people filled gourds, pails and canteens to see them through the following day. The water was turned off on different days in different sections of town. If they had not planned correctly or suddenly needed water desperately, Managuans in a dry section would wait for hours to catch buses to a section where the water was still running.

If there was little water for people, there was almost none for the trees. By late afternoon of a hot day, everything was so dusty and dry it was hard to understand why the malinche and jacaranda trees, along with the bougainvillea vines, did not give up and blow away. Then the sunset would draw a pink curtain over the western end of Managua, and the sky would be velvety enough to become a prediction of humidity. Perhaps the trees knew something.

Managua still had virtually no street signs. Directions, when they were given, were rendered in terms of buildings and trees that once were present but had ceased to exist after the earthquake fourteen years earlier. Follow this road until you come to the corner where the Gran Hotel used to be, turn left for three blocks to where the jewelry store was, go right toward the lake until you come to the place where the oak tree fell, then you're there. With everything a reference to the past, if Managua had nothing else it had a collective memory.

On the way to an embassy party, a journalist driving several of us got lost. The journalist knew Managua well, sort of, having lived there for more than two years. The fifteen-minute drive took over an hour and a half because the journalist had been to the embassy official's house only once and could not find her way back there. Half a dozen times we stopped people in the upper-class neighborhood where the diplomat lived. They were friendly and eager to be helpful. They pointed out the Venezuelan and Polish embassies. They showed us the residences of the ambassadors from the United States and the Soviet Union, who lived across the street from one another. But even lifelong residents of the neighborhood could not tell us where the street was that we wanted. "The problem is," the journalist who was driving said, "no one in Managua can find where he's going unless he already knows how to get there."

"Memories of underdevelopment," said a diplomat at the party, commiserating with the woman who had lost her way. The party was thick with journalists from *U.S. News & World Report,* the *Wall Street Journal, Esquire* magazine, CBS News, *New Republic, Atlantic Monthly,* and Cox News Service, among other publications and outlets. Most were regulars, but some had come down for the current crisis, which this time was a combination of events. There was a Congressional debate over aid to the contras. There were the current Contadora negotiations, pushed by eight Latin American governments, four of them in Central America, paradoxically being stalled by the only two countries that genuinely needed them, the United States and Nicaragua. There was a recent Sandinista "invasion," "incursion" or "border crossing" (new arrivals could pick the one fitting their prejudices) into Honduras against a contra camp.

Most of the journalists were glad to be in Nicaragua, still part of what one described as "a great moment"—a moment attenuated now for the better part of the decade with no end in sight. One journalist had just been fired, but he was having an affair with a Sandinista official and planned to stay near her. Discreetly, she did not come to the party, as he did not go to Sandinista parties. A wire-service reporter said a friend of his, from a rival news agency, was used up, his moment having extended too long. Another reporter swore that the American ambassador who replaced Tony Quainton, Harry Bergold, was now also used up and eager to be recalled. The story went that Bergold was sick of opposing aid to the contras privately but having to tell the State Department what it wanted to hear in his cables, in effect becoming the Administration's mirror image, rather than its eyes, in Central America. "We coexist all over the world with governments we don't like," said an embassy official at the party, inevitably insisting on being identified as a Western diplomat. "Why can't we coexist with the Soviets and Cubans in this part of the world? The situation is not hopeful. Both the United States and Nicaragua are so stubborn, so committed to their points of view, so reluctant to lose face, it is hard to see anything changing for the better. Things are not black and white here, but neither side admits it's partly wrong. Lines are tightening toward a snapping point."

The sharpest criticism I heard of the Sandinistas was from a journalist who had just watched them walk out of the latest Contadora meeting in Panama. "It wasn't only that they were bellicose, they were stupid," he said. "They could have had a treaty that at least linked them with the other Central American countries in opposing regional war." "Oh well," his date said, "they probably thought signing a peace treaty while the United States continues to fund the contras is like buying a car wired to explode when the ignition is turned on."

When it got late, someone remembered that Halley's Comet was due to appear over Managua that night. "Let's stay up and look at it," he suggested. The comet was not scheduled to appear until after four in the morning. "We'll watch this gray blur focus into a dart of light, and we'll see it as a beacon of hope in this beautiful tropical villa besieged on every hand by Communist tyrants." His wife said he couldn't have any more *Flor de Caña*.

After the party, some of the Americans went to the backyard of one of their homes to wait for the comet. They wondered about the death of the sexual revolution. Several remarked that a few years earlier, this time of night would have found them all paired off.

"AIDS is what killed it," one said.

"No, herpes," another said. "AIDS won't get most people. Everyone can get herpes."

Others had their own choices.
"Penicillin-resistant gonorrhea."
"Chlamydia."
"Gardinella."
"Yeast."
"Crabs after you've had them four times."
One journalist had had a gastrointestinal infection and was sent by a friend to a Cuban doctor. He cured her and told her about his previous service with the Cuban army in Angola. It was a strange existence, he said, since the Cuban troops who went were mostly black and identified with the Angolans, while the doctors were all white and tended to identify with the few Portuguese left in Angola. During the affair they had after the doctor cured the journalist, he seemed more furtive than necessary, since he had no wife in Nicaragua. He confided to the journalist that Cubans could be punished for having American lovers. He continued to sneak in and out of her life, and her room, until she returned to the United States.

No one waited until four o'clock for the comet.

Cardinal Obando's church was in the upper-class neighborhood where the embassy party had been. White adobe outside, with cream-colored plaster walls inside, the church gave a feeling of space and tranquillity even when full. The congregation was lighter skinned than others I had seen, and the sanctuary seemed to hold the last contingent of those who can dress nicely in Nicaragua. Most of the Sunday worshipers brought their own Bibles and followed the service in them. There was a small band featuring a guitar, bass guitar, drums and a piano.

The priest assisting Cardinal Obando announced that during the past week the Sandinista security police had come to a publications office belonging to the Catholic Church. They had confiscated a printing machine, two typewriters and a photocopier. On the way out, they noticed an air conditioner. To make certain the office could not function anymore, the priest said, the Sandinistas took the air conditioner, too.

After hymns accompanied by the band, Cardinal Obando gave

his sermon. The Gospel of the day was from St. John, with the lesson taken from the passage in which Jesus, after being crucified, appears to the disciples at the Sea of Tiberias. "Simon Peter suggests to the others that they go fishing, and that is what they do," Cardinal Obando said. "But after fishing all night they catch nothing." The cardinal looked down at his Bible. " 'When the morning was now come, Jesus stood on the shore,' " Obando read, " 'but the disciples knew not that it was Jesus.' "

The cardinal looked out at his congregation. Most of them could have been from Spain. Unlike them, Obando y Bravo was originally a Nicaraguan peasant, a mixture of the New World and the Old, his forebears including Indians as well as Africans and Spaniards. "When Jesus asked them if they had caught anything all night, they said no," Cardinal Obando continued, "so He gave them another way to go, a new direction in which to fish. 'Cast the net,' He told them, 'on the *right* side of the ship, and ye shall find.' Look in your Bibles, that's exactly what He said. The *right* side. So the disciples did cast their net over to the right, and they were rewarded with such a multitude of fish they were barely able to bring in the net. It's utterly clear, isn't it? Christ told them to go to the right and they would find what they were looking for. Being on the *right,* my friends, implies faith, dignity and abundance. As soon as they had brought their catch to shore, the disciples knew it was Jesus who had appeared to them, and they shared a wonderful breakfast of fish and bread with Him."

The congregation murmured in appreciation, and the cardinal repeated his moral a final time. "They went to the right, and they got what they wanted. They got so much that when they finished their own breakfast Christ told them to serve everyone else. If they truly loved Him, they would share the abundance with all their brothers."

His lesson over, Obando became jovial and confidential. His red cassock, imposing when he first took the pulpit, now looked brightly Central American instead of sedately Roman. He said he was glad to see everyone there and made a little joke about the television cameras at the back of the church. Many in the congregation chuckled when the cardinal praised the cameras for seeing everything and then criticized them for distorting so much. The cardinal's audience knew he was referring to a famous incident in which one of his monsignors was filmed running naked from the home of a woman whose husband had apparently come home unexpectedly and did not appreciate the form the pastoral visit had taken. The church has officially declared that the monsignor was set up by the Sandinistas, forced by the thuggish husband to disrobe, and then shoved into the street, where cameras were waiting to record his embarrassment. The Sandinistas, who showed the incident on their news broadcasts, staunchly maintain that the camera crew simply happened to be filming a demonstration in the next block when they were rewarded with a naked monsignor to make their afternoon more interesting.

Serious again, the cardinal said the church, as always, needed money. "We are a poor church," he said just before the collection was taken, "and we need all our friends now. At the old seminary a few days ago I saw walls still cracked from the earthquake, prayer books from the days of our grandparents. Please, my friends, the seminary is supported by your donations." Obando asked the congregation to help him buy new typewriters and a photocopier to replace those confiscated by the government from the church publications office. "We don't link ourselves to a political party," he said, "but we would like to have freedom of religion, and that means freedom to disseminate our views on such matters as the military draft which is forcing our young men into battle. We aren't supporting a war against the Sandinistas, but I don't agree that President Reagan is the head of the contras the way they say he is. This is a struggle between Nicaraguans and should be settled by negotiations between Nicaraguans." Several members of the congregation spoke out to agree with their cardinal, and no one in the audience of approximately three hundred expressed disagreement.

"There are those who call themselves the people's priests," Cardinal Obando said, referring both to the "Popular Church" of the liberation theologists and to the priests in the Sandinista government, "but they are in error. The true priests should not be in politics. The true priests should be with the Holy Father. Only the Pope can direct the religious energies of the populace. Any priest who does not have communion with the bishops is not with the Pope." Obando finished and was applauded by virtually the entire congregation.

"Let us pray," he said. "God listens to our people in their difficulties. We pray to you, Almighty Father, to hear our lamentations."

"We will return to Jesus Christ," the congregation responded together.

Across Managua on the same day, the second Sunday after Easter, another Catholic priest also read the Gospel of the resurrected Christ appearing to the disciples. Father Uriel Molina is a leading advocate of liberation theology in Nicaragua, blending Marxian social goals with Biblical teaching to hold that the most important mission of the church is to follow Christ's preferential option for the poor. Like Cardinal Obando, Father Molina told of the disciples having fished all night without catching anything in their net. Neither Obando nor Molina mentioned the possibility that nighttime might not be the right time for finding fish on the surface of the Sea of Tiberias.

The resemblance between the two services, however, ended there.

"In the morning, Jesus appeared to the *campesinos* and told them to keep on trying," Father Molina preached. He was from Spain, taller, graver, more European than Obando. Like Obando, Molina contrasted with his congregation, which included many darker-skinned mestizos as well as a scattering of Americans attracted to the Popular Church's mixture of revolution with religion. " 'And the other disciples came in a little ship,' " Father Molina quoted. " 'Jesus saith unto them, Bring of the fish which ye have now caught. Simon Peter went up, and drew the net to land full of great fishes, an hundred and fifty and three: and for all there were so many, yet was not the net broken.' The disciples had stayed together even during the long night when they caught no fish. They made a collective effort and they persevered. They did not know it was Christ talking to them from the shore, advising them to continue trying, yet they kept the faith. They came in finally with a full net, enough fish for everyone. The church itself, like Jesus at the Sea of Tiberias, cannot remain isolated from the people but must go among the faithful to stimulate the work that needs to be done. In this way the poor can freely transform their misery into a shared life of plenty.''

The juxtaposition was normal in the spring of 1986 in Nicaragua, a country having an argument with itself. The man of peasant stock, Obando y Bravo, becomes a cardinal and preaches to what remains of the old aristocracy on the virtues of moving to the right. The Spaniard of aristocratic bearing, Uriel Molina, emigrates to the former colony, antagonizes the church hierarchy and preaches to the peasantry about liberation and collectivism.

Having drawn his radically different lesson from the same passage used by Cardinal Obando, Father Molina let the band in his church take over and lead songs about fallen soldiers, revolutionary martyrs and the salvation of the poor. The church itself, known as the Iglesia de los Pobres, the Church of the Poor, was lined with murals celebrating the revolution. One was of Sandino; another showed Nicaraguans putting up new buildings (with a caption reading, ''The Poor Will Reconstruct the Church of God''); another memorialized a little boy who worked with the Sandinistas against Somoza's National Guard until the latter caught him and killed him.

During the singing, a little girl in a torn dress carried a crying baby out of the thin-walled church, uninsulated from the heat as the cardinal's adobe church had been. Two little boys flipped coins beneath the crowded pews at the back. A drunk wandered to the front and stumbled past the altar to shake Father Molina's hand. Molina was a little awkward with the intruder but finally persuaded him, as the last song was ending, to take a seat in the front pew, from which the drunk stared at the priest for the rest of the service. When the collection was taken in a basket made of straw and hardened tortillas, the drunk stared at the basket as if he might take something out of it or possibly lose his last meal into it. After a long moment, the usher passed the basket on to a sunburned old man in a suit and tie.

"The meaning of God," Father Molina said as he came to the heart of his message, "is that we must all work so that the poor can have a better life." He then made as strong a defense of the revolution as Cardinal Obando's criticism had been. "This revolution is reviving Nicaragua," he said. "The contras who try to destroy the revolution must make amends for their attacks against the people. While the vanguard continues to pay with their lives to defend the triumph, the rest of us must learn to live in this difficult situation. God has sent the message to all men and women: 'Live in the flame of the candle, and it will not hurt you but will transform you.' This is what we do in the revolution."

Father Molina carried his argument about the Sandinistas to the church hierarchy, whom he accused of forgetting the masses. He also linked the hierarchy to Washington. "None of us wants to be unfaithful to the mother church or to the faith itself," he said, "but the faith doesn't mean we have to be counterrevolutionary, as some would have us do. President Reagan talks of God to try to manipulate the meaning of God. He leads those who would make God an instrument against the people. They ask for reconciliation with the killers of men, the rapists of women and despoilers of the land, who are the contras, but they refuse reconciliation with those of us in the church itself who happen not to agree with them that the revolution is evil. Where is it written that the faith requires us to be anti-Sandinista? Our people are hungry and thirsty, but as good Christians they continue walking toward freedom. Let us pray: for an end to the conflict in which we live, for unity in the church, for peace in the international community."

Outside the church itself, the domestic opposition often described itself to be without mooring. "We flounder now," an opponent of the Sandinistas said in Managua. "When they told us not to participate in the 1984 election, the United States destroyed us as a credible opposition. We are now outside Nicaraguan political life. I can give a speech to a poorly attended rally and scream about oppression to foreign journalists, when I can find them. I can go to Honduras to join the contras and work for the CIA. If I'm too old for fighting I can go to Miami and complain for the rest of my life. Those are my only choices."

Though she had sent her son to live with a friend in Costa Rica so that he could not be drafted, Azucena Ferrey continued her own fight, helping to lead the Social Christian Party in its many criticisms of the Sandinistas. In her office under a large blow-up of a photograph showing President Ortega's wife ice-skating with several of her children in Rockefeller Center, Azucena Ferrey had inscribed a scolding: "While Nicaraguan mothers suffer the loss of their children in the war, while the children are dying due to lack of medicines and food, the wife of Daniel Ortega, Rosario Murillo, enjoys herself with her children in the country that is the enemy of humanity."

Harassment by the Sandinistas had declined, Mrs. Ferrey said, adding that her disagreements with the FSLN were even stronger than in 1983. She blamed the economic situation and the increased scarcities on the country's leaders, she felt the war could be ended if the Sandinistas would negotiate with their enemies, and she wanted far more guarantees of personal liberty and private property than were provided in the ruling party's proposed constitution. Her family was divided by more than geography. Mrs. Ferrey herself believed in staying in Nicaragua and working within the system for changes she wanted, but her favorite brother had moved to Honduras to take charge of a human-rights commission for the United Nicaraguan Opposition, the umbrella organization of the contras.

"My party is *not* an internal front of the contras," Mrs. Ferrey said, "but we want a society with equal rights for those who are not Sandinistas. Every time the Social Christian Party suffers by being denied the opportunity to hold a rally, the contras within the country take advantage by pushing their own cause, which I strongly disagree with. I will never want the United States to invade or to support an invasion of my country. But the FSLN has made Nicaragua into the ham in a sandwich where the two pieces of bread are the United States and the Soviet Union. We know the United States is interested only in its security, not in our well-being. We know the Soviet Union is interested only in another power base, but the Sandinistas do not understand this. What the Social Christians must do is to break the vertical structure of the government here, a structure where the state is the party and the party is the army. That is why I remain to fight in Nicaragua—and also because this is my home."

She was leaving for Chinandega to meet with colleagues and followers. The Social Christians, with a numerically small but vocal constituency, had boycotted the 1984 elections but were planning to field a full slate of candidates in the next balloting for the National Assembly. In the long argument over the future of her country, Azucena Ferrey seemed ready neither to be silenced by the Sandinistas nor bought off by the CIA.

At the end of 1981 and the beginning of 1982, Enrique Dreyfus spent four months in prison for being coauthor of the famous letter of criticism to Daniel Ortega from prominent businessmen. By 1986 his family lived abroad, but he remained in Nicaragua. With a Nicaraguan mother and a French father, he was brought up in Canada and has two brothers in France. He is a distant relative of Captain Alfred Dreyfus, whose trial and imprisonment on false charges of espionage were the anti-Semitic scandal of *fin de siècle* France.

Enrique Dreyfus in 1986 still had coffee, cattle and produce farms in Nicaragua, but he said he was not permitted to change his cordoba profits into dollars in order to buy supplies on the international market or even to pay his daughter's college tuition. "My mother lives here and I stay here holding the fort," he said, "but I work as a consultant for the investment bankers Lazard Frères to earn dollars to keep my daughter at Georgetown. The situation gets worse. All information on purchasing power, agrarian reform, any criticism of the government is heavily censored. Even an organization's internal newsletters must be submitted to the censor before they can be printed."

I wondered what he wanted to see the United States do.

"If you're number one you have to take some risks. A president or chairman of a corporation has to fire people sometimes if they aren't doing their jobs or they continue making mistakes. When I hear people say the United States can't act without the consensus of all Latin America, that means in effect the United States is not number one. If you're number one you can act for yourself."

With his education and sensibility more European than Central American, Dreyfus was afraid that peace negotiations might virtually concede Nicaragua to the Communists. "Contadora could become the next Yalta," he said. "This is not a matter of gripes, it's a question of values. How do you define freedom and democracy? This is the point. We should start by using the same dictionary. Nicaraguans have to decide what dictionary we want to use. They don't kidnap or kill here, so it's different from El Salvador. But by the time we decide what dictionary to use for our definition of freedom and democracy, we'll have more dead in this war than were killed in the insurrection against Somoza."

I asked if he was tortured in prison.

"Prison was not such a bad experience for me. My cellmate was a Communist. It was worse for him. The biggest problem in prison is depression. I can be depressed and recognize the feeling as depression. That is much harder for a poor uneducated fellow from the countryside like my friend the Communist. He and I got along beautifully, and the conditions weren't so bad. I had friends and many people on my side. There were demonstrations on my behalf, and these kept my spirits up. The Communist felt more alone, and for a time he did not know he was depressed. He had never seen toilets before, and we had them in jail. It was a great problem for him to go to the bathroom, because it seemed unnatural. I taught him to climb up on his bunk and look at the sky so he would feel he was outside under a tree. After doing that he was able to come down and defecate. For me the experience was not so bad as for others. Dreyfuses know how to handle prison."

Marina Castillo had been teaching history for fourteen years, which meant she had passed roughly half her career during the Somoza government and the other half after the revolution. "Although this is a state school and not a parochial one," she said, "my problem as a teacher before was less Somoza than the church. The priests were very powerful, and religion was inserted everywhere. If you didn't teach that the New World was discovered because of divine intervention, someone would tell a priest, and the priest would tell his bishop, and the bishop would tell your administrator. The administrator would have to talk to you about this whether he wanted to or not. So you would always have to say that God willed the voyages of Columbus."

In the class she taught to fourteen- and fifteen-year-olds from a working-class *barrio* in Managua, Mrs. Castillo traced the political, economic and social reasons for exploration of the seas by Europeans. "You will see we have some emphasis on the existence of classes and class interests, but it is hardly fanatic Marxism," she had said. Given Nicaragua's historical ties to Spain, Mrs. Castillo's tilt toward the Iberian Peninsula was not surprising. "By the end of the fifteenth century," she lectured, "Spain and Portugal were losing the important Far Eastern markets to Venice and other Italian cities that were in league with Arab traders. Spices, drugs and dyes were monopolized by Italy and Arabia. Spain and Portugal grew weaker and poorer. They had to have a new route to the East and new markets for trade to free themselves from the Italian and Arabian monopoly. This is what brought about the voyages of discovery and the scientific improvements in shipbuilding and navigation. Christopher Columbus' inspiration to look for a new commercial route for trading with India brought him by accident to the New World. Of course, this led to the decline of city-state feudalism in Europe and to the rise of mercantile capitalism. New products, new businesses, new inventions sprang up in Europe and jumped the ocean to North and South America. Now who do you think benefited most from these developments?

"La burguesía," the students replied.

The choleric "foreign businessman" who in 1983 had wanted the United States to drop an atomic bomb on Nicaragua was curiously mellow and rather sad in the spring of 1986. His harassment by the Sandinista *turbas* had stopped, and his anger, so vituperative before, seemed spent. I was surprised he was still in Nicaragua, but he said his company could not get anyone else to take the job, so he had stayed on. "My family is scattered; it doesn't make much difference now," he said. "My twenty-one-year-old daughter came down last summer to plant trees for the Sandinistas. She's a peacenik or something, I guess. Got duped by the Sandinistas. Anyone who thinks this place functions well is out of his mind. I get along all right in my business relationships with the government's commerce people here, but they treat their shortages very selectively. When they want someone to get water, he gets it. I can't stand the soldiers everywhere. The good things that have happened here in the last few years have nothing to do with the Sandinistas. Well, damn Reagan, too. I find the environment here *simpático,* not the damn Communists."

That was as far as he would go.

I looked for Stanley Atha, the old Marine who had come down in the 1920s to chase Sandino and stayed on all his life. There was no answer on his telephone, no one living at his home when I tried to visit. After a number of wrong turns, I finally located his daughter. She said he was staying now with another daughter outside Managua. She was sorry, but it was not possible to speak with him, since he was no longer living in the postrevolutionary era even part of the time. He was well physically, she added, but his imagination took him back every day to the distant past. The last Marine in Nicaragua was hearing the bugles and watching the campfires of an eternal patrol that kept closing in on Sandino but could not quite draw the knot around him.

In the streets around Bello Horizonte, one of the few sections of Managua that manages a thriving night life despite the usual vacant lots and unrepaired earthquake damage, the lower middle class of factory workers, clerks and civil servants were moving through their leisure hours with a mixture of enthusiasm and apprehension. Roberta Lichtman, who had been so helpful during my earlier visit and was back in Nicaragua after an absence of over a year, often went with friends to the cafés around Bello

Horizonte. "A woman wouldn't come here alone," she said, "because the revolution hasn't yet shaken the average Latin American man's conviction that a woman by herself in a café is basically soliciting."

Prostitutes do in fact look for business in Bello Horizonte. The government has tried to provide other work for them, but with the economy depressed and jobs scarce because of the flood of refugees into Managua, prostitution remains a vigorous little industry. "This revolution is the best thing that ever happened to my business," a prostitute told us proudly. "Some of the *comandantes* are my best customers."

"Don't listen to her," said a jitney driver drinking beer at an outdoor café whose tables sprawled onto the sidewalk. "She can't even get an old pensioner to go home with her on a Friday night."

It happened that this *was* a Friday night, the busiest night in Bello Horizonte. "Watch this, *estúpido*," said the woman, and she wiggled a knee out of a slit in her tight black dress. After she had batted her long fake eyelashes at the next ten men who walked by, she landed a shy-looking fellow with sloping shoulders and a look that seemed to indicate he would rather be somewhere else. On one of his shirtsleeves was a black armband. As they went off together, the jitney driver said he saw the man every Friday night in Bello Horizonte. "He is an accountant who had a wife and mistress," the jitney driver said. "On Friday nights he always saw the mistress. About six months ago his wife died. Right away he broke up with the mistress. But after a couple of months he still needed his Friday nights."

We asked how the jitney driver was getting along. Any such question from a foreigner is all it takes in Nicaragua for someone to begin talking about the revolution.

"Up and down like a jack-in-the-box. The terror is gone. You can't know what it was like to live here under Somoza unless you were here or you saw how happy people were to get rid of him. The revolution gave a chance for everyone to start over again, and we needed that. It is a great transformation, and most of us will fight to preserve it. But seven years later we are still at war, still so poor. The government does this and that. Sometimes a program works, sometimes no, but the war and the poverty are always with us. I don't know if we're going to make it."

What about freedom?

"How free is a man who doesn't have enough to eat and whose life is endangered by an army of traitors? I don't like censorship, but all our newspapers have always been institutions of agitation, not information. The Sandinistas are great liberators, but we'll never know if they're for freedom as long as the war lasts. The rain will come soon and slow the war. When this year is over Reagan has only two more dry seasons to destroy us. After that he's no more Mr. President."

In another café a young woman whose hair was up in curlers sat with her boyfriend. She rocked a little boy back and forth in his stroller. He had a paper cup of orange sherbet in his hand, but he was going to fall asleep before he finished it. "My husband left for Honduras in '83 right after Rico was born," she said. "I heard he was with the contras, then I heard he was killed, and after that someone said he had seen him in Miami. I work in the land-reform program, though I'd like to be a radio announcer. My boyfriend Eddy makes spare parts for old American cars, and we're trying to find a place to live together right now, since it looks like my husband is not coming back. Oh, Rico, I get to finish your sherbet." Deftly, she scooped the cup of sherbet from Rico's hand just before it fell to the sidewalk. She gave Eddy one lick of it and ate the rest herself. "The problem is, this is the only sweet I've been able to buy Rico all week," she said.

The silver spoons were gone from their glass display case in Ramiro Lacayo's comfortable home. In their place was a Chinese Ahka automatic rifle, presented to Ramiro Lacayo on his seventieth birthday by Comandante Humberto Ortega, the defense minister and brother of Daniel Ortega. "My country is at war," Lacayo said, "so I show the gun. I hope to show the spoons again one day."

Ramiro Lacayo was the retired businessman who in 1983 had

proudly proclaimed his support for the Sandinistas and had shown me his backyard bomb shelter. He was no less a Sandinista supporter in 1986, perhaps even a little firmer in his progovernment stance. He had become a member of the National Assembly and was president of the National Committee on Human Rights. In this capacity he had recently visited prisons in Nicaragua, Honduras and El Salvador. He had also inspected conditions among the Miskitos on the East Coast. "The efforts made by the Sandinistas in partnership with the Miskitos to improve the situation on the East Coast are very significant," Lacayo said. "They are bringing results, and although the Miskitos are still suspicious, these results—the land to the *campesinos,* the schools, the medical care—are the reason there is less fighting there now. The Sandinista prisons are not where I want to spend the weekend, but neither are the prisons in the United States. In comparison with prisons in Honduras and El Salvador, the prisons in Nicaragua are picnic grounds. The human-rights group here that criticizes the Sandinistas are great inventors. They are fed their 'information,' if you want to call it that, by the U.S. embassy. Your allies in Central America still maintain dungeons. We have nothing like that here."

Aside from the war and poverty, the National Assembly's most important business, according to Ramiro Lacayo, was the writing of a constitution. "When I come to the United States, I don't see this in your newspapers," he said, "but we are studying your own Constitution very carefully. We have sent delegations to talk to your constitutional lawyers, and many groups are involved, not only the Sandinistas." Lacayo had been in the United States earlier in the year because his wife needed medical treatment. "Get sick in your own country, not ours," he said, laughing, giving advice I understood better later. Lacayo estimated that only about a quarter of his old business friends had left the country. "This is no bed of roses for the rest of us," he said, "but the difficulties businessmen have here come from the U.S. aggression, not from the government. If a person does his job and pays his taxes, the revolution respects him. We are a poorer country but a happier one than when I saw you in 1983. The revolution was still in an experimental stage then. Now we know it works, and it works for us."

If the revolution was working, what accounted for the discontent, why were the contras still able to recruit followers?

"When the United States tightens the screws on us, things get worse. When things get worse and the scarcity is everywhere in almost all consumer goods, more people suffer. When more people suffer for long enough, some of them join the contras. As a businessman, I can say that your policy is most of all bad for business. If you would be our friends, we would have no contras, no war and fewer shortages. How would that hurt the United States? Since you will not be our friends, my bomb shelter is still ready."

Two twelve-year-olds flailed at each other beneath a bare light bulb in the headquarters of the neighborhood CDS, the Sandinista Defense Committee. Their boxing gloves, meant for adults, looked as big on them as watermelons. The man teaching the boys how to box danced around them, shouting encouragement and instructions, considerably lighter on his feet than the boys were on theirs. A world or two away from Spanish Harlem, the scene could be reproduced in any gym in any city with a sizable Hispanic population. As hard as it seemed for either of the twelve-year-olds to mount an attack while wearing watermelons, one of them finally did haul off with a right uppercut that raised a welt beneath the eye of the other.

The CDS was in a former shoe factory in Barrio San Luis. Its main economic function was the distribution of scarce goods such as rice, beans, sugar, cooking oil, soap and eggs. In 1983 some of the residents complained they were forced to attend CDS meetings in order to qualify for rationed items. In 1986 new rules stated explicitly that the only criterion for a CDS card, and therefore a share of rationed goods, was to be a resident of the *barrio*. Other CDS activities included the usual "revolutionary vigilance" against possible contra agents, civil defense (which meant digging trenches and organizing first-aid squadrons in preparation for attack), taking the neighborhood census, stopping crime, operating a preschool play center, vaccinating the *barrio* children, keeping the streets clean and running the neighborhood sports program that included the young boxers with the oversized gloves. A description of the CDS made it sound far more organized than it was. In fact, the struggle of the CDS in Barrio San Luis was to bring a little order out of the general chaos of poverty, dislocation and the stream of refugees.

In the category of "revolutionary vigilance," any undemocratic excess was possible, from the settlement of old personal scores to the blackballing of residents who disagreed with one or another Sandinista policy. For an American, this was reminiscent of loyalty oaths, veterans' organizations against dissenters, and the House Committee on Un-American Activities of the 1950s. The excuse for this function of the CDS was the claim that wartime conditions made *vigilancia* not an abuse of freedom but a necessity for survival. There was no prospect in the Nicaragua of 1986 that peace would break out to test this claim.

When the twelve-year-olds had gone three rounds and looked ready to collapse, the light bulb above their heads was unscrewed and a movie projector was plugged in. A crowd of almost two hundred, most of whom were children and teenagers, watched a Soviet documentary about an international youth congress held in Moscow in 1980. The biggest cheers were for the ascendance over a stadium of several thousand balloons, for a troupe of African dancers and—raucously, mockingly—for a parade of marching chickens. The second film, also a documentary, dealt with the lives of Argentine cowboys. Bronco busting, cattle herding, rope tricks and target practice with six-shooters, home on the range in the Southern Hemisphere; the film drew more rapt attention than the Soviet documentary. Cowboy fantasies proved more deeply seated than floating balloons and marching chickens.

The children were cleared out, adults filed in, and the main event of the evening in Barrio San Luis was ready to begin. Two different factions fought a brisk, bitter contest over who would be elected as the CDS delegate for the *barrio*. Eight candidates narrowed quickly to two: the neighborhood power broker, named Roosevelt Funes, and a noisy insurgent known as Dona Marina. (Four decades after the collapse of the Good Neighbor Policy, "Roosevelt" was not likely to become again a name Nicaraguan parents would call their offspring with unalloyed pride, but Roosevelt Funes was well into his fifth decade.) Since Roosevelt Funes was running the meeting as well as promoting his own candidacy, he began with a long-winded appraisal of his qualities. A slim man with a trim mustache, he saved his bombshell for the end. He hated to be the one to bring this up, he said, but it was a known fact throughout San Luis that Dona Marina had robbed the CDS of both cooking oil and millions of cordobas.

The outcry over this accusation was drowned out by Dona Marina herself. She was a small, round woman whose roundness appeared to be all muscle. "Liar! Pig! Traitor!" were among her gentler responses. She stormed from the old shoe factory with a few of her followers while the debate continued. Roosevelt Funes had a hard time keeping order both among his own supporters and those of Dona Marina. The fragility of democracy in Nicaragua was displayed by a partisan of Dona Marina's who arose during the debate and yelled for silence. When she got it, the woman shouted, "The election is unnecessary! We don't want to vote, we only want Dona Marina!" She was cheered more loudly than either candidate all evening.

In a few minutes Dona Marina returned with two police captains and a sergeant. "I demand that you exonerate me from the false slander of this demented bureaucrat, Roosevelt!" she yelled at the policemen. One of the captains said they could have nothing to do with politics. "This is not politics!" Dona Marina shouted, blocking the captain's way as he tried to leave. "This is crime! I am accused before my neighbors and *compañeros* of a crime I never committed. Tell me, tell all of us, *compañero capitán*, has there ever been a particle of evidence or even a serious charge that I have misused the cooking oil or any of the goods that the CDS distributes, or that I have stolen money from anyone?" Sheepishly, the captain had to admit he had never heard anything bad about Dona Marina, and the other captain and the sergeant, equally intimidated by the fierce candidate, nodded. At this point it would not have seemed out of place for someone— either Dona Marina, Roosevelt Funes or the policeman—to break into an air from Gilbert and Sullivan. Instead, Dona Marina permitted the constabularies to leave, and the balloting began. As it would have occurred in the Nicaraguan version of *The Mikado,* Dona Marina beat the machine candidate by taking 70 percent of the votes.

At last the audience with the cardinal was at hand.

He was as informal as his simple, undecorated office, wearing a short-sleeved beige shirt with a white clerical collar but no gown or hat. Behind his informality, however, was the cardinal's agenda. Whether this was religious or political was what all Nicaragua debated.

Cardinal Obando himself saw a political message neither in his official pronouncements nor in his interpretation of Scripture. As far as he was concerned, his sermon quoting Christ instructing his fishermen to cast their nets to the right was the common sense of trying a new direction while keeping the faith. If it sounded otherwise in church, that was the slant his listeners chose to put on it. When I reminded him that he had associated dignity and virtue with the right, he earnestly denied any ideological intentions. "We are pastors who don't push any political party," he said, "because that would divide the church even more. Preaching the evangelical Word is political only in the broadest sense, not in the sense of militating for one party. We don't want totalitarianism of the right, nor do we want totalitarianism of the left."

Obando reflected that the church in Nicaragua was in open disagreement with the past regimes under which his countrymen suffered. During the war against Somoza, he had helped a group of ransomed Sandinistas get to Cuba to continue their struggle on one occasion, and on another had helped a different group get to Panama. Given the historical context of his—and the church's— role in society, I asked what the relationship was between Christianity and revolution.

"This is so difficult to decide," he said. "We denounced the old oppression as a sin. We wanted a more humane, fraternal system with a narrowing of the gap between rich and poor. But we cannot support the absolutization of the revolution we have here. We don't want to see the revolution raised to the category of idolatry, and we don't want hatred between classes. We encouraged the revolution, but now I think the people of Nicaragua find themselves in a complicated situation where they are asked to become fanatics. One should try to coexist, right? And the church does try to coexist. But we cannot identify the teachings of Christ with the way the government is acting here. Christ does not preach hatred. Christ is not going to expel priests for being against conscription of young men to become killers. In Christianity we talk about reconciliation and pardon for our enemies. As Christians, we hate sin, but we don't hate the sinner. For Christians, the end does not justify the means. For Marxists, the end does justify the means. So I am forced to see a certain incompatibility between Christianity and what is going on in this revolution here."

He did not mean to denounce all Sandinistas as Marxists, Obando said. But there was enough Marxism in the fomenting of class hatred, the restrictions on personal liberty, and the hostility to private property to make him suspicious of the power of the state. "The church must denounce injustice where we find it," he said. I asked why, since he was so critical of the Sandinistas, he had never spoken out against the activities of the contras when so many human rights organizations, including those sponsored by Roman Catholic groups, had done so.

"We have criticized injustice on both sides, because this is inevitable when blood is spilled."

I pointed out that aside from his detestation of war in general, in fact the cardinal's specific criticisms were always directed at the Sandinistas.

"If someone slaps you, you're going to say that he slapped you. It is not the contras who have closed down our radio station and our magazine. It is not the contras who insult the church in their newspapers. They didn't surround my car and damage it, or block my path when I was attempting to enter a church once.

They have not taken priests into custody and fingerprinted them. It is not the contras who censor my pastoral letters and search the social service office of the diocese. I'm not saying I'm in agreement with the contras, but it's logical that if someone steps on you, you will protest against the person who has done this."

The church itself remained divided about the revolution, did it not?

"The priests who are in the government are in defiance of the Holy Father. The priests they call people's priests, the ones who preach in what they call the Popular Church, are attacking the traditional teachings of the church. They divide the church and try to deteriorate the inbred sense of religion in the Nicaraguan people. But we resist. We are disciples of Christ, and we have to suffer through persecutions because we have to follow His footsteps. One has to look for a more humane system for the poor, but liberation theology is not workable. The proponents of liberation theology have fanaticized it."

Although Cardinal Obando did not feel he himself, as the titular leader of the Nicaraguan church, was political in any but the broadest moral terms, he criticized the priests in the Popular Church as decidedly ideological. They had taken their stand with the Nicaraguan government against its enemies. I wondered if he judged the government to be religious.

"*Sandinismo* itself is becoming a religion, and at the same time the government wants to meddle in our internal church affairs. Often when we want to make a change in the assignment of a parish priest who is with the Sandinistas, they interfere and cause tensions. Imagine what would happen if the church meddled when they want to change *comandantes*!"

Did the cardinal think the government now had taken on the power the church itself once had in Nicaragua?

"Never. The government could not take on the role of a bishop because the people would not stand for it."

Yet the church was being squeezed into a smaller place in Nicaraguan life than it had ever occupied. Cardinal Obando did not wish to dwell, he said, on the possibility of further erosions of church power. Similarly, he knew that his proposals for the government to hold talks with the rebels only inflamed the Sandinistas, who had frequently maintained there could be no dialogue with murderers, especially murderers they felt they were beating. Under the circumstances, the cardinal was cryptic about the church's role in trying to bring peace to Nicaragua.

"We can make suggestions, but the responsibility for political solutions does not rest upon the institution of the church. We are a power of God, we try to shed light upon the situation. If the hatred continues, the economy will get worse and people will be hungrier. But you know, we also must continue to promote and defend life."

Cardinal Obando said repeatedly he did not like to think of the situation's getting worse than it already was. When he remarked that life must be promoted and defended, he conveyed an almost Rotarian sense of the improvability of unfavorable circumstances. But he found himself enmeshed in complexities not easy to fathom. The war was draining his people, with no foreseeable end, and the poverty he had known all his life was deepening. The policies of the Sandinistas were bothersome, especially where government edicts affected the church. But as a pastor having trouble keeping members of his flock in the orthodox fold, he was visibly more hurt and more bothered by dissident priests than by the Sandinistas themselves. Ronald Reagan had said he could not permit Obando to become the Cardinal Mindszenty of the Western Hemisphere, referring to the Hungarian cardinal whom the Communists imprisoned after coming to power. Obando y Bravo discounted that possibility—"The circumstances are completely different"—but the prospect of liberation theologists in his church was another matter. "They abuse the faith," he said, "and they shame the mother church." If the Sandinistas remain in power, I asked, did he anticipate a role for the church similar to that in Eastern Europe.

"Ah, but in Eastern Europe," he said wistfully, "there is no Popular Church." He shook his head. A moment later, like a ship stabilizing after a wave's buffet, the cardinal's constitutional optimism returned. "We know we will survive, though, because our faith is not tied to temporal concerns. We endure in Christ. The church has to exist until the end of time."

Tomás, who did his fighting in the north near Ocotal, had been angry for a year after he came home. "But now," he said, "I only get mad when people call me *lisiado*. Don't call me *lisiado, call me *deshabilitado*."

Between Cardinal Obando's faith and the Sandinistas' determination, the Nicaraguan people carried on their struggle in various ways. No one in Nicaragua was far away from this, but for those caught directly in the conflict, there were special problems. At the Organización de Revolucionarios Deshabilitados Ernesto Ché Guevara in Managua, those problems were irised down to the question of how to get around without usable legs. *Lisiado* means crippled, which was not how Tomás preferred to think of himself.

In training to become an electrical appliance repairman, Tomás came to the rehabilitation center on days he did not have classes. The center was in Bolonia, a formerly middle-class neighborhood that by 1986 principally housed foreigners and government offices. Bolonia, as arid as the rest of the city, did have a few oleanders lining its dusty streets.

Three years earlier a bullet had found its way into Tomás' spinal column. He stayed in bed for a year, at home with his family. Some of his old friends came to see him, and some would not. Of those who came at first, some soon stopped. "I was totally angry one day, totally depressed the next. I knew I was becoming a piece of squash. After a year my father said I would have to leave because he couldn't watch me destroy myself. I did leave, but I started to play basketball with other disabled veterans. Soon I was going to the classes to repair televisions and washing machines. Now I can take care of myself."

Tomás, who preferred to keep his last name to himself because he still had not reconciled with his parents, sat in the rehabilitation center near two other paraplegics, the three of them in their wheelchairs. They were all still in their early twenties, each with

the torso of an athlete, each with the spindly legs of an old man.
I asked Tomás how he felt about the war.

"It was important to defend *la patria,*" he said. "I am no
longer sorry for going to fight or for myself, though I was at first.
I'd do what I did again. Just don't call me *lisiado.*"

"There was no choice," said the man in the chair nearest
Tomás. He backed his wheelchair away and picked up a newspaper.

The third paraplegic looked out the window. He swatted at a
fly on the windowpane with a rolled-up magazine. The fly was on
the outside of the pane and flew off.

"I want only the opportunity to develop my full potential
now," Tomás said. He was very good-looking; with a corona
of black curls, a neatly trimmed beard and dark, round eyes,
his face was delicately cherubic. "Next week I will go with my
team to play basketball against the disabled of León. By autumn
I will be able to repair the simple appliances most Nicaraguans
have."

Mistaking his friendliness for an eagerness to talk personally
about himself, I asked Tomás if he expected to have a family of
his own.

He turned away and looked out the window at a cyclist going
by in the street. "I could be a father," he said, and was silent.

The three paraplegics took turns on a machine that was something like a Nautilus. Pushing with his arms against handles connected by cables to lead weights, Tomás was able to do more
repetitions than the others. Soon the three left for lunch. They
were going to meet two more disabled friends at a café.

Outside, the three wheeled their chairs down the street as
though they were flying. At the corner two soldiers, their Ahkas
strapped to their backs, were buying pineapple chunks and sweet
cassava from a pushcart vendor. Tomás stopped to look at the
soldiers, and they looked at him. It was a neighborhood of easy
sociability, with several noontime card games going beneath the
oleanders. Hi there, our unfortunate *compañero,* the soldiers did
not say to Tomás, you are our worst nightmare. I was what you
are, and you can become what I am, Tomás did not reply to the

soldiers before hurrying, flying, to catch up to his friends in their chairs.

Early one Saturday morning, Roberta Lichtman and I rode a small bus to the interior. Along with a half-dozen journalists and a few other travelers, we left Managua at six-thirty for a five-hour trip to Santo Domingo, a village deep in Chontales province in south-central Nicaragua. Later in the day Daniel Ortega was going to Santo Domingo for a kind of town meeting known as Cara al Pueblo—literally, "Face to the People." The contras had been active in many parts of Chontales and in Santo Domingo itself, attacking Sandinista followers and recruiting followers of their own among religious villagers and conservative landowners. An army sweep made the area secure enough during the presidential visit; leading Sandinistas held regular Cara al Pueblos, where they heard suggestions and often complaints about government programs.

The countryside was even drier and hotter than Managua. We passed through lowlands where there was little sagebrush and climbed into hills where the heat shimmered off the pavement that rose ahead of us. The pavement ended and we bounced along dirt roads through back country.

On the rocks above a gully that still had some water running along its bottom, a bony cow and a spavined horse watched a young woman wearing only a red skirt wade into what was left of the stream. Lifting up her skirt, she washed her legs and thighs, and then knelt down carefully to scrub her breasts. She did not seem to notice the bus as it swung in a long arc around her, or she ignored it as a way of preserving her privacy. Under an oak across the stream from the horse and cow, a small boy sat on a donkey holding a basket of laundry his big sister or mother had finished doing before she washed herself. The boy looked up at the sky, less interested in the bathing than in the *zopilotes*— buzzards—that rode updrafts as the early sun heated the mountain air. From the industrial point of view, the bus was surrounded by underdevelopment; from the biological, by nature in parched but undisturbed harmony.

As the bus wound us deeper into the interior, I could not avoid the thought that in Nicaragua the United States might face the prospect of much the same kind of victory and defeat we endured in Vietnam. We won virtually every battle in Vietnam, we succeeded in making large portions of the country unproductive for the enemy to the point of being unlivable, and we effectively destroyed the economy. We lost, of course, in failing to bring Vietnam the freedom and democracy we said we fought for, in failing to prevent the forcible reunification of North and South, and in failing to leave the country with a government or political system we approve of. Nicaragua and Vietnam were different in history, geography, custom, religion, population and culture; only poverty and superpower policies could make them similar.

What a missed opportunity the Nicaraguan revolution was becoming. A missed chance for the United States to befriend revolutionaries with anticapitalist roots before they became dependent on the programs and ideology of the Soviet Union. A missed chance for the Sandinistas to have a powerful neighbor helping with their country's transformation from feudalism to an approximation of a contemporary agri-industrial state. A missed chance for American conservatives to see economic progress in some model other than what can be produced by savings and loan associations. A missed chance for what remains of the American left to debate the relevance of the socialist ideal.

The continuing invasion scare not only unified most Nicaraguans. It also paralyzed most of the opposition in the United States. Nicaragua became little more, for Americans, than a depopulated focus for the rhetoric of Cold War II. On the right, the Sandinista government was pictured as a direct extension of Muscovite tyranny. Unless the United States rushed in soon to apply a military remedy, the infection would spread south until it reached our vital interests in Panama and north until it reached our vital organs themselves along the Rio Grande. It was a vision that terrified liberals into silence. Faced with the theory of revolution as gangrene, what liberal wanted to be accused again of being soft on Communism? Another question, with a slender seventh of a fractious century remaining, would be: What kind of revolution can an impoverished and oppressed society hope to have that the United States will find desirable and supportable?

In arming and pushing the contras into battle against the Sandinistas, the United States was creating a scenario. If we support the contras, we place our national interest in their hands. If the contras could not win, as no one in Washington or Managua expected them to do by themselves, sooner or later the United States would have to send troops to their rescue or sacrifice our credibility as an ally. If we rescue effectively, we would have to invade. If we invaded Nicaragua, we would have to win or lose. If we lose, we lose big, as in Vietnam, but more humiliatingly because of where Nicaragua is. If we win, we conquer the territory. If we conquer, we have to administer. If we administer, either by ourselves or through a new creature of our imagination and potency such as Somoza was, we would turn Central America, Mexico and much of South America into potential enemies and therefore into—by our own definition of enemy—Communists.

On the left, the rhetoric about the Nicaraguan revolution was as insidious in its way as the right-wing scenario, since it ruled out thinking about the Sandinistas. If you were not with the Sandinistas all the way—judging their "mistakes" against human rights to be nothing more than responses to far worse "mistakes" of aggression and brutality on the part of the United States—you were against them. With anything less than genuflection you stoked the fires of American intervention, helped create an atmosphere where crushing the revolution was acceptable. How strange that poor, weak, underdeveloped Nicaragua became a magnetic compass for the True Left.

The doctrine of criticism as heresy stifled inquiry on the shrinking American left, where argument could have been invigorating. The Nicaraguan revolution offered the left an opportunity to debate the progressive course, as it is called, into the next century. What were the possibilities for a program on the left that neither debased itself into totalitarian dogmas of social engineering nor compromised itself into yuppie extinction? Why have so many revolutionaries who proclaim themselves socialists suddenly discovered on coming to power that disagreement is treason? Is this the nature of institutionalized socialism? If not, is it the nature of revolutionary regimes in pretechnological societies where capitalism has equaled piracy? Is it the ultimate essence of Marxism to be antidemocratic, or is it the form Marxism inevitably took when Lenin brought it to his own antidemocratic—and defeated —country? What does Marxism offer a developed democracy, or is it irrelevant? Is a bourgeois culture, with an entrenched middle class, a requisite for freedom of expression? What do the new technologies do to traditional socialist impulses to protect labor and preserve jobs?

In much of the Third World, capitalism has not solved but deepened poverty. But where governments composed of self-described Marxists have come to power, they have frequently suppressed dissent, jailed poets, accused critics of being CIA collaborators and—most telling from their own viewpoint— failed to solve basic economic problems. Meanwhile, they have installed their own elite class, the one entity they all abominated while fighting for power. Looking at Managua through the pronouncements of the Sandinistas, it was possible to see not only a feisty band of patriots straining for independence from the American imperium but also a group of leaders as susceptible as any other to the fatal contagion of power.

Earlier that day, even earlier than the bus left Managua, Daniel Ortega had called a press conference. By five in the morning in the auditorium of the government's press building, six television cameras were ready along with fourteen tape recorders, twenty-one still cameras and thirty-seven journalists, not counting technicians. When the meticulous security checks were finished, the journalists were somewhat pacified by scrambled eggs, somewhat awakened by the Nicaraguan coffee.

With cameras whirring and two-thousand-watt "deuces" blazing away powered by more electricity than many entire Nicaraguan towns have, President Ortega strode onto the auditorium stage at six A.M. Predictably, he was there to rededicate himself and his country to the battered Central American child known as Contadora. Predictably, he talked about his firmness in defending

the sovereignty of Nicaragua combined with his flexibility in the search for peace. "Nicaragua was the first Central American country to support Contadora in 1984," he said, "and we now reaffirm our support for a Contadora agreement as the path to peace. We cannot, however, be tied to the *modified* Contadora that permits the United States to continue financing the same . . . " And so on. Either President Ortega had come to believe he could drown opposing arguments in a sea of rhetoric or else the CIA had lodged one of its agents snugly enough inside the Sandinista establishment for the mole to have convinced the *comandantes* that an early morning news conference with no news was the way to transmit their resolve to their enemies.

When the bus reached Santo Domingo the day had become so hot that the mules of the town were not bothering to flick their tails at the flies on them. For their part, the flies were so still on the mules' backsides as to appear dead, neither crawling nor taking wing. Santo Domingo was in a valley between brown hills, and the village itself recollected Spain. Houses of yellow and white stucco, small and well kept, led up a hill to a plateau where the church was. The town was poor enough not to be able to afford any roof but one of corrugated tin for its church, and inside it would have been possible to bake bread.

The meeting between the Sandinista leaders and the citizenry, the Cara al Pueblo, was to take place in the scorched plaza outside the church. Farmers had been trucked in from the surrounding countryside, most of them (as indicated in a few chats) from small private farms of their own and not from cooperatives. The local agricultural union had provided the trucks, giving the meeting its public-relations aspect as well as providing the farmers and their families with a ride into town for Saturday shopping after the meeting. As a magnet for the townspeople and a signal that a public occasion was about to commence, the sound system in the plaza was filling the blazing noon, in English, with "Say You Say Me" by Lionel Richie, for which he had just won an Academy Award. Roberta Lichtman said she could hear this anywhere and went off to find a cold drink.

In the plaza I stood talking to the leader of the National Union of Farmers and Ranchers, Daniel Núñez. More a poet than a bureaucrat, he was well known in Nicaragua for his willingness to criticize the Sandinistas when he felt they abused their power. Though loyal to the government, he had not hesitated to point out, in the earthiest terms, what he felt should be done with two Sandinista soldiers accused of raping women in a northern village. In Spanish, Daniel Núñez introduced me to a friend of his as a man fluent in six languages. There was nothing for me to do but compliment the man, and there was nothing for him to do but say, in English, "Ah, but I speak rubbish in all six."

Suddenly, my head felt so light I knew I was going to faint. The Cara al Pueblo was about to begin. I excused myself and ran a few yards to where a couple of journalists from the bus were. They asked what was wrong. Next, I recall a lump already forming on my head when I came to. Falling, I had hit the only patch of concrete in the grass-and-dirt plaza. Roberta had returned and said I had been unconscious less than a minute. Good, I said, sitting up. A Sandinista army doctor materialized immediately with a stretcher. With the president of the country about to arrive, it made sense there would be a doctor around. He asked if I would like to get on the stretcher. Why would I want to do that? I asked.

Then they were carrying me on the stretcher. I had fainted again. This time Roberta caught my head before it hit and helped the doctor roll me onto his stretcher. The doctor and a medic carried me up an embankment and put me down in an empty hut just off the plaza. The hut was a schoolroom and on the blackboard was written *"Bienvenido Presidente."*

I felt quite tranquil on the stretcher in the classroom, but Roberta looked pale.

"I'm pale? You're green!" She was shouting. Her pallor, it developed, was the friendly reflection she cast at me. "This time you were out for a couple of minutes. You were convulsing, for God's sake. Eyes rolling back like marbles, trembling all over. I'm wondering how I'm going to tell your wife and trying to keep you from shaking yourself off the stretcher."

I asked if perhaps we could hold the instant replay until I felt a little stronger.

"Hypoglycemia," the army doctor declared. "I see it all the time. We must get sugar into you."

Outside in the plaza, the meeting was beginning with music by a local band of bullfight quality and with warm-up speeches about crops.

It was hot in the classroom hut, but I felt better to be out of the sun. The doctor, a nurse, and a medic all hovered attentively. They talked about how to reverse the hypoglycemia and get more sugar into my bloodstream. As a principal crop, sugar is revered in Nicaragua almost the way the Virgin is. It has the force of sacrament, a cure for any ailment. Accordingly, Coca-Cola is the chicken soup of Nicaragua. They began to pour more Coca-Cola into me than I had ever looked at. No sooner had I finished one sixteen-ounce bottle than another was popped open and placed in front of me on the stretcher. The nurse held my head up so I could drink more of it. I wondered why the American trade embargo had not been expanded to include Coca-Cola; perhaps they had it transshipped through a neutral country like Switzerland. The only recess I got from Coca-Cola in this classroom was when the doctor decided I should drink some straight dextrose he had on hand.

A helicopter flew over the plaza. Daniel Ortega was arriving. I thought about asking whether the Nicaraguans would let me go back to Managua with him and avoid the bus ride. They might not be too fond of medevacking an American in their Russian chopper. What if Ortega was not going back to Managua but on to the front? Or to a military base, a secret lair swarming with Cubans and Soviet advisers? They would not want a Yankee listening to them while they were computing the number of hours it would take them to get to the Rio Grande, then arguing about the best night spots in San Antonio or where to find girls in Denver just before they blew up the headquarters of the North American Air Defense Command under Cheyenne Mountain.

The dextrose was sweet but milder than the Coca-Cola. A new

medic came into the room and said he was certain I had heat prostration. He saw it frequently in battle. I was angry that the heat had gotten to me so quickly while the crowd in the plaza was now well into its second hour of swelter. The doctor gave me more Coca-Cola.

The sound amplification was powerful enough to send the entire program into the classroom. Daniel Núñez, the agricultural official, was advising the crowd, which Roberta estimated at four to five hundred, to get every inch of good farmland planted before the rains started. "Nature will be kind to us only if we do our own job properly," he said.

I got off the stretcher and sat at one of the small children's desks. Immediately I felt very weak again, so I lay back down on the stretcher. The doctor, who was giving me so much of his time I began to hope no one else passed out to take him away from me, was not pleased. He said he would have to give me fluid intravenously. For an instant I had a vision of his mainlining Coca-Cola into me; I would either granulate or turn into Arnold Schwarzenegger.

But he meant only the dextrose. He poked a needle into several veins in my arm and was disappointed. "I can't find a good one because you have very fragile veins," he said. This worried me not because it was true but because a lifetime—well, I hoped *half* a lifetime—of medical examinations had given me the certainty that it was not true. What did that mean about the rest of his diagnosis? He took my other arm and after more pincushioning discovered a vein he liked.

A local politician was telling the crowd that hoarding and speculating were delaying economic recovery. He praised the town government, of which he was part, for getting more goods to more people than other towns in the area did. "Buy only what you need, please, and all of us will benefit," he said.

After fifty cc of dextrose, I felt stronger. I also felt extremely grateful to the doctor and asked him what I could possibly do for him. American gratitude has the vigor of prayer. "Nothing," he said. "That is what we're here for." I considered giving him my watch, then I glanced at his and realized it was far better than my own. I considered my beloved binoculars with the motorized zoom lens that I had let the Sandinistas use at the border two years earlier. No, I couldn't part with them. Besides, I rationalized, the doctor would only give them away to some point man on a patrol, and then neither of us would have them. I asked him where he was from and whether he had done much traveling. He paused before answering. "Managua," he said, laughing a little. "No, not much traveling."

Something about his pause or his chuckle made me want to know more, but he went outside. Roberta said the doctor had told her, in the manner of the Caribbean, that it was a little after two o'clock—*dos y pico*. Nicaraguans generally say that it is a specific number of minutes after the hour, as in *dos y cinco*, five past two. Other usages had made Roberta wonder about the doctor's nationality. He had dismissed an aide with a *"come mierda"*—literally, "eat shit," though the doctor laughed as he said it—that is characteristic of Cuban slang. I reflected that sugar was also a principal crop of Cuba, Coca-Cola also a favorite drink. I thought it might be interesting to talk to him about Angola. "The gift you can give him is to respect his privacy," Roberta said, shutting me up.

The doctor let me take a classroom desk outside and sit in the shade where I could look down the embankment into the plaza to watch the Cara al Pueblo proceed. Daniel Ortega had by now joined the group of officials that sat at a long table on a raised platform at one end of the plaza. The schoolchildren from my classroom did not chorus *"Bienvenido Presidente,"* if that is what the sign on the blackboard had taught them to do. Completely unlike his performance at the sunrise press conference earlier in the day, Daniel Ortega was very modest at this town meeting. He did no talking at all for well over an hour after arriving on the platform. He only listened.

A man in a baseball cap that said "Pandle & Sons" came to one of the microphones that had been set up among the crowd. He worked in a small lumber mill and complained that the pay there was based on an eight-hour day and they often had to work twelve hours. Why was there no provision for overtime? A rice farmer was irritated because his pickers were drinking on the job. A cotton grower pointed out that fumigation of his fields was going badly because planes were not permitted to fly before six in the morning and the best time for spraying pesticide was five, when the weevils were out but the bolls were still closed. A cattle rancher complained he could not get enough fodder for his stock, and when he was ready to take his steers to the slaughterhouse he could not get them there. "The fact is," he said, "we've had no new trucks since 1978. We can't meet any basic production goals without decent vehicles." A slaughterhouse manager had the same complaint; he had no trucks to take his beef to Managua.

On a hill possibly three hundred yards away from the meeting, beyond the last shacks at the edge of Santo Domingo, a white horse watched the crowd. People moved around the plaza, left their seats to buy tortillas and crushed ice flavored with orange or pineapple or grenadine, all heavily sugared, then came back to the Cara al Pueblo. The horse, immobilized perhaps by the sun, perhaps by curiosity, stared at the meeting all afternoon.

A *campesino* complained about the big landowners that remained in Chontales province. "Why should one family own so much when hundreds of us can barely exist on our tiny farms?" More farmers asked for machines, boots, machetes. "And by the way," one said, "we need a thousand rifles in my region to defend ourselves against the aggressor." He was cheered. A woman in a Boston Celtics T-shirt rose to agree with the farmer. "If a Yankee crosses the line in our village," she said, "he'll lose his private parts." Another woman quickly grabbed a microphone to say, "That's the spirit. When a woman gets going there's no man who can hold her back." The crowd, ready for a break, laughed and clapped for her. But a construction worker, burly and grim, said if his crew didn't get better materials and a couple of cranes, they would never finish the warehouse they were trying to build. "We're already five months behind schedule," he said, "and I have to report that industry in our area has pretty much collapsed."

Several officials briefly answered specific questions about

overtime, shortages and farming problems, then gave way to Daniel Ortega. The president of Nicaragua was a different man in a different world from the hectoring speaker at the press conference that morning in Managua. "Our problems are not so bad," he said, "that they won't get worse. They will get worse. We have a survival economy. We have not adjusted our economic plans to this survival economy, and we must do that. Our needs are so great we have to look for outside help, and yet no foreign country can bail us out. In the end no one will save us but ourselves."

Basically, Daniel Ortega was telling his people that the situation was more desperate than the leadership had realized. It was a wartime pep talk about working harder and making greater sacrifices, but it was not primarily about blaming the United States. Ortega even mentioned a mistake no one else had. "Because of the world market slump in cotton," he said, "we decided to cut back this year on cotton production. But we didn't do this until after the new crop had already been planted. This was terrible planning—the worst."

Fidel Castro often harangued Cubans for hours with the mistakes his government had made; he was known for delivering arias of breast-beating. But no Nicaraguan leader had ever confronted his people with simple admissions of inadequacy. Ortega had nothing like Castro's charisma; he had approximately as much charisma as Senator Bob Dole of Kansas. Both men had total self-possession and an appealing power of concentration, but neither Dole nor Ortega would ever be asked to give Mark Antony's funeral oration in *Julius Caesar*. If crowds could still be described as rabble, Dole and Ortega were not rousers. They were, perhaps, the ultimate high school commencement speakers.

Daniel Ortega faulted his government for not giving workers enough alternatives. "If we close a plant or decide to make a shift in crops, we have to provide opportunities for jobs in other areas," he said. "We must readjust our planning to better utilize the few resources we have. The problem of consumer goods is serious, and we have not been consistent in our production. For example, today we have enough soap and cooking oil, but last month we did not and next month we may not again. We must organize ourselves in production and in rationing so there can be a steady supply of scarce goods even if it is a very small supply."

He had exchanged his six A.M. bravado for a measured candor in front of the hometown crowd. Cara al Pueblos were videotaped for later broadcast throughout Nicaragua, which meant the criticism and response became in effect an exercise in citizenship for the whole country. Not until late in his reply to his fellow Nicaraguans did Ortega mention the United States. "The cause of much of our difficulty, well, I won't repeat it," he said, "because you know what it is. You know there is a war going on between the United States and Nicaragua. You know who is killing your brothers and sisters and children. All that is left is for the United States to declare war against Nicaragua. We wonder why they don't do that, since they are so intent on destroying us."

Back in Managua, I had to deal with whatever had made me faint in Santo Domingo. I was not hungry, which was strange. The consensus on the bus was heat stroke, which sounded logical to me until shortly after midnight at the Intercontinental, when I had a bowel movement filled with blood. Not yet asleep, Roberta Lichtman hurried to my room with the information that the Baptist Hospital was the best in the country. "We have such fun on our Saturday-night dates," she said, remembering the huge spider, the Muzak of gunfire, and the Wallabee salesman in Jalapa two years earlier.

At the Baptist Hospital, we were told it was not wise for an American to be sick in Nicaragua. Only one doctor was on the premises in the middle of the night, an attendant said, and he was busy performing a Cesarean section. No one knew when he would be finished, and in any case he was an obstetrician, not a bleeding specialist. "Whatever that means," Roberta said. "But where can we get help for my friend right now?"

The attendant recommended another hospital, and we set off.

"Wait a minute," Roberta said when the cab driver had gone only a few blocks. "This time of night we're going to get the runaround everywhere we go, but I know one place where they deal with bleeding twenty-four hours a day, seven days a week." She headed the cab for the Sandinista Army Hospital.

When the guards outside the military base refused us admittance on the grounds of our being foreigners, nonmilitary foreigners, and worst of all, Americans, Roberta used some of the most vivid Spanish that can surely have been uttered since the death of Federico García Lorca. After listening to her a few minutes, they begged her to be quiet so they could call the hospital's main office. Waiting in the cab, I heard only the word *loco* before the corporal in charge of the guard station waved us inside. "One of them told me we can't be the bleeders, since we're the cause of *their* bleeding," Roberta said. "At least we know the milk of human kindness is not filling *his* veins." I was happy enough to get into the enemy compound.

In the emergency room I was asked to lie down on a gurney next to a soldier who had been wounded in the shoulder. He had already been bandaged and was hoping to be released in the morning so he could go home to Matagalpa. Managua did not suit him. A doctor attended me so quickly I could not tell whether they thought what I had was serious or simply wanted to get the Yankee off the premises as quickly as possible. He took my blood pressure and said it was fine, and indeed I felt fine. As decorously as possible, he then inspected a stool sample and immediately said two words to me in English: "Go home."

When I asked why, he said I had a bleeding ulcer. I told him I was in no pain at all, and he said that made no difference; in all likelihood I had a bleeding ulcer and had fainted earlier from loss of blood. I might require transfusions, and blood was extremely scarce in Nicaragua. Blood was not handled there with the hygienic standards he assumed were normal in the United States. He was confirming Ramiro Lacayo's advice about getting sick in my own country. Ah, where was Somoza's old plasmapheresis center—the one whose exposure got Pedro Joaquín Chamorro murdered, whose murder galvanized Nicaraguans into destroying the center and supporting the revolution that had come to anger the United States so much—now that I needed it?

As if in apology for not keeping me at the hospital, the doctor gave me about five dozen Tagamet pills. Tagamet inhibits the stomach's production of acid and is the drug of widest choice in the treatment of ulcers. He told me to take four pills a day. I said if I was going home I would hardly need several dozen pills. "Good luck," he said, pointing to the door.

The two flights scheduled to leave Managua for the United States the next day were canceled. Roberta asked the American embassy to send a doctor and a nurse to the Intercontinental. They arrived at the hotel together, but the nurse got to my room first, because the doctor refused to ride in elevators and insisted on walking upstairs to the seventh floor. The nurse said ulcers happened in the spring. The doctor, a middle-aged Nicaraguan, heard the symptoms and confirmed the bleeding-ulcer diagnosis. He launched immediately into a diatribe against the Sandinistas. "We are going to throw them out very soon," he said. "If I were younger, I would be in the mountains so fast with my rifle."

"It's the same card game as ten years ago here," said the nurse, a middle-aged American. "The same card game with different players."

"Take only liquids now," the doctor said. "Drink lots of Coca-Cola. That will stabilize you."

"No, no, dearie," the nurse said to the doctor. "Coca-Cola has caffeine in it, and that's bad for an ulcer."

"Oh, right," the doctor said.

The nurse said the embassy had recently flown out an American labor official who had a heart attack in Managua. But the medical plane had to be summoned from Fort Lauderdale and it took fifteen hours to get to Nicaragua. Hold on here, I said, what about the great U.S. Army hospital in Panama? Hasn't it been there seventy-five years, didn't it help get the Panama Canal built? "We have lost faith in Gorgas," the nurse said tartly. "Things have gone to hell there." Poor Gorgas. The conqueror of yellow fever and malaria, Dr. William Gorgas, memorialized in the hospital in Panama, had now been humiliated beyond redemption; a nurse in Nicaragua wouldn't trust his hospital to handle a puny little ulcer. She concluded I should go to the United States on the first commercial plane the next morning.

"But let me see that Tagamet the Sandinistas gave you," she said. "Hmmm. Can't tell."

What couldn't she tell?

"I can't tell where it's from. The Nicaraguans don't manufacture their own medicines, so everything they have is a donation. If this Tagamet is from Budapest, it's better than ours in the States, because the Hungarians have sharper quality control than we do. But if it's from Bulgaria, where they have virtually no quality control, your Tagamet could well be canary shit."

With that, she was off to the U.S. embassy to fetch me some Tagamet from Smith Kline & French.

I once heard an ulcer described as the stomach's attempt to digest itself. Neither the food I had been eating nor any tensions associated with being back in Nicaragua quite seemed to account for my springing this leak, and doctors are reluctant to ascribe ulcers as directly to diet or stress as they once were anyway. I wanted to stay in Nicaragua, but obviously I had to go. The anagram for "ulcer" that most readily occurred to me was "cruel." Later, when I had stayed a week in the hospital at home and saw the bill, the anagram changed to "lucre." At this point, however, spending my last day in Nicaragua in the Intercontinental, which still presided in its shabby eminence over the landscape, I felt I had less to fear from Nicaragua than from myself.

The nurse bustled back quickly from the U.S. embassy, bringing American Tagamet. The doctor was still with her, having ambled down seven flights to talk to friends in the lobby and ambled back up again. "The contras don't matter," the doctor said, puffing only a little, "because very soon we Nicaraguans will rise as one man to throw these skunks out. It will be bloodier than the war against Somoza."

"Four a day," the nurse said, and they were gone.

I asked Roberta if she thought there were elements of a soap opera present here.

"As the Third World Turns," she said.

Roberta helped me to the plane the next morning and remained in Nicaragua herself to see what developed.

American visitors to Managua continued to protest outside the tall vertical iron bars surrounding the U.S. embassy. Twelve Vietnam veterans wearing green caps and golden T-shirts led a chant one morning against American policy:

> "Ronald Reagan is no good,
> Send him back to Hollywood.
>
> Sound off, one two,
> Sound off, three four.
>
> If he had been in 'Nam back then,
> He'd never made it back again.
>
> Sound off . . . "

"Yesterday, as I stood at the anti-contra protest and heard their crimes described," a woman of about fifty from San Francisco announced to the demonstrators, "I was ashamed to be an American. I came down here ten days ago a liberal, but I'm going back a radical!"

Three of the Vietnam veterans pricked their fingers, adding their blood to what had been lost in Nicaragua by villagers, farmers, students, contras, Sandinistas, teachers, doctors and, with such casual inadvertence, myself. "May these drops," one of the veterans said, "become the last blood spilled in Central America."

Across the street from the embassy the Sandinistas had put up a billboard. Lettered on it was Sandino's reply to a U.S. Marine captain who demanded his surrender in 1927. "I have received and understood your communication of yesterday," Sandino wrote. "I will not surrender and I await you here. I want a free country or death. I am not afraid of you. I count on the patriotism of those who are with me." Managua's newest shantytown squatter settlement of refugees from the countryside was spread out down the road from the billboard.

Recovering from my ulcer in the hospital, I saw a headline that the rains had begun in Nicaragua. *Las lluvias,* the Central American monsoon, had washed out both a contra offensive on the northern front and a Sandinista counterattack. In Washington, Congress debated how much and what kind of aid to send the contras. President Reagan postponed again his final decision on an American invasion of Nicaragua. "1986 is the year when the book will be closed," the counterrevolutionary leader Arturo Cruz said. "If they are still in power by the end of 1986, that's it." In the mountains above Estelí, both sides were bogged down in the mud. Roads were washed out, and it was hard to evacuate the dead and wounded. Both sides regrouped to wait out *las lluvias.* Then they would start again.

ACKNOWLEDGMENTS

MY SPANISH BEING INADEQUATE to Nicaraguan conversation and nuance, I have relied on a number of translators and interpreters. Roberta Lichtman was foremost among these; the last chapter, in particular, is hers as much as mine. I am also grateful to Luis Estrada, Gretchen Sleicher, Laura Enríquez and Rebecca Morales for their translating. Susan Baum and Katie Davis provided invaluable research help. A small portion of this book, in different form, was originally published in *The Nation*. *Esquire* magazine has also published an excerpt. In addition to my editor, Alice Mayhew, the Latin American specialist George Black has provided astute criticism and advice during preparation of the final manuscript.

It is customary for authors to thank their families, and I do this knowing that thanks are far from sufficient. For this book to exist, my wife and children have had to put up not only with my absences but with a continuing sense that I was not at home even when I was physically present. My youngest child has no memory of a time when her father was not thinking about Nicaragua.

ABOUT THE AUTHOR

Peter Davis is the author of *Hometown: A Contemporary American Chronicle*. He was an Emmy and Peabody award-winning writer/producer for CBS News, and he won an Academy Award for his film "Hearts and Minds." He has contributed to *Esquire* as well as other journals.

Foreign Affairs From Touchstone Books